A LISTENING WALK

A LISTENING WALK
...and other stories

GENE HILL

Illustrated by Tom Hennessey

NEW WIN PUBLISHING, INC.

ACKNOWLEDGMENTS

The story entitled "Some Things Never Change" originally appeared in the *Gun Digest Hunting Annual*, First Edition (1984), copyright © 1983 by DBI Books, Inc. All other stories are reprinted from *Field & Stream*, 1978, 1979, 1980, 1981, 1982, 1983, and 1984. The author thanks DBI Books, Inc., and *Field & Stream* for permission to reprint this material.

Library of Congress Cataloging in Publication Data

Hill, Gene.
     A listening walk—and other stories.

     1. Hunting. 2. Fishing. I. Title.
SK33.H6585 1985   799   84-27080
ISBN 0-8329-0385-X

FOR JIM RIKHOFF
who has enriched my life in all the ways I consider important and
given me both comfort and laughter when I needed them. Although
he has been largely responsible for my not leading a normal,
respectable life, we have, in his own words, "passed a good time."
Our companionship has taught me the meaning of many things, but
the two that have been most outstanding are *loyalty* and *hangover*.

CONTENTS

A LISTENING WALK

ONCE A SALMON
SANG TO ME

I am the noble salmon, sir, and before you look for me,
There are certain things to ready when I seek the rivers from the sea.

A couple of hundred hand-tied flies might start you out—I think;
If someone mentions Bogdan, you could produce one in a wink.

Your cap should come from Scotland, like the contents of your flask,
And you can demonstrate the Spey cast, if anyone should ask.

If you are a mere beginner, then four rods or so will do—
Bearing Orvis and Hardy labels, and perhaps a Leonard too.

Your waders should be custom-made; your staff, unblemished cane;
Your necktie from the Anglers' Club or some regiment of fame.

I assume you know the Moise and the Restigouche as well;
You can name the pools on the Mirimichi and tales of Iceland tell.

The Tay and Dee are second homes; you know them beat by beat.
If the Cascapedia is mentioned, you ask, "Grand or Petite?"

From early June to Late July, we'll make attempts at rendezvous,
But I might be feeling sulky and just make a swirl or two.

And if you're casting 4/O's, I might have my mind on 8's ...
Instead of your Hairy Mary's I'd prefer a Col. Bates.

I know you've studied Kelson and can quote Lee Wulff and Phair;
You think you know when feathers work or wings tied out of hair!

It's amusing to us salmon to see such innocent belief...
Which is why we'll hit a cigarette and now and then a leaf.

But we couldn't be here without you and we thank you, gentlemen,
For cleaning up the waters where we travel back to spawn.

So we'll roll to you in passing as we make our way upstream—
Just a little flash of silver to add color to your dream.

We'd miss you on the rivers, so please don't overdo;
Take lots of time for fishing—but do a little spawning too!

NO, I HAVE NOT THANKED
A GREEN PLANT TODAY
—I'VE BEEN BUSY

In the last year or so I have been requested to help save the Hudson, to help save the Yellowstone, to help save the tuna, the striped bass, the Atlantic salmon, Silver Creek, the Pine Barrens, ducks in general, whales, wild horses, burros, and enough other creatures and places to make me more sympathetic than ever with the Lord resting on the seventh day.

I contribute time and money to DU, TU, FFF, the Gamecoin, African Safari Clubs, the NSSA, ATA, NSSF ... and oh yes, the NRA.

Not to mention license fees, big-game permits, and special duck, woodcock, pheasant, and trout stamps. I clean up beer cans on streams, I build wood duck nests, I teach kids gun safety and how to fish. I release almost all the fish I catch and try not to shoot my limit on waterfowl (which is easy). I plant bird cover, dig ponds, and create sanctuaries. I hunt with a trained dog to help save game. I douse my campfire and pack everything out that I packed in.

And every so often I most humbly, in my very small way, emulate the Lord by looking at what I've helped do, and say to myself, "That is good." I am delighted to have seen the antelope increase to vast numbers, to know that there are now more whitetail deer than when Columbus discovered the continent. I am pleased that the salmon fishing is getting better, that I can see Canada geese by the thousands where not too long ago there were few. It's been hard and costly work—but I can't imagine anything more worthwhile. I am anxious to do more and I will.

I am simply a man who likes to hunt and fish when I have a little free time. I am a typical, average American sportsman. I consider myself one of America's great natural resources; I have helped save, clean, reclaim, guard, and propagate as many things that I believe to be precious as I could. And my children believe as I believe; they understand what I have given them and they will work to do even more.

There seems to be only one little thing that not too many people are willing to help save: Me.

Every year there's more and more pressure to prevent me from gunning. The town close to where I live forbids the discharge of a firearm ... even at a backyard clay target. National television shows portray me with bias and prejudice. Every major newspaper carries advertisements from various groups saying that I not only shouldn't hunt, I shouldn't even be allowed to own a gun. A kid who wants to earn a little pocket money running a farmboy trapline is dismissed as a torturer.

Some people who canoe on the rivers I have helped clean up try to intimidate me when I'm fishing. They are starting to shout, "Fish have feelings too!"

Some backpackers and cross-country skiers are taking pride in burning our hunting and fishing camps; no doubt the fish and game are most grateful.

These are the same gentle people who put bumper stickers on their cars asking me, *Have You Thanked a Green Plant Today?* Well, no I haven't. As a sportsman I've been too busy sowing wild celery, willows, multiflora, and rice, and asking farmers to leave a few rows for the bobwhite and pheasants.

It seems that more and more people today find it hard to be for the environment and all that it stands for without being against those of us who like to hunt and fish. I don't really know why it has to be that way, and I'm hurt that these well-meaning people won't take the time to think the problem out; won't see or understand my side of it.

We sportsmen have done a magnificent job of educating each other. We work together and talk our problems out. We write articles about the fine job we've done in bringing back the wild turkey. We show films about the reclamation of wetlands. We count ducks and regulate ourselves on seasons and bag limits. Our good works are legion—but in a way we've kept them all to ourselves. I think we should do something a little different; we're not asking for love necessarily, but for understanding.

I know there has been some effort in this direction, but we need more and we need it soon. I'm not quite willing to put a sign on my van saying "Last year I spent X dollars to support our wildlife," the way the big truckers advertise that "This vehicle pays X dollars a year in taxes." But I want to find a way to constantly remind the anti-hunters, bird watchers, and "I Brake for Animals" crowd that I'm one of the sportsmen who are basically the source of the abundance of birds and animals. And I didn't do it just by sending a dollar or two for a bumper sticker.

Maybe our fishing and hunting clubs ought to take ads in the local papers saying that "The pheasants and quail you enjoy seeing and hearing were made possible by the following local sportsmen," and run a list of names. Maybe someone will ask one of you about this program and you can tell them some of the facts about wildlife and its management. Not emotions—but biology; about feed, cover, propagation, and harvest. People have to learn that wildlife is no longer a purely natural circumstance, anymore than a field of corn or a herd of Herefords is. Somebody has to care for the land and tend the crop, whether it's trout or tomatoes, ducks or soybeans.

You have restored the deer herd, brought back the huge flights of ducks, cleansed our rivers and lakes, replenished the plains with antelope, and made the seas safer for gamefish. You have won a few fights, but the biggest one lies ahead.

There are many millions of well-meaning, but ingenuous and unknowledgeable people who are violently against your enjoyment of hunting and fishing. They will agree, if forced, that a certain amount of culling and harvesting must take place—but they want the professional game manager to do it, not you in your blaze-orange vest. A great many of the wildlife professionals believe that underneath this sentiment is a prejudice against the sportsman—rather than a great sympathy for our wildlife. One major survey revealed that when the facts of starving deer herds were explained, a widespread reaction was, "Well, that's nature's way; I don't want an army of hunters milling around in our woods." Frightening? It should be.

Even more so when we admit that this emotion might be so irrational as to be impervious to education or logic. Part is an overreaction to what seems to be an increasing climate of violence. Part is a collection of emotional half-truths about what constitutes conservation.

The fact that much of what is feared is neither true nor real isn't going to make the struggle any easier. The sportsman—meaning you and me—must adopt a personal code of ethics, every one of us, that is as close to being above reproach as we can make it. We must come to our own defense "with clean hands."

I'm a great believer in the lessons of history. I have great faith in our ability to deal with the great numbers of undecided, the "I don't cares," and to change the attitudes of the violently opposed just as we have reversed the destinies of so many of our precious wildlife resources.

And it has to work, for we are the last and the most important resource of all—the totally concerned, the totally committed. The sportsmen.

LOW ROD

Now that fishing season is just around the bend on the calendar, I have to face the fact anew that my peers with fly rods are many, and united by the common fact that they are not the ones who forced the adoption of "no kill" stretches. Given the natural abilities of the average fly fisherman, "no kill" is an apt way of describing what is likely to happen, no matter where or what. To label that goal as intentional is, to be honest, dishonest.

This year to liven up the (justly deserved) feelings of inadequacy in those of us who describe flies by color ("the brown fly or the gray one?") and who know only three sizes (all right, maybe, and the hell with it if that's what they want), I propose the following competition for the title of ... Low Rod. Since merely not catching anything would never separate us in ranking, we have to look further for the qualities that distinguish us from each other.

What about a point system? Let's say 20 points for a fly box irretrievably dropped in fast water; 15 points for a fly that comes untied the moment a fish touches it; 10 points for leader knots that come undone; and 10 points for a knot that's too big to pass through the tip guide. At agreed-upon intervals tippets will be checked for wind knots; all those with more than three will get 1 point apiece. No points for being hung up in trees or bushes unless the fly and at least half the leader are sacrificed; then 5 points. Hooks broken on back cast, 2 points. Hooking self in jacket or hat, 1 point; ear, cheek, or neck, 3 points. Burning line or severing leader with lighted cigar or cigarette, 5 points. No points for falling in unless a creditable witness testifies that water depth is less than 18 inches and of virtually no measurable velocity; then points will range from 1 to 5 depending on degree of clumsiness.

When pure ineptitude results in lost pipes, wet sandwiches, or breaking the tip of a one-tip rod, points will range from 5 to 10. Rods broken in screen doors, car doors, or rear windows of station wagons will be 2 or 3 points, depending on circumstances. Rods broken by stepping on them, or by flailing water in anger or frustration, rate somewhat higher.

Reels falling off reel seats, 10 points, unless fish is lost; then 15 points. Line not tied to backing, 10 points. Backing not tied to reel, 10 points. Loss of fish due to either is an extra 5 points.

One-point credits will be given for such things as improper threading of line through guides, upside-down reel, cutting wrong section of leader after attaching fly, tying one clinch knot or blood knot more than three times before it will hold, having wrong reel and line for rod used, and asking someone else to tie leader or fly, or to select fly, streamer, etc. Any normal fisherman should be able to accumulate 5 to 10 1-point items in a single day.

Putting rising fish down with inept cast, careless wading, etc., is to be expected and earns no points whatsoever. Likewise losing fish from not checking leader or hook, or fumbling net procedures.

You cannot win Low Rod if you are found actually matching the hatch—either in size or pattern—unless all concerned agree that this was purely coincidental and occurred without any deliberate intent whatsoever. Catching fish, however, does not absolutely disqualify you, providing you admit it was accidental and the size falls below a keeper. On the other hand, to be fair, catching chubs, dace, or other unwanted coarse fish should be to your credit; hooking and then losing such fish should earn 1 point each time.

A real effort for Low Rod can be made by using flies you tie yourself, providing they fall apart after only a few casts and/or cause audible laughter from at least two other fishermen no more skilled than yourself. This is a real test of character.

In the common case of a tie or near-tie for Low Rod, I think we can use our common sense. Tearing waders or boots more than once an outing on barbed wire, normally only a 1-point incident, can be awarded extra points if the tearee carries no patching material or if his patches refuse to adhere. Having absolutely no yellow or gray flies when that's all the trout are taking, again, though not ordinarily worth more than 1 point, can earn more if this is agreed to be indicative of the Low Rod's span of trout fly knowledge in general.

Let's look at how a born Low Rod approaches a typical situation. We see a moderately wide stream with a bend creating an undercut bank on the far side. Underneath a tall but overhanging willow, a much-better-than-average trout is rising to the occasional insect. The type of rise, the time of year, indicate that he is feeding on grasshoppers; indeed our Low Rod has seen hoppers in the grass along the bank at this time of the season for years.

To start with, he, of course, has no hoppers. But this really doesn't make that much difference, because there is absolutely no way he can cast far enough and with the proper curve to drift any fly over the trout. But having been in this situation before, he knows it. He will use his wits. He first considers going upstream, stripping the whole fly line from the reel, and finding a small stick in which to lightly imbed the fly. When the stick is just above the rising trout, he will pull the fly loose and make a nearly perfect presentation to the trout! There is a *possibility* that this will work, but in all probability the fly will remain imbedded in the stick, or the tippet will break, or he will pull too hard and the fly will hang up in the willow. He reconsiders.

He might have been able to merely strip line from above and hope for a miracle, but he has brought the reel with the sinking tip line.

However, genius is not to be denied. He will cut off the sinking tip portion of the line and follow Plan B. In considerably more time than it takes to tell it, the deed is done. He has tied his leader to the shortened line with what he assumes to be a variation (his) on the nail knot, re-threaded the remaining line through the guides (missing one on the tip), and begun to strip line. As he approaches the backing on the cut line, he is only intent on the rising trout. His fly, spreading oil from too liberal an application of flotant, approaches the trout. The trout circles warily by the edge of the bank, and then takes!

At this moment several things happen more or less at once: the tippet breaks or the clinch now comes undone; he is not sure which because his backing knot has just released the fly line. Thus, in a matter of seconds he has accumulated nearly 30 points—more than enough to tip the day's honors his way. Is he chagrined? Not at all, for in the final analysis his scheme did work; the trout did indeed take the fly. To the true sportsman the other events are inconsequential, and in this instance, unavoidable.

He is left with a story of a superb trout, and evidence of being down to the backing, and after a classic struggle, the glorious fish has rightly maintained his well-earned freedom. All in all, not a bad day.

Needless to say, these are just illustrations or suggestions. Should you choose to adopt such a rating system, you should take into account local conditions and other such variables as you see fit.

If one of your companions wins Low Rod several times and seems unlikely to ever be dethroned, it should be no problem to disqualify him from competition and encourage others to come forward. After all, how many fly boxes does one have to lose before he quits carrying one and resorts to small plastic pill bottles? (The correct answer is four.) And how many expensive rods does he have to step on before he learns to watch where he's putting his felt soles? (The correct answer is two—I hope.)

No doubt some enterprising tackle catalog will have a Low Rod pin like the one that's offered for doubles on woodcock or grouse. Fine. Our society is too advanced to restrict our plaudits for the few born with fine reflexes and coordination. There are those of us who need, desperately, credit just for trying. Who is to say that we are not the bravest of the brave?

I hope that you, knowing or guessing that I have fished with the likes of Lee Wulff, Len Wright, Ed Zern, and others who would rather not have their fishing ability linked with mine, believe that I just made these potential mishaps up out of my imagination. For this kindness, I thank you. But let me remind you of the time when outdoor writers used some clever pseudonyms like Hawker, Jock Scot, 20 Bore, and the like; not that they were actually embarrassed to be identified with this profession, but they wisely felt that a little anonymity might be a prudent thing. So, along these lines, were I to adopt a pen name for my fishing career—one that would be honest, descriptive, and catchy (!)—none other would be quite as apt as Foul Hook.

UNPACKING SOME
MEMORIES OF AFRICA

Just about this time of year, a few years back, I was happily packing
for Africa. After I got home I never really unpacked. I played at
staying ready to return at a moment's notice. I kept a few things in
my little tin trunk and a lot of things in my heart. But now that my
part of Africa is closed to hunting, I guess I might as well shake out
most of the things I put away.

I wish I could tell you about the dawns and sunsets, but I can't.
I could attempt to describe the colors of the sky, the way the light
shifted from dark olive to orange to yellow to blue-white, and the way
the air went from bone cold to suffocatingly hot, but I can't really do
them justice. I can close my eyes and see the colors change, but I lose
the intensity when I open them.

What I would like you to hear most are the sounds of morning—
a pair of shrikes, a male and a female, calling so melodiously to each
other that you could cry from the beauty of it. The baboons setting

up an early leopard watch with their angry, vicious barking. And until the morning heat sends everything into a modest quiet, the rising sursurrus of sounds; an animal newspaper with everybody reading his items aloud to everyone else.

And then evening comes on and the sun hangs there just the way Cezanne would want it to, framing a perfect acacia tree so long you'd think it was stuck. Then suddenly it's dark and the night orchestra tunes up: one animal small-talking to others of its kind; another just bragging and shouting; others still going about their nightly business of getting supper and rounding up the kids.

But, as I said, I can't do it justice and I won't try. I can't even get across to you one of the things that I still dream about. It's a simple thing to say but something else to feel all around you. It's space, or distance, or horizons, and it's really no one of these things—it's all of them; it's Africa.

Perhaps more than anything I liked riding up in the back of the hunting truck with the trackers, trying each other's tobacco and snuff. You'd look out in front as the truck topped a hill, and there was Africa *everywhere*—and you'd smile because that was just what it ought to be. You'd turn around and there it was, even more of it, all spread out behind you. And no one was there, except for a few Masai or Wakambas who you didn't see unless you went looking, or got on one of the real roads—the kind that didn't have trees and brush growing up in the middle.

Off in the distance you'd almost always see something: a band of ostriches, giraffes, oryx, zebras, gazelles, or—where we were—rhinos. It was an experience just being there, being part of Africa, part of something so right, so big, so exactly what I could never get enough of that I didn't want the truck to ever stop. In my mind we just keep driving on and around forever ... Katheka and Josie and me, poking each other in the ribs whenever we see something, or chunking a little snuff under our lip to make spit. Together we form a kind of African Flying Dutchman.

I can't really explain how this vastness drew something out of me, rid me of some emotional paralysis, and made me feel as free and as natural a part of that landscape as the Masai or the oryx or the impala. But I have never been happier.

Another of the memories I didn't want to unpack was of lunch time: cold meat from yesterday's super, maybe a kidney or a Tommy liver, along with a chop or two, some sardines, fresh-baked bread, and a semi-warm bottle of Tusker beer. I'd lie on my back and watch the clouds play through the leaves of fever trees, or the giant figs. I'd watch the weaver birds in their sort of upside down nests, or the blue rollers doing their aerial chandelles. Then I'd sleep in the heat until Josie woke me for a cup of tea, and we'd be off again, sailing over the sea of Africa.

In the evening, or more often well after dark, we'd spot our campfires and begin wondering what we'd have for supper, what the others had seen or shot, and whether to have a scotch or a gin. At camp a huge fire would be warming our canvas chairs. We'd have a quick drink and chat about the shooting, and then a hot bucket shower, clean clothes, a down jacket, and one or two more drinks before dinner.

It was always early to bed, snuggled under three or four blankets, wish-dreaming like a child for tomorrow's lesser kudu or a better-than-30-inch oryx. The now-familiar night sounds were a touch of home. It was always a great temptation, now and then indulged, to sit up and listen until the small hours and marvel that even the fire smelled like nothing else but Africa.

I would be up early with the ripping sound of my tent zipper being opened by one of the kitchen men bringing me my pot of tea. He'd light the gas lantern as he left so I could see to dress and shave. Then I'd have 15 minutes or so to lie in bed and drink my tea before getting up. No king ever enjoyed such luxury more!

Then breakfast: oatmeal, more tea, toast, and bacon. Afterwards I'd check the rifles and ammo and be off into the chill of a 6 o'clock African morning, my fluting shrikes going slightly off-key in the cold and dark. I would have given anything to be able to whistle just well enough to join them for a minute, but was never tempted enough to risk spoiling it.

A day's note from a most inadequate diary typically reads: "Morning hunt was a five-hour walk. The .375 tends to get heavy. Shot very good impala 88 kilometers from camp. Watched vermillioned Masai women building hut. Perfect day to see top of Mt. Kilimanjaro. Cannot believe I am camped virtually on a side of it. Never want to go home. Watched four kongoni who seem to be practicing sharp turns. Shepherd's pie for supper. Up tomorrow at five as usual. A lovely day."

MY LOVELY days went into a notebook with a few words designed more to jog the memory than to attempt to capture the uncapturable.

There are little notes like, "Saw fourteen fine heads of different species today: rhino, elephant, eland, lesser kudu, etc., etc." Already I'd gotten too blase to finish the note. But now I remember some of the others: cheetah, a pride of five that we literally stepped on and flushed, like so many brown-spotted, golden, land-bound birds; a red-maned lion that was far too elegant to shoot—and too smart to come to our bait for a closer look; a leopard at mid-morning that sat a half-mile distant and coldly stared into my eyes until I flinched and looked away.

There are those who will go back without a rifle, but I am not one of them ... not yet. I like to hunt. I like to stalk, the tracking mystery, the shot, and the skinning. I suppose I could go without shooting, but that's a decision I can only make with a legal rifle in my hand. I want both the right to shoot and the privilege of not doing so. I could see Kenya again without my heavy rifles—but I couldn't experience it.

What I ought to do is keep my tin trunk packed, after cleaning out the despair and the regret, with a fresh notebook and a new pen. Add a box or so of .375s, my old walking shoes, some fresh chewing tobacco and snuff, and a few pictures to show Josie and Katheka when I get back.

An artist once said that his eyes were stuck to a point and would bleed if he turned away. Just so, my heart has been pierced by the turning of Africa, and bleeds for it.

WANTED: TEN-YEAR-OLD

I like to find somebody, come April, to walk the brooks with me. A somebody who likes string, pocketknives, wet feet, and the sort of interesting-looking dog that comes along with it all. Somebody who likes the squish of mud between bare toes. Somebody who always has an eye out for that elusive, almost nonexistent perfect fork to make the ideal springtime slingshot. Somebody who has an eye out for jack-in-the pulpits and lady slippers (somebody who also prefers the names *Indian moccasin* or *whipporwill shoes*). Someone who has an eye out for skipping stones, pussywillows, arrowheads, and similar treasures that give an added purpose to an April wandering.

Someone who likes to fish for eels because they're exciting, slimy, and have lots of scary teeth; who appreciates the fact that once you've learned to handle an eel from beginning to the skinning you've learned a lot—including some words that won't appear on the next sixth grade spelling test.

I want someone to show about taping a bottle around an apple bud and watching it fill with fruit through the summer. I'd like to show someone how to plant a willow shoot so you'll have something else to visit to see just how it's taken hold. I need to show how to reach under a rock and feel a fish and rub it with your fingers until you can just pick it up by the mouth; bearing in mind that now and then the fish will turn out to be a watersnake, which often tends to dampen your enthusiasm for the sport. I'd like to show someone how to live off the land, beginning with watercress and sassafras and ending with chewing spruce gum—which is just the right start for a ten-year-old.

I want someone to share with me the mystery of hexagonal honey-combs, the tunnels of ants, the labyrinths of groundhogs, the giant paper acorns of hornets, the adobe of dauber wasps, the tiny jeweled caddis cases, the almost random layers of sticks that eagles feel proud of.

I need someone to wonder with me at the strength of the ant dragging a dead "bumblebee," the bravery of a blackbird pecking at our heads to save her nest; the front-end design of a black snake that lets it ignore the diameter of a rat; the glorious coloring of butterflies and moths.

I want someone to ask me (someone who rather wants to believe) about horsehairs becoming snakes; about bats and your hair; about severed turtle heads not dying until sunset; and can an eagle really carry off a small boy?

I'd like to hear a thin, piping voice recite, with feeling and hope, *"Star bright, star bright, first star I have seen tonight, I wish I may, I wish I might, have the wish I wish tonight."*

I'd like to teach someone who'd rather whittle a whistle that works than go buy one.

I'd like to walk along with someone who'd listen to my stories about wolves, Indians, ghosts, and the possibilities of treasure. Someone who loves the thrill of being scared and the comfort of being protected. Someone who's concerned with knowing buck rubs and coon tracks, counting tree rings, predicting weather, and what we would do if we really saw a bear.

Someone about ten, give or take a tooth or two, would be just about right. Ten is the age that usually produces just the right blend of wonder and sophistication. A ten-year-old is someone who is usually honest, funny, polite, and interesting. It's about the last year that someone can listen to you cuss without wanting to immediately imitate it. They won't criticize your sandwiches or your clothes and, since this is the last year they will make mistakes for a while, they'll understand yours and be kind enough to treat you as an equal.

They'll trust most of what you say—with few exceptions, those being the depth of streams and the climbability of trees. Being wet and dirty is still a natural condition and they still retain their ability to talk to animals and be understood. April and ten-year-olds should spend the month together. They're both youth at its best, budding in every direction.

You can teach ten-year-olds the song the brook sings, and chances are they will improve it. They'll have some idea of what the dog dreams about, why the crow is chatting, and what the possum might be thinking. You can talk about insect and animal cannibalism, fratricide, battles, and mayhem and they won't pale or get queasy. They are above all realists—right now.

They'll understand game management, controlled forest fires, and other complexities better than most adults because they're not prejudiced against learning something. It's one of your last chances to be with someone who doesn't know everything about anything. And maybe with your help the ten-year-old will stay that way.

A ten-year-old is sort of a puppy you can talk sense to. Maybe even show off a little by starting a fire with a piece of glass, whistling to quail, or showing how to get an oriole to weave a piece of string into her nest.

Ten-year-olds have just the right sense of size. They know that ponds are as interesting as lakes and that brooks can be gotten into better than rivers. This is the age where one fish is as good as a limit; where leaving something today so you can have something left for tomorrow makes sense. Now is when attitude is more important than equipment, enthusiasm more important than know-how, and the adventure itself more vital than its success.

With someone along to walk April with, it becomes the first month of spring rather than the last month of winter. A rain is something to go out into rather than come in from. A lingering patch of snow becomes a showcase for myrtle and crocuses, which together make a perfect tradeoff at home for wet and muddy clothes.

And you know for sure that the pot at the end of an April rainbow is most likely to hold a pocketknife, a piece of string, some fishing hooks, and a handmade, off-key, wooden whistle—part of the treasure of still being partly ten years old.

EQUIPMENT TIME

There's a short time in the between-seasons stretch of late spring that I reserve for myself with the greatest of pleasure. You might call it "equipment time." Your wife and saner, more grown-up people might refer to it as something else, like "playing with his toys."

I admit to a certain small self-indulgence in the area of knives, reels, rods, extra barrels, lures, flies, and the slow but sure accumulation of items akin. But if someone wants to refer to my Bogdan and Hardy reels as "toys," they can look for their bourbon and water at some other refreshment stand. If they can't understand why I have more than two or three fly rods and want even more, then they are not welcome to smoke my tobacco or dip my snuff while watching me wax and polish them. And anyone who wants to take a look at my trap gun has to be a little more specific; does he mean my current favorite, the one that I've got hopes for, my old doubles gun, my up-for-trade over/under, one of the guns that is too short now, or any one of the two or three that just don't feel quite right?

Now's the time that I consider breaking in a new fly vest. Only someone who's never done it would be puzzled by the fact that you don't just dump all the stuff out of the old one and jam it into a new one. A real fisherman knows that this is generally a gradual performance. Adapting to a new fly vest is a very tentative undertaking. You put it on while you clean a gun or sort the mess of flies you have in a box. You might take a few practice casts in it or wear it while you fool with bluegills in the pond. But you don't suddenly abandon the one you've worn for years just because it's a little smelly, the zippers don't work, the pockets are held together with rusty safety pins, and it's so heavy you can barely lift it.

You have to remember with a new coat that the upper right-hand pocket has a pill jar of nymphs in it, whereas in the old coat the nymphs were in the inside left-hand pocket. These are not adjustments to be lightly considered—otherwise that greatest of all tragedies may happen: you will *forget something that you might possibly want to have along.*

The non-sportsman or the casual now-and-then gunner or fisherman doesn't understand why a plug caster has a tackle box that ought to come with a built-in hydraulic lift. They don't realize that nothing is ever thrown away—not a rusty or broken hook, not a diamond-hard strip of pork rind. It's all there—right down to the mashed split shot and the four sponge rubber weedless frogs that everyone has, but no one has ever taken a bass on.

What kind of trapshooter would go further than hand trap practice on the lawn without spare trigger springs, firing pins, moleskin, screwdrivers, pliers, three colors of shooting glasses, gloves, and an assortment of hats? I'd bet damn near anything that there are more assorted tools and accessories at a fair-sized trap shoot than you'll find at a manufacturers' hardware show.

Equipment time is sorting all this stuff out, admiring it, trying to remember what certain things are for, and putting it where you have a 70/30 chance of finding it.

Equipment time is putting new 20-pound backing on your salmon reels. The miserly may remind you that you just did that last year. The true fisherman knows that you are doing it to make sure the knots are right, and that you just get a great deal of satisfaction from fooling with line cleaners, glues, and oil: also that this might be the year for the big one and you want to know you're ready for anything; and above all, that there's something most satisfying about sitting back and listening to the click of a fly reel while the mind carries you back to that golden day when the rod first bucked in your hand; you were scared and did everything wrong and got lucky, and you couldn't have been happier.

Equipment time is when the Labradors watch you shake out the hunting coat pockets, put the leftover shells in empty Edgeworth cans, and pick the bird feathers out of the dog whistles. They watch, with an excited, wishful thumping of their tails, as you swing the little Greener a time or two before you wipe it down and slide it in the rack. You tease them a little more with a highball or two on the Olt before dropping it in the pack basket with the hand warmers, the mittens, and the heavy camouflage parka. The big 3-inch magnum rests across your lap and you remember that one last goose that came again as you softened the call and whispered *now* to Jimmy—and then one more season was over.

Equipment time is checking what you have against the new catalogs, and finding out what you can order that you don't have, or do have but know you can't find. It's looking over your leaders from last year, remembering that you forgot to sort them and realizing that you'd better throw them out and tie new ones. It's steaming flies and looking for holes in your waders. It's finding a box of bass bugs you forgot you had and discovering a reel you spent all summer accusing your daughter of losing.

This is a time to fool with what a non-thinker might charitably call "stuff": an old single-action reel that cost a dollar when it was new and working, about thirty years ago; a hand-whittled bass plug covered with faded barn paint that a kindly old man once gave to a kid you remember well; one of the ugliest fly rods ever made that was, no doubt, a thing of beauty to whoever it was that made it. Some decoys—a Maryland canvasback, a New Jersey black and a tailless pintail with toothmarks all over it from an old friend of mine who liked to carry it around when she was a puppy.

A shotgun stock that I once sawed off for a little girl who's not little anymore. Stuff you sort of pick up, look at, and then put back— and in that little moment remember something... see a face... hear a laugh... or imagine a scratching at a door. Stuff that doesn't mean a thing to anyone in the world but me, and nothing that you could ever persuade me to part with.

This strange assortment of odds and ends is part of the fabric of my life. Every so often I have to wrap it around me for warmth, when I feel the coming of the cold that touches us all at the closing of one season... and just before another begins.

TOO MANY LEADERS

There are so many new books around on the subject of self-improvement: how to invest $1,000 and become a millionaire; how to look and act 20 years younger; how to intimidate your boss; to be thinner, stronger, break 200 straight, be irresistible to the opposite sex, and so on. I'm sure the topics are almost completely covered. None of that stuff for me, however; not on your life.

I'm at the age and close to the intelligence that says go for camouflage, fade into the pack, be average or less if you can make it. You may think it's mere coincidence that people are clustering around Dan Bonillas and Kay Ohye at the big trap gatherings and not around Hill, but it isn't that simple. After all, I shoot the same kinds of guns they do, I use the same kind of shells, I wear the identical shooting jacket and the same color shooting glasses. I even know how to scowl refusing a slow pull. The truth is that I don't want to be one of the high average leaders. I don't want to toe it up at the 27-yard line with Gene Sears and Frank Little.

When I want to have a cold beer and a sandwich I can go have one; no one is tugging at my sleeve to watch them shoot right angles from the five post on the practice field. No one has ever asked me about the set on my release trigger or if I prefer an ivory front bead or a red one and why. *Au contraire*, as the French say. If anyone should ever go up to one of the shell company representatives and ask him what shells Hill shoots, he will answer right back, "Not ours, I hope!"

There are too many leaders, experts, and irresistibles already. What they need is you and me. They can't peddle their ideas and theories to each other; they have to find new markets, and that's what the rest of us are for. What good is being a leader if you don't have anyone behind you? I'm probably worth a lot more laughs at a shoot than ten 27-yarders. I can make more mistakes in a round of twenty-five than they make all year.

Somebody has to play the role of the bad example, and I've volunteered.

Why does everyone want to be the AFTER in the BEFORE & AFTER questions? What we've got going for us is wishing, hope, and a sense of adventuring into the unknown. Ray Stafford knows he's going to break 199 or 200. I don't have the faintest idea how I'll do, other than that it's not going to be 199 or 200. No way you can compare the challenge we face with the lack of it that John Muir contends with. All he's got to worry about is matching his shirt, pants, and jacket. He *knows* how to break good scores. With us it's a constant learning, or unlearning, process.

Same with fishing. Poor old Lefty Kreh goes out and sees a trout rise, ties on a 22 Quill Gordon, makes a perfect cast, gets a perfect float, and one more trout has a sore lip. We see a trout rise, tie on the smallest fly we can handle, which is a 14, false cast a wind knot or two in the leader, come up 3 feet short, and put the trout down smirking and smiling to himself. A successful cast is one where we don't have to get half undressed and tear a hole in our clothes to get the fly back. A fine day on the stream is one where we're not bleeding afterwards. Lefty doesn't have any imponderables left to speak of. We've got them by the hundreds. Now who has the most to remember ... the most to look forward to next time?

A Bubba Wood can go out and shoot virtually anything and run 250 at skeet. Not us. We have to have a gun that weighs 7½ pounds, with 1 degree downpitch, 1¼ × 1¼ Monte Carlo and slightly butt heavy, four points of choke, and hopefully twenty-four lines to the inch of checkering. Who has the more enjoyable evenings by the fire poring over gun catalogs? Bubba doesn't much care if his sneakers match, while we're seriously debating between Gokey or L. L. Bean shooting moccasins.

I don't say something even approaching a grudging "good" would destroy my pleasures, but I'm having a fine time right now. The delicious decisions about bead color, the shape and texture of recoil pads, the mind-wrenching that goes along with choosing light or heavy eights should the wind come up, are part and parcel of the whole scene. I'm as reluctant to change as I am likely to.

Give Lefty a fly rod that's soft, fast, heavy, or weepy and he'll just alter his casting stroke. Hell, I don't even have anything to alter. I have to remain a believer, despite facts far to the contrary, that somewhere exists a rod which fits what I do, however awkward and mirthful others might view it. Rod companies and collectors' lists don't exist for the likes of Kreh—whereas they'll end up getting my daughter's dowry and a fair chunk of our food money. I'm a consumer; if I'm perfect at anything, that's got to be it. I've got to believe that the staffs of all our sporting goods companies are tirelessly working toward the day when they'll produce something that will see me through a 50 straight or a 60-yard cast that doesn't look and sound like a tree falling; maybe even two back to back, if that's possible!

No doubt (as has often been mentioned by a relative by marriage) if I spent more time learning how to use what I've already got as opposed to constantly searching for something new and/or different, I'd possibly be better off. But to be honest, nothing so amazes me as the fact that one of our very finest trap shots, Vic Reinders, only has *one* and only shoots *one* trap gun and has used it for hundreds of thousands of rounds. An absolutely superb trout fisherman—a man whose approach on a stream to a rising trout has held a group of us spellbound and who, when he caught and released the fish, got a well-deserved round of applause—this man owns one trout rod: an ancient, crooked, broken-and-mended time-and-again Hardy. I asked him if he ever wanted something different or newer. He just sort of smiled, indulgently, and said "What for?"

I won't say I'm an equipment malcontent, but you'd be hard-pressed to find someone who is more anxious to try a new idea in a trap gun or fly rod than yours truly. Sure, I've got a couple of favorites, but except for my bird and duck guns, you could color me fickle. And to make the self-revelation even more confusing to those with more common sense, I have hardly ever sold or traded a gun or a rod that sooner or later I didn't regret losing. I have hardly ever sold or traded something and not gotten a little stung either, but I can't blame anyone but myself for that.

I'm like the shooter or fly-caster who's always "practicing." Or almost so. It seems that I'm always trying out something new. If it's not a shotgun or rod, it's a new way of using one. No doubt one of the reasons I never get bored at a gun club or on a stream is that nothing is ever really the same as far as I'm concerned.

I've never really grown up (as the same relative by marriage has also often mentioned) and the kid who constantly imagined himself to be Tom Mix or Flash Gordon or Tarzan has only found new and different heroes in his life. I spend a day shooting with Kay Oyhe and then I spend a week imitating him—in everything but his scores. I spend a little time casting with Lefty Kreh or Phil Wright or Gardner Grant and I'm imitating them, or at least trying. But the fish know who's who, the same way that the clever clay target does.

They say that inside every fat man is a thin man trying to get out. Or, "Show me what a man laughs at, and I'll show you what he fears or envies." I think these things are likely true. No doubt, inside this flinching, gun-stopping shooter—unquestionably in this wind-knotting, fish-lining caster—there beats the heart of one who dreams, alas fruitlessly, of the day when at some gun club or fishing camp he'll hear someone whisper in awed tones, "Who was that masked stranger?" as he mysteriously rides away.

BASS ARE NOT
BUCKETMOUTHS

As long as I can remember I've always felt uncomfortable, and often queasy in my stomach, with writers who name and create fictitious and fulsome family relationships about wild animals and fish. Long before the unfortunate Bambi syndrome, well-known and widely read outdoor writers and naturalists were going on at distasteful length about Reddy the fox, Lobo the wolf, Tiger the musky, and so on until, to paraphrase Dorothy Parker, this constant reader almost threw up.

At the risk of being stoned at some outdoor writers' gathering (here I use "stoned" in the Biblical sense, not the current vernacular) I must add that I am also tired of reading about bass being "hogs,"or "bucketmouths." I hope to never again see "hat-racks" for antlers, "doodles" for woodcock, "bulls" for drake ducks, or any firearm named "Old Betsy." I can happily live without ever again seeing a pump referred to as a "cornsheller," a .30/30 spelled "thutty-thutty," or a reel described as one "screaming in protest." Not only are these literary crimes, but they reek of mental poverty, laziness, and denigration of both the English language and the sports and game involved. The list is, sadly, virtually endless.

In my opinion, impressionable minds, age notwithstanding, have enough to cope with without being burdened with the philosophical falsity of confusing instinct with either bravery, rationalization, or a complicated thought process involving multiple choices that would confuse an Ivy League Ph.D.

Too much of this nonsense and these erroneous "facts" are coming back to haunt the sportsman as it is. No doubt much of it is an effort to avoid unpleasantness; but it has led. I'm afraid, to such widely spread pseudo-scientific propaganda as "Man is the only animal capable of cruelty or wanton killing." And much more of the like.

Almost all animals and many fish fight their own kind, and kin, as well as other threatening or nonthreatening species. In a time when the front page of every newspaper is filled with a variety of murders, thefts, bombings, hit-and-runs, child abuse cases, and other mind-staggering indecencies, I see no reason why we can't live with the fact that lions will eat their young—as well as the young of a variety of other creatures—as will dogs, fish, and many birds.

Whitetail deer do not name their fawns Spot and Russet. Atlantic salmon are not baptized Silver or Leaper. The leader of a wolf pack doesn't lose any sleep over who's missing at roll call. And even Shakespeare can't convince me that "where a Queen cries, there rue grows." Our human community has enough problems with the passions of love and hate and understanding without putting all that on the other creatures who have enough problems of their own as it is.

I would have liked to discuss Hemingway's 300-yard kill of a running lion with him. Some 90-yard waterfowl shots I've read about and, with one or two exceptions, I'd like to stand at streamside and watch those guys laying out 100-foot casts with their fly rods. I have known and witnessed some truly remarkable feats involving outdoor skills. I have seen African trackers do what I would have called impossible had I not been there. I know of a couple of highly skilled rifle shots who could duplicate what Hemingway wrote about but wouldn't try because they knew better. I also know one or two wingshots who, with precision, care, and common sense, can gun a day very successfully without leaning too heavily on the second barrel. But these are very rare people indeed—rare in the fact that they possess extraordinary skills, and rare that they constantly practice them. I have never heard any of them brag or boast about it, by the way.

It's not that I'm devoid of sentiment, nor am I a born skeptic. I enjoyed stories about witches and trolls. I would love to believe (and maybe I do a little) in the Loch Ness monster, Yetis, Bigfoot, and UFO's. I delight in the mysterious and the unknown—but I'd rather we leave them like that than try to categorize the lifestyles of other creatures in a soap opera scenario.

Nor do I fault hyperbole, imagination, wishful thinking, or dreams, idle and otherwise. Poetry, imagery, allegory, and fiction all have their functions in writing of any sort. But not at the total sacrifice of good taste, common sense, realism, education, or wisdom.

Our literature is myth-ridden from the first recorded tale of Beowulf. We have expanded our minds on classics that dwell on the ancient gods, the supernatural, and the struggle to define the awesome unknown. We know that many early mathematicians, astrologers, physicists, and anatomists insisted on debunking myth and speaking what they knew as truth even when it meant ostracism, ridicule, physical punishment, or even worse. Those who first insisted that the earth was round, that the sun was the lifegiver of our universe, or promulgated such a simple thing as sanitation in caring for the sick, did so at tremendous peril. But today, in a time when we live casually with the phenomena of nuclear devices, interplanetary travel, DNA molecular structure, and the like, why should so much outdoor writing be cluttered with so much romantic nitwittery, shallow exaggeration, self-aggrandizement, and pseudo-naturalism... all couched in language and dialogue that comes off sounding like a Hollywood version of Indian and illiterate trapper talk?

The television shows that feature man/animal friendships are no doubt the worst offender. But, I suppose, given such a ridiculous premise to start with, where do you decide to draw the line?

The frequent dishonesty, philosophically and biologically, of Cousteau, Disney, Amory, and a vast number of others who have so untruthfully portrayed the sportsman and wildlife, should serve as an ugly reminder to us of the gullibility, unwillingness to be realistic, plain ignorance, and stupidity of so many easily influenced people—adults and children alike. Those of us who know better have the unceasing responsibility not to let this sort of thing go unchallenged. We have to start being heard more often and more loudly.

The increasingly strict laws regarding truth in advertising, and manufacturing responsibilities in product safety and wholesomeness, ought to be applied in some degree to the media. I'd feel a lot better if I saw at the start and conclusion of some shows a disclaimer that read: "None of the situations in this show are true—or could be. The grizzly is, in fact, an extremely dangerous animal and should be treated with the utmost caution. Last year X deaths and Y serious injuries occurred involving people who came too close to these animals...

I'll add sort of a "trailer" myself: None of the above is meant to suggest that I'll never sit and swap a yarn or tall story with you, or that I'm going to write with one hand on the Bible. But if I ever tell you that my reel sounded as if it were in pain after some bucketmouth erupted like a geyser—or that Old Meat-in-the-pot fetched me three honkers out where it took them 5 minutes to fall—I'll give you my 400-yard rifle, my pet grizzly, Silvertip, and the rod that will always cast the whole fly line.

IT'S NOT JUST FISHING,
IT'S FATE

One of the favorite themes of outdoor fiction (or what ought to be called fiction) is that of destiny. The old mule deer that eluded the old man for years until finally they met again, for the last time, and either it got away or it didn't. It doesn't matter, because it always turns out that this is the last hunt for one or the other.

No doubt things like this do happen, although rarely. I'm not one to attribute more to wild animals than a sense of self-preservation and the instincts that support it. I refuse to believe that an animal can recognize a hunter from one season to the next and am rather skeptical about the other side of that coin as well.

But, on the other hand, it is sometimes pleasant and imaginative and a little romantic to mull over the destinies, or fates, that put you in various places at specific times.

You know for a certain fact when you're fishing a salmon river that the salmon was born and raised here, and that it left and spent the next year or two or three in the ocean. I can't help but dwell on the distances traveled, the predators encountered, and the almost unbelievable factors that return the fish to the place of its birth. We know that the locator systems of the fish deal with an incredible sense of smell; but it's still a bit spooky to convince yourself that the Matapedia and the Upsalquitch and the Restigouche are as different to the salmon as peppermint and cinnamon and licorice are to us.

I've watched a salmon in its lie for hours. After a while it represents even more of a mystery than the biological curiosities it embodies. I can understand, to a degree, that it has ceased feeding when it reaches freshwater. I can cope with the knowledge of its sense of smell. I can imagine its migratory route—from Canada's Gaspé Peninsula across the north Atlantic. I can, in some small way, appreciate the tremendous instincts for reproduction that will carry this fish to the edge of destruction if need be. But add all these complexities of nature together and the whole becomes much greater than the sum of its parts.

I think of the mathematical odds against a salmon becoming the full-grown creature that I watch lazily finning against the water flow. I know it's waiting for something to send it upstream—a change in temperature, a rain to raise the stream level, or something else—a combination of circumstances that I can't ever know. I measure its instincts against mine and come up with the comparison of an abacus to our most sophisticated computer.

And yet I can stand there and tie on a Jock Scott or a Blue Doctor or whatever my simple mind tells me might be a likely choice and, with some persistence, a great deal of care, and no small smattering of luck, the fish is mine. I, who am so much less competent than a seal or an otter or an osprey, so much less deadly than a seine or a long line, have triggered something I know not and have interrupted the course, the destiny, of this incredible thing, this mysterious machine.

The Atlantic salmon is a haunting fish. It is a fish of theories, suspicions, and guesses seasoned with insecure knowledge. It is the subject of some of the loveliest books I know, as well as some of the most palpable nonsense.

Most salmon rivers in North America lie in areas of our most beautiful countryside. The rivers of the Canadian Gaspé thread in and around the Chic Choc mountains, rewarding you with at least a change of scenery if the salmon are their usual dour selves. And with the rivers go the traditional big canoes. For the most part they are locally made, the most famous being the Sharpe and the Miller. You'll find others, Chestnuts from Maine and an occasional Old Town, but just as many are nameless from anonymity or age. Typically they're at least 20 feet long, broad of beam, and as stable to cast from as a boat dock.

I don't know of any fishing that has so much consecrated tackle. Here you'll find (in my canoe as well) a goodly number of the old giant two-handed rods: The Paynes and Leonards and Sharpes and Hardys of 12 to 14 feet, beautifully balanced with the silver fittings of the almost lost Zwarg and Vom Hofe reels or the exquisite, contemporary Bogdan. Along the smaller rivers, or later in the season as the fishing turns mainly to dry flies, the 9-foot graphite and glass rods have made some inroads, but many anglers will end their days attuned to the powerful, sweet rhythms of a Garrison, Orvis, or whatever, as long as it is bamboo. Ah, tradition!

One of the greatest arts in the search for salmon is that of reading the water. Although it's possible to make a pretty good guess in a little river, it's almost impossible to be sure in a huge one. Since the salmon doesn't feed, his lies serve the functions of rest and security. Also, they change as the water drops or rises. An experienced guide is priceless.

Now the stage is set. Here you are on the awesome Matapedia, sitting in the bow of a 22-foot Sharpe. Carefully laid to one side is a net with a handle made of 1½ - or 2-inch pipe with a circumference that looks as if it could hoop a horse. It's a little scary to imagine a fish that calls for such an instrument. You have threaded the line through your rod, checked the knots on the leader—which ends in a tippet of 18-pound test—this is the middle of June, and in the back of your mind are many tales of 40 pounds and up, or three-hour battles with fish so big they never showed....

Here we are in the fly box. You stare at the battery of 2/0's, 2's, and the fragile-looking 4's: Durham Rangers, General Practitioners, Orange Blossoms, Green Highlanders, Thunder and Lightnings, Dusty Millers, Rusty Rats, and Silver Doctors. You wisely pass the box to the guide, who very carefully pulls out a Green Highlander, muttering "Dark day, dark fly." Most likely he'll want to tie it on himself and he'll use a knot you haven't seen and (if you're like me) will never learn. He'll ask you to put it in the water by him so he can watch it swim. If it's satisfactory, he'll show you where and tell you how he expects you to fish the first drop—first with a covering series of casts, then gradually extending line until you cover the whole section as if it were marked out on a grid.

Your guide follows each cast with his eye, looking for a slight disturbance that indicates a following fish or a roll. When one area has been covered to his satisfaction, he'll move the canoe and the whole coverage will begin again.

You know the salmon are in the river. Now and then you might see one leap high into the air, slapping the water like a plank. As you cast, wondering, as we always will, if maybe the Silver Doctor would have been a better choice, your mind will follow this fish from the ova that were dropped somewhere near where you are now, to the alvein, the parr, and the smoult that one became. You'll wonder at what moment, at what mysterious urging, it decided to leave the river and take to the sea. You'll see the fish on its transatlantic journey, and watch it grow from a mere few inches to the three- or four-year size of 30 pounds or more.

You'll imagine it sniffing up through the Bay de Chaleur, into the mouth of the Restigouche, pausing for a day or so at the great junction pools where the Matapedia joins in ... until, sure now, it turns upstream toward home.

The guide calls to you and points out a spot where he's just seen a fish roll. You check your leader for wind knots, tug the fly and run a hone over the point, then stand up and begin the false casting to lengthen the line. Then, in just the right spot, you drop the fly, quickly mend the line to get the drift right, and wait, your rod hand poised like a trigger ready to strike.

I like to remember a guide taking my wife's first salmon ashore, washing it and placing it back in the canoe in a bed of freshly picked ferns. When he'd gotten it all to his liking, he turned to her and said, by way of explanation, in case one was needed, "It's not just a fish ... *this is an Atlantic Salmon.*"

L O S T

One of my favorite sayings and beliefs is, "If you don't care where you are, you ain't lost." I have spent so much of my time either dead lost, confused, or, as it is sometimes more kindly put, just a little turned around, it's a wonder that the people I've hunted with haven't spent more time hunting for me than hunting.

Sure, I know all the tricks: landmarks, moss, looking backwards so you'll recognize what things will look like when you're coming back out; how to find North with a watch face, and so on. But they really don't help much.

I don't even like to remember how many times I've crossed what I *knew* to be the last ridge, the one with the funny-shaped rocks in the background, only to find out when I'd climbed over some sheer rock face that they'd moved the whole camp, horses and all, to a spot about five miles back.

I wish they'd quit going to all the trouble of shifting highways, making creeks run the wrong way, and hiding bridges just for the sake of making me nervous.

The whole trick is to be cool. Like the afternoon I spent on an absolutely unknown mountain mesa in Colorado in a dense fog. I didn't have the vaguest idea where I was or where the camp was, except that we were both in the same state. I *was* sure of that because I'd been walking in circles and hadn't veered off to Wyoming or New Mexico, Suddenly I saw one of the wranglers walking ahead of me in the timber. I broke into a little trot which not only got me up to him in a hurry but gave me a good excuse to be sweating. "Hi, Virgil," I said. "See anything?" Note that I did not throw my arms around him; tears of relief were somehow halted in their flow; my voice didn't crack; nor did I get down on my knees and give thanks for an answered prayer. I was cool.

The big worry here is that Virgil is going to say "Why don't we hunt back toward camp? You make a little swing left for about half an hour, then head kind of southwest and I'll meet you where the creek forks." No way I'm going to let Virgil out of my sight until I see the kitchen tent, because if I do I'm right back where I was a little while ago—lost.

"Waste of time, Virgil," I say, shortstopping any ideas he might have of our hunting the way back. "I've been all over this area with a fine-toothed comb ... climbed over to where the big poplars are, down to that meadow and around past the beaver pond and never saw a track," I tell him, knowing that there's always a big poplar stand, a meadow, and a beaver pond around somewhere and he won't be likely to ask me any hard questions. My immediate motto is, "Where goeth Virgil, so goeth I." And I do—right back to camp, which usually turns out to be an easy 20-minute walk—in the right direction. The way I'd been headed it would be about 24,000 miles.

Later that night when we discussed plans for the next day, I never blinked an eye when Virgil said, "No use to head over that way; Hilly's been clear down to the beaver pond, the big meadow, and where them heavy popples are." Heroes are made, not born.

The old mountain men were legends in large part for their ability to map a huge territory in their head and then draw near-perfect directions in the dirt for newcomers. Little good that would have done me, since I probably wouldn't have known where I was when the drawing was going on. I always hate the morning directions the guides give. They go on the order of "I'll just mosey over towards Hayfork Creek for a couple of hours and then cut around and meet you on the edge of that big stand of spruce. Now don't you cross over the south

branch of Cougar Brook—just make a big swing and stay this side."
And off he goes. An hour or so later you admit to yourself that you
don't know spruce from oak by now; that you've crossed what surely
must have been Cougar Brook about four times, and that the next
face you're likely to see is a rescue party … in about two days. The
urge to go straight into a screaming panic is overwhelming, but you've
got to stay cool, right? Wrong, but somehow you manage. And somehow—divine guidance is as good a reason as any—you find what
looks like spruce, and somehow the guide turns up—or at least he has
so far. (Here I knock on wood.)

Guides have a way of assuming that you've spent the past thirty
years, as they have, memorizing the local landscape of a state you've
never seen except from the window of an airliner. And I always neglect
to ask for directions specific enough to see me through, not wanting
to seem as hopeless as I really am. And there's always the ultimate
misunderstanding when the guide is following you under the assumption
that you've been here before and know where you are—and he hasn't
and doesn't. That happened to me once, hunting quail down in South
Carolina, and it is just starting to seem funny—after about six years.

I've lost people who were hunting with me in covers I knew like
the back of my hand. One of the worst cases was an airline pilot who
wore a wrist compass and carried another in his pocket. We were in
a really heavy mess of blowdowns, but only about 15 minutes from
the car. I told him to walk straight out until he came to an old dirt
road, then turn left, and he'd come right to where we left the car. He
checked his compasses, both of them, and I didn't find him for over
two hours. When I did, he was headed in the opposite direction. He
had some explanation for all this, but I never understood it. What I
did get out of it was a feeling that when I hunted with a man who
wore two compasses, I should not let him out of my sight.

Any feat of navigation leaves me in deep admiration. And I have
tried to get a handle on it, really, but it's just not my destiny to be a
homing pigeon. I have about as much understanding of how people
have sailed the seas with pierced gourds for star finders as I do of
anti-matter or black holes in space. Navigators have spent countless
hours explaining the science of chronometers, sextants, astrolabes,
and other arcane devices to me. I have actually plotted theoretical
courses and wrapped my mind around the complexities of drifts,
winds aloft, and magnetic deviations, yet when I'm in a mountain fog
or snow squall, I am odds-on to be looking for Virgil or his equivalent

a lot more seriously than I am trying to figure just how I got where I am....

I rather like the word "lost." We use it to indicate things past, things irrecoverable, and to portray a philosophical or temporary avoidance of the immediate—"lost in thought" or "lost in memory." So, no doubt, we have all been lost, happily, in a duck blind, drowsing on a deer stand, or idling away a little time in a high-country meadow reflecting on all the things men have always sought comfort in—from an idle musing on the shape of clouds to the tangents of life and circumstance.

In order to find ourselves, we now and then must get a little lost. As I've said, I do it fairly often, but never with more pleasure than in a sun-drenched haven in the mountains where I can still faintly hear the play of hobbled horses and, when the wind is just right, smell the smoke from the cook tent, small but visible, in the valley below.

THE TRAPSHOOTER'S
CODE

One of my neighbors was watching me on a Sunday morning load some shooting odds and ends into my van for a few hours of recreation at a local trap club.

"Going away for the fall?" he asked.

"No," I answered, "we're having a fifty-bird event at the club this morning."

"Well, I guess I don't know anything about trap shooting," he said, "but when I was a kid we'd hunt all year for ducks, geese, quail, partridge, and rails with the same gun. Shoot a deer with it too, come the season!"

Well, rather than take up too much of a know-it-all's time at that moment, it occurred to me that maybe I ought to write it all down for those of you who don't understand trap and, for those of you that do, to hand out to your neighbors when you start getting bombarded with silly questions.

Other than guns, which we'll come to in due time, there are several small inconsequential items of a personal nature that you need for safety, convenience, and comfort. Starting out at the top, you'll need a long-brimmed cap if you're shooting in the morning on a field that faces east, or in the PM on a field facing west. If the field is set in between, you'll need a short-billed cap, unless it's terribly cold, in which case you'll need a stocking cap or a ducking type with ear flaps. In summer you'll need a visor or sun shade. Best to always travel with an assortment. The trapshooter's code among the real veterans is: Leave nothing to chance; leave nothing at home.

The ears require exterior muffs or sound baffles. Some prefer the custom-fitted, moulded plugs, others, one or another of the plastic foam inserts now available. Sooner or later you'll end up with one or two of each kind, so you might as well start buying them all now. Another precept of the trapshooter's code is save yourself trouble later on.

A great deal more important than hearing, as all of us veteran trapshooters know, is to be able to see. Since it's very possible that your fellow shooters have been experimenting with anything from face powder to cornmeal in their reloads, you'll find that the air is occasionally a touch gritty, so you'll need a pair of lightly tinted, gray or tan glasses for when the visual conditions are otherwise perfect. And since light qualities are rarely perfect, you'll also need yellow glasses for dim light, green glasses for bright light, and vermillion glasses for light that is neither really bright nor really dark. You might as well get the whole bunch right now because you'll need them sooner or later. Trapshooters are very sensitive to light, unless it's neon and it's after dark. Also you might as well drop the extra buck or so for side blinders that fit over the side pieces. They don't help a lot, but Dan Bonillas wears them, so does everybody else—except for wealthy and very old shooters who use the top flaps off shell boxes.

You'll need shooting vests, so you have something on which to sew gun club patches, the name of your store, or witty remark emblems. You'll also need a place to pin on pins to show that this is definitely not your first day on the line. Vests have leather recoil pads on the outside and some sort of cushioning on the inside, which will always be too thick or too thin; this can't be helped. They also have pockets that shooters once used to carry shells in, until leather shell bags came along with compartments for new hulls and empties. You've probably already guessed that one vest simply will not do. You realize that we shoot in warm weather, hot weather, chilly weather, and very cold weather. We shoot in rain and wind. Obviously one vest won't get the job done. But before you settle on four or five basic ones, don't let it slip your mind that some gun clubs are fairly dressy, so you'll need a nifty-looking one, and others are very much vice versa— meaning that the membership looks as if they all spent the morning changing flats on a semi. Either way, the trapshooter's code holds that you are never too conspicuous.

Pants need to be purchased by category to parallel the vests, with but one or two exceptions: in summer the very young and very good shooters wear cut-off jeans, and the very old wear a versatile trouser that covers such other demands as milking and cleaning up cow residue. Pants are not really all that important beyond modesty, comfort, and the concealment of varicose veins and mismatched socks.

Shoes are something else. If you are a Westerner, you have little choice but pointy-toed cowboy boots, unless, again, you are young and sport an AA average—then you opt for gaudy running shoes and no socks. You will need different shoes for rain, snow, cold, and the relatively dressy club. You can buy an accessory pad that covers the shoe you would normally rest the gun barrel on, so the tops don't end up looking like someone had at them with a biscuit cutter; on the other hand they flap when you walk, and you may forget to change them from one pair to the next. Saving your money for the important things is part of the trapshooter's code.

Gloves are tricky. Naturally there are gloves designed to keep you hands warm, which come with a number of unsatisfactory exits for the trigger finger. More favorable are gloves which remind the opposition that you might, in another time and circumstance, have been a gun-fighter. If you wear just one glove, you can wear it on either hand; it makes little difference. I suggest you buy a pair of sleek black ones and find out which hand needs one, or whether you come off looking more sinister-looking with the pair. A regular golf glove will get the job done but looks a little effete. A bit of practice in front of a mirror will make the whole glove thing come off more forcefully.

Now that you have a few things, you'll need something to carry them in. Remember that a good deal of this stuff is always with you on the line—temperature changes, light modulations, shifts in wind direction, and the usual fluctuations in weather demand it. You'll see a wide variety of carriers, ranging from valises designed to hold a plumber's biggest Stillson wrenches, to posh shopping bags, and a variety in between. I take off my hat (my Red Fox Chewing Tobacco hat) to one shooter I saw using a roll-around wire basket like the ones you see in supermarkets, only a little smaller. Do not make the mistake of buying one too small; you'll regret it. The trapshooter's code holds accumulation in very high regard. If you've won one and it says so on the outside, by all means use it, even if it means you have to carry another one as well.

This short list includes just the basic, day-in, day-out necessities. Bedrock, so to speak. You'll encounter local customs and faddish variations, and your own personal tastes and needs will dictate certain plusses and minuses. Don't be afraid to experiment; part of the trapshooter's code is that if you don't try it, you'll never know.

As soon as I've polished up the details, we'll go on and cover other facets that interest the beginner or the curious: guns, stocks, chokes, beads, ribs, recoil pads, spare parts, day-to-day alterations, emergency alterations, devices to block out the off-eye, and devices to bring the off-eye into play—just to skim the surface and whet the appetite.

The day will come when you may, like one shooter I know, after breaking a 200 straight, go directly to a choke specialist and begin questioning him as to why you were taking tops off so many targets. Should the interior of the barrel be altered, or would just a touch of bending get it right where it belongs?

Remember, the trapshooter's code involves the basic philosophy, Never be satisfied!

ANNUAL REPORT (SUBMITTED IN A BYGONE YEAR)

It's time for the presentation of my Annual Report. (Sounds of muffled yawning and the restless adjustment of chairs.) Although I'd hoped for a better balance on the positive side, a few last-minute circumstances that I had not foreseen have affected the ledger. We might as well get those over with first.

One of the more costly items was incurred with the introduction of saltwater fly fishing and the necessity of obtaining a few items of equipment not already in stock. In self-defense, I must point out that I had mentioned this probability to the Chairman more than a year ago. Back then prices were a good deal lower, but she was determined to repair the furnace at a cost far above the sweater or two that might have seen us nicely through, and my chance for a wise investment of venture capital was, once again, lost. Management and I do not always agree on what constitutes forward thinking or what diverse uses our present stock of tackle ought to serve. However, you will be relieved to know that our inventory now covers the basic rods, reels, lines, and at least the foundation of necessary flies and assorted paraphernalia. I trust that you see the need for this—and that, in time, the Chairman will see her way to complete agreement.

Although I am not *always* in conflict with Management, I did go ahead and purchase a new 20-gauge Remington, rather than cut down one of the extra stocks for an old one, now that one of the younger members of the company has shown a decided interest in and some talent for skeet shooting. I'm not exactly sure how or when this will show a dividend. Only time will tell.

On the brighter side, we have again upped our production of Canada geese on the pond. Also, I am most pleased to announce the addition of at least two clutches of mallards and a handful of wood ducks. As for the ospreys, they are still with us, and I think I noted some new and tentative baritones singing with the great horned owls.

The pheasants held about even last year, but with our addition of a few acres of corn I believe that next year's census will show a decided gain. The Turkey Coop covey of quail were once more heard but not seen all through the summer, so I will mark them down as remaining on inventory with no change. The deer herd has continued to grow, necessitating some expense and a great deal of personal labor. This was supervised by the Chairman in person, and involved transferring the garden plot to what was once a portion of the front lawn. Since very little cash outlay was needed and the crop was all that could be expected, Management is pleased to the point at which we are no longer reminded that the move should have been made some years previously. (Hindsight and total recall are among the Management's stronger points.)

Several of the old apple trees were lost to a summer cyclone, but this assures us of a plentiful supply of my favorite kind of firewood. Somehow, the soft memories of our most pleasant journeys are made even more sweet in front of such a fragrant fire. The Chairman has been contemplating a new planting, but I hasten to remind you that the time to spray and prune apple trees falls, unfortunately, at the time when the early trout season peaks; or when the first flight birds are due. I may have to call for a show of hands on this at the next meeting, so please, the few of you that are keeping notes, bear this in mind.

The past season was all that I had hoped for—even a bit more, when it comes to our winter supply of ducks and geese in the freezer. To those of you who voiced skepticism at the purchase of two new Olt goose calls, I can produce witnesses (who had come to scoff) to testify that I managed on several occasions to bring birds in over the decoys. While I cannot, in the honesty you have come to expect from me, claim the same for the duck calls, I can point to the coming season with great optimism for improvement in this area.

Again our trap and skeet scores were not all that I had hoped for. I ask you to remember, with charity, the severity of our past winter and the trouble we have always experienced with crossing birds in high winds. No doubt a new single-barrel trap gun that has recently been introduced would go a long way to correct this, but I hesitate to approach the Chairman at this time; no personal sacrifice is too great in the effort to maintain harmony between labor and management. I further insist that the time spent moving the garden, when I might have benefited from a few practice rounds instead, not be part of the record. I am among the first to agree with the Chair that there is a great deal more to life than hunting and fishing, shooting trap and skeet, and messing around with bird dogs.

In light of Management's view on this topic, I will say that at the present time, we anticipate no major capital expenditure in this area, beyond the purchase of a case or so of factory ammunition for special occasions. I might add as another note of good news that two trap jackets, once considered lost, were found at the gun club on the closet floor, and the replacement money will be diverted, wisely, to a pair of the new vermillion shooting glasses. A sharp rise in average is expected immediately.

At the insistence of Management, a new category, "Carelessness," will be entered, but all expenses will remain personal. I am obliged to note that several pipes, a fly box, my good camouflage duck hat, and a pocketknife come under this heading, as do a few trifling losses at the poker table and a good-hearted wager or so on the outcome of a few rounds of trap and skeet. No rods were broken and the one missing reel is around somewhere. It will, no doubt, turn up.

I had every intention of ending this report with a demonstration of the double-haul and the showing of a few slides from a fishing trip. However, I entrusted the reel and the film to the Chairman, and she informs me that they were accidentally placed in another pocketbook and left at home. (Murmurs of approval mixed with scattered applause and sighs of relief.)

SOME OTHER TIME

In my small, but highly prized, collection of prints and paintings I have several showing idyllic settings in quail country. The landscape is soft, with knee-high grass punctuated by exclamation points of high-branched pines. In the background there is always a sun-washed cabin reeking of peace and tranquillity, or a tilted corncrib standing as a memorial to past and better times.

The sun is never in the gunners' eyes. The gunners' clothes are never torn, sweaty, or something to be ashamed of in public. On the contrary, the colors blend artfully, the twills and tweeds have known the touch of a tailor. Even though you can't see them, you know that the boot laces aren't a rat's nest of knots, and the trouser cuffs aren't held together with iron-on tape or crude stitching with heavy black thread. No one is wearing overalls.

The dogs are actually standing still—one locked to perfection on the covey and the others backing like statues. They aren't rib-sprung, burr-matted, or wild-eyed. Never do you see one peering around his shoulder to see what he might get away with, or one three feet off the ground snapping his teeth at the tail assembly of a flushing bird.

The guns are almost always side-by-sides; no friction tape on the stock and plenty of blueing still visible. We are left to see the fulfillment of this dream scene in our imagination: the gunners walk in very casually, the birds flush into just the right amount of sunlight and turn away from the heavy cover into the clearing as each gunner makes a perfect right and left. Two of the dogs are sent on and both make a perfect retrieve of two birds each—at the same time.

I absolutely love these paintings and never tire of gazing on these exquisite scenes, knowing full well that this is the only place I'll ever see anything like it. There is, of course, a great deal of reality in these works of art; only they don't all get together in the same place at the same time in real life.

Just for example, put yourself in the place of one of the gunners. In the background we have our thinly spaced pines, and you have just walked in to flush the birds. Sweat is running down your face, your hands are bloody and torn, your eyes are red and strained from searching every step for canebrake rattlers; and every time you raise your gun, the rip in the back of your jacket opens up another inch or two disturbing what little concentration you can still muster. Now that the birds are in the air, which one do you take first? If you chose the one in the left center that's just about to cut behind the tree, you've been reading my mind. Now swing back for the second barrel to the quail that's right in the middle...except that by now he's swung behind the other tree on the right and you've joined me in another of our famous doubles on jack pine. This is especially guaranteed to delight your host who has been saving this log cabin covey to welcome you in the nicest way he could.

What possesses a man who can get all the way around to low 5 on the skeet field without a miss, to stand here like a stone elk on a B.P.O.E. lodge lawn and fling 818 No. 8 shot into the small patches of air that scarcely separate fourteen quail? There are, of course, many good reasons, but one that's a gold-seal guarantee is to be behind a pair of perfectly superb pointers with a guide who is known to regularly pick up twenty-three birds or better from a box of shells using a wired-together shotgun that you wouldn't turn into a lamp, while remembering that you spent the better part of the night before rather modestly bragging about your natural-born gifts with a shotgun.

In the bull ring they call this "the moment of truth." Here in this sun-dappled arena I, too often, have justly deserved being gored by a cock quail.

Usually this scene is followed by a moment of silence, the hollow, mocking ring of two fresh shells being dropped into your double, a kind, soft voice telling Rip and Lady to go on, and then that same voice launching into a tale (that you know he just made up) about how he once had a whole day just like that—where the weather and light were perfect, the dogs impeccable, and it took him almost a whole day, a dozen coveys, and nigh on to a box of shells before he could get the hang of it.

This revelation, topped off with an exchange of Red Man or Beechnut, helps to settle you down and then he says that Lady's found a single. Back in the spotlight you make a magnificent hard left on a driving bird and it drops in the little clearing where the old cabin garden used to be. You shift your chew very casually and thank him for his kind words. You realize as Lady drops the bird in your hand, that the first covey business could have happened to anyone, and that this single was absolute proof that your born destiny was to gun quail.

As this becomes an ideal day, you suddenly stop listening for the clicking of rattlers, your ripping coat decides that enough is enough, and now and then a bird flies on this side of a pine tree and not the other. It's just breezy enough to keep Rip and Lady busy, but not too windy to make the quail hawk-shy. A small, light cloud comes between you and the sun and so silhouettes a pair of birds that a perfect double fells. There is, as we would fully expect, the occasional miss that could happen to anyone. But there's still a comfortable heft to what's left of the box of shells you had in your pocket to start with when your guide tells you to be extra careful and not take but one more pair, and then a single, so you won't be over your limit.

Along about dusk, when your thoughts sort of drift to bourbon and branch, collard greens, cornbread, pan-roasted birds, milk gravy, and some sweet potato pie, you might be fortunate enough to come back by way of the old garden plot again. You stand there for a minute imagining what the cabin must have been like when it was new. You see a long-ago young man and his wife resting on the porch from the evening garden chores…listening then, as you are now, to the evening song of this small brown bird. Rip and Lady stop and listen too, asking a question with their eyes. Your friend smiles and very softly says it for all of you, "Some other time…some other time."

DUCK HUNTERS' WIVES

When the time comes for a young duck hunter to pick a wife he becomes deeply troubled. It's like a man with his first bird dog; he's not really sure what he expects it to do. He's not really sure what he wants himself.

When you choose a dog, you look at the females in its ancestry. The ladies are where the class will show over the long haul. And when the young man looks for a wife he should exercise the same intelligence. Pretty often it happens that the swain will not have the imagination or sense to believe that he can get good looks and function in the same package. It's been my experience, philosophically speaking, of course, that good-looking girls work as hard as any and are just as easy to train. Neither does the young man realize that a girl who might not qualify for movie stardom or a magazine cover may very well end up as one of those exquisitely handsome ladies in the age group of, let's say, forty and over.

But remember, if you will, it wasn't all that long ago when a suitor was shown (to a modest degree) what sort of stuff his fancied was made of. Daughters were exhibited at various functions, and the young man who'd had his eye on Martha since fourth grade could keep track of her accomplishments right up until the time he or some other lucky fellow asked for her hand.

A girl of six or seven already knew the basics of simple sewing and cookie making, took care of some chickens, and had a row or two of the vegetable garden to herself. As she grew older she would appear at school dances in dresses that were stitched by her own hand; she carried in a three-layer cake that she made herself for the refreshment table; and it was not too unlikely that her permitted drop or two of perfume was blended from one of those closely guarded old family recipes.

In her late teens she would have hand-raised a calf to exhibit at the local fair or 4-H show, was a better than average horsewoman, an excellent amateur veterinarian and could, if no one outside of her immediate family was watching, use a hay fork and split wood with amazingly accomplished skill.

The young man would be selected by some mysterious process of which he would usually remain unaware—an aunt at a church social would spy him, another cousin would remark at his promise, and so it would go until the invisible web brought him to Martha's home for Sunday dinner. In those days dinner was served sharply at 12 noon, and it was both festive and ceremonial. The invitation was really, as everyone knew, to give Martha a chance to parade some of her accomplishments and her family to touch lightly or not too lightly on others.

Chances are that Martha's marvelous complexion came from getting up at 5:30 or 6 in the morning, chopping some kindling for the kitchen stove, taking care of the chickens, making breakfast, cleaning the kitchen, putting some bread out to rise, and then walking the two miles to church—arriving slightly before 8 o'clock to familiarize herself with the hymn selection; her soft, sweet voice being one of the leading attractions of the church service.

Dinner was one of those multiple-course affairs that are for the most part seen only in old photographs. Some of the basic standbys, the season of the year permitting, were turkey or chicken, pearl onions, turnips, mashed potatoes, and homemade bread and rolls. Nobody took any credit for preparing basic fare; it was the little embellishments, like the fine engraving on a shotgun, that the suitor's attention was drawn to: special secret-recipe relishes, succulent jams and jellies, exotic pickles; if any of these had won prizes at fairs, this was mentioned over Martha's blushing protests. Later, her fine hand was detected in the dessert area: divinity, marzipan, éclairs, cream puffs of such delicately layered pastry as to defy imitation or sufficient praise, cinnamon apple pies that scented the whole house and made it officially Sunday…and the list went on and on and on.

After dinner, Martha might (you could bet on it) be prevailed on to sing, play the piano, or both. Then the women went about their leisure-time activities—dishes and then crocheting, knitting, tatting, or whatever they fancied. The men gathered to smoke or chew tobacco and talk—and the talk would circle once around the farm affairs, then head toward gunning. Dogs were recalled from their graves, retrieves were made over and over again, in annually worsening weather. The legendary shots were exhumed and, although it wasn't often necessary, their daily bags were enlarged by a few brace and the always-remembered long shot was again witnessed. First-hand or fifth, it really didn't matter.

Details were lovingly argued over: Audubon Ducking Powder versus Laflin and Rand Orange. Hard shot versus drop. And then finally, the unsolvable, the never-ending dispute or debate over O's and BB's for geese versus 2's or 3's. What a pleasant way to spend a Sunday.

Martha and her young man were allowed to walk together and chat about the things such people always chatted about; in code of course, the small talk of lovers that meant something else to both. "How do you feel about duck hunting?" he would ask, meaning "Are you willing to get up all season at 3 A.M., make breakfast, pack my lunch, and pick what I bring home and be joyous about it, and understand why I love it so?" And she would answer "I think a man ought to get out away from work whenever he can," meaning "My father and brothers are gunners, and I wouldn't even consider a man who didn't enjoy something I was brought up to appreciate."

So, after a decent interval, the cycle began again, Martha and her husband bringing forth another generation of duck hunters and duck hunters' wives.

But society changed and the softness of those old days has gone to rest in our memories, coming to life every so often when someone mentions better times. It's not that the Duck Hunter's Wife has disappeared into the realm of endangered species, it's just that so many of them changed habitat and lifestyles for so long that some of the basic instincts have become dormant. In reality, the dream of being a duck hunter's wife is the ambition, however subliminal it may be, in hundreds of thousands of our finest ladies. Unfortunately, nature has a strange and unpredictable way of balancing these things out. For a while when there were quite a few male duck hunters, the young women who ought to have been yearning to spokeshave a decoy or sculling oar all wanted to become airplane pilots, neurosurgeons, or corporation presidents. This was a pity, since these professions are already overstaffed and a young woman ought to aspire to higher things. Now, when the rise of the national urge to fill in all the swamps, tidelands, and marshes to create shopping malls has contributed heavily to the decline of the male duck hunter, women are clamoring to return to the lifestyle of their forepersons.

However, there is a trend back both ways. Virtually all the available land for shopping centers has been filled (hopefully) and we have been left a little room for both duck and duck hunter to co-exist, and both have been noted to be on a population upswing. So those would-be Duck Hunters' Wives are going to be able to realize most of their fondest dreams.

But just where do we start? The society that spawned them by the thousands has nearly gone. The duck-hunting mothers and fathers and brothers have diminished to the point of being conversation pieces in many parts of the country.

No doubt it would be hopeful if our school systems added duck calling to their music curriculum and the coloration of widgeons and gadwalls could be studied in art classes. The differences between a Harry Shourdes and an Elmer Crowell decoy could be taught and early math might wisely include the calculation of shot patterns, lead, and velocity.

What a marvelous world it would be if a young bride could adjust a double-reed call to perfection and was familiar with the pros and cons of choke boring and forcing cones as well as being able to recite houses and vintages of the preferable red wines.

Who among us would not sing out in joy to read in the local paper that "the bride was exquisitely veiled in camouflage and her bouquet was borne by Misty, her black Labrador retriever..." I guess I'm just a sentimental old fool, but the thought of heart-shaped decoy anchors and a honeymoon blind makes me wish I were only twenty again.

LETTER TO AN ANGLER

My Fishing Friend:

I expect this to be your first summer of real fishing, so I am going to give you a good rod and reel to learn with. I don't believe you'll catch as many fish as you did last year in the pond with your worms, but I think it's time to find out what sort of fisherman I believe you really are.

I've always liked your attitude. You've been patient, persevering, anxious to learn, and just plain fun to be with. You never kept more fish than you should have and never complained when we didn't take any. I've often been proud of what you've done when you didn't think anyone was watching—I think you're a fine sportsman and I treasure the time you share with me.

But now we're going to go further; you might say take the first steps of a long journey that will really have no end. We are going to learn about the hidden corners of the woods where the Lady Slipper grows. We will watch the ones that must fish to live—like the osprey and the otter. We will learn the names and songs of the birds and some interesting things about trees and berries and snakes and thunderstorms—we are going to go from fishing to being a fisherman.

We are going to discover, hopefully, which parts of the water fish are in and which parts they are not—and why. We will learn the complicated structure of lakes and bays and flats and tides. We will learn what the surface of a brook or river can tell us about the middle and bottom. These are some of the things a fisherman should know...this will be the knowledge and the lore that lets you *see* where others merely look.

I think you'll find it exciting to become part of a world where a slight change in temperature or a shift of wind or a different light can alter everything around. In time you can come to see as the fish sees and feel as they feel. A stone to you will be a vital thing; creating a resting place here, a feeding area there. A log will come to mean a cooling shadow or a place to hide.

Questions will beget more questions and answers will grow weak and changing, and lead to further discoveries and theories and—now and then—knowledge.

We will learn the mechanics of our tools. The matching of rods and lines and lures. Knots and splices and why some work with certain things and not with others. How to take care of lures, sharpen hooks, clean reels, patch boots, hone knives and, no doubt, how to build a quick fire to dry ourselves out when we've made a mistake or been careless or just unlucky. You might even learn how to swear a little—but don't let on where you picked it up.

Now if all this is beginning to sound as attractive as algebra, I apologize. There are already too many fishermen who seem to have forgotten that the whole idea is to have fun. They might be masters but somehow they have put the cart before the horse. Fishing is a part of living for us and if we don't make a lot of mistakes and do our share of foolish and hard-headed things we won't have the humility to tell ourselves and who ever else is around that we were wrong or just dumb. It'll be the rare day when we do about half the things right— the trick to it all, life or fishing, is not to be ashamed of errors, but to learn to laugh at ourselves and maybe learn something in the process.

You see, with you and me, we're the ones keeping score, we're the ones making our own rules about pride and honor and self-respect. And if we come out caring about the right things—having the right attitude, then we've caught what we've really set out to take home. I don't know anybody who has fished or hunted that hasn't done something every so often that he's ashamed of later on, but the trick is to not do them again and not forget that we weren't meant to be perfect.

All of us go through the "how big" and "how many" stage of fishing. I still do, as a point of interest or curiosity, but I've been around long enough to know that there isn't too much I can do to have the 3-pounder hit my plug or fly when the one that hit yours was only 2½. And I know that there will be plenty of days when you just plain outfish me. That's alright too. There's nothing wrong with you outfiguring me and taking few details into account that I was too lazy or careless to figure out.

All men being created equal is a fine philosophy for a politician, but most fish know better. You'll learn that no matter how good you get you're pretty likely to meet a man that can shave you. But the point of all this is that 99 percent of the time we're not in any kind of competition except the most friendly. Competition fishing always seemed a little off-base to me anyway, and I expect we'll talk abut that some other time.

I'm also afraid that you might pick up some of my bad habits (I don't count chewing tobacco and swearing, but some people do). As you already know I have very little resistance to picking up a new rod or reel or a handful of flies or a new plug or spoon or what have you. I admit that this is a little weakness. And I admit that I'm not getting any kind of real control over it. Maybe I had too little as a kid and I'm trying to make up for it and maybe I just love fine things and maybe it's that and some other reasons. Maybe I'm still enough of a kid to want to try out something brand-new that nobody else has ever had his hands on. But you'll have to cope with that all by yourself. I'll advise but I won't vote. I will say that I've found out that there are precious few bargains in the world, and that good stuff is a joy and a lot of bad stuff is tempting and you might as well resign yourself that you're going to make mistakes but I hope not too many. A knife that won't hold an edge is dangerous junk. A reel that won't run smooth is going to cost you fish and a rod that won't cast makes you use all those words you shouldn't. I've got a collection that keeps me from feeling too smart. I used to call them trade goods but nobody who knows me will trade!

Anyway, we're about to start out. I hope what we learn we can put to good use in our everyday life and I suspect we can. I believe that a man who can get some kind of a handle on when to persuade, to coax, to challenge and even threaten, can use it in more places than fishing. I believe that a man who learns to respect the privacy of a bird's nest or a muskrat burrow and thinks to plant a willow where it will do some good might act the same way around people.

And when you meet a man who might intimidate you, stop and think—before you get scared—about all the things you know that he doesn't: about how you can whistle up an oriole; point out Orion and the Pleiades; tell a fox track from a dog; tie a fly from sweater yarn; curve a cast into the wind and predict rain; that given a knife and a hook and a piece of string you could get along just about anywhere. Remember the storms and the rivers you've shoved against and you'll have a pretty good idea of who you are; that you've been a man where and when it really mattered. These are some of the things I'm trying to give you with this fishing rod.

I might as well confess to you now that there are a lot of these things I don't know to well myself and I thought you'd be just the right person to learn them with. I hope that someday you'll pass them on. It's not enough that we move rocks to create pools and plant trees for shade to preserve our fishing—we have to build the right kind of fishermen, too.

WATERFOWLING

Over the last few years we've all been put to the task of answering questions about our pastime of gunning. Since we are more or less on the defensive, it would benefit us as a group to work toward a standardization of answers. Such a mass, or unified, response would only add to our solidarity—as well as reinforcing the high moral level of our sporting attitudes. To this end I have made a general list of questions and answers that closely reflect those I have encountered in my travels and I offer them to you to use as you see fit and as they apply to your own circumstances.

Q: *Why do you get up at 4 a.m. to go duck hunting?*
A: Mainly to have breakfast with my pals in a diner. The food is good, the waitresses don't wander around in soiled wrappers with their hair up in plastic rollers and we can put our cigarettes out in the saucers.
Q: *Do you really get a kick out of it?*

A: Most of us used to back in the days when we all shot pump guns. Now most of us have switched over to autoloaders. I've even gone to using a Pachmayr Triple Magnum pad and a recoil reducer in my 3-inch magnum and it really helps.

Q: *What about the poor ducks?*

A: Actually, today there aren't any poor ducks anymore. Most waterfowl have extensive land holdings in Canada, and the U.S. Government has been setting aside homesites here in this country. Plenty of food, housing, and recreation facilities are open to any that want to look them up. The mallard *is* a bit of a spendthrift—they tend to carry on with several females at a time and that's expensive as we all know. The pintail and teal do go a little overboard on travel, but by and large they're all doing handsomely.

Q: *I don't see how you can justify it at all!*

A: Neither do I. Last year I spent weeks working for two different DU committees, at my own expense. I spent over eighty dollars in out-of-state licenses and more than I want to even think about in motels, restaurants, sporting-goods stores, and travel expenses. One friend, who's an accountant, gave up keeping a record when he discovered that various DU functions and sportsman's dinners and that sort of thing cost him over forty-five dollars in Tums and Rolaids alone.

Q: *I don't mean that—I mean the shooting.*

A: There are lots of theories. Some of us believe in the Churchill theory of "automatic lead." That's where you just look at the bird and as you follow it with your eyes the gun will automatically work out the right lead. Others sort of spot-shoot—they pick a place where the bird will be and go right there. But I'd say the majority swear by the swing-through method. That's when you come up behind the bird, swing through to establish your lead, and then touch it off. A few use what they call a sustained lead. You start your gun out ahead of the duck and keep it there. I can do that on skeet targets but not in the field.

Q: *You're just giving me smart answers.*

A: Well, I've given it a lot of thought. But actually there's a whole other side that you ought to take into consideration. Like heavy loads versus light loads, shot sizes and pellet hardness. Whether you prefer a full choke or something a little more open. I'd be glad to explain my theories on choke boring if you'd like, but it would help if you read Brister and Oberfell & Thompson first.

Q: *How do you explain all this to your children?*

A: The hard thing to explain to children is to start out with both eyes open so they get in the habit of using binocular vision; they all tend to squint or close one eye.

Q: *I mean what do they feel about you bringing dead ducks home?*

A: The older ones hope I'll give them a glass of red wine. The younger ones like them breasted out and pan broiled in a little butter. I do that more with geese but in general I don't think anything is better than a whole roasted bird if they haven't been into eel grass or sea cabbage; then we have to marinate them overnight.

Q: *How can you treat hunting as if it were a calling?*

A: Calling is something else entirely. With ducks, for example, it depends a lot on local custom. Mike McLemore, he's the four-time national champion, likes the Arkansas type—they've got a nice tone and a good range and for all around they can't be beat. But you get out in the midwest—Iowa for example—you want something a bit louder. I take a couple of calls at least. One I like just for the highball or come-back call, and the other has a great reed for the feeding chuckle and the lonesome hen.

Calling is a real art and you've got to work at it constantly to be any good. You'd be surprised at the discussions over plastic reeds versus brass—even the type of wood and the shape of the barrel. I can listen to a good duck caller for hours—if you ever have the time I can bring out my tapes and records. And there's almost the same controversy over goose calling. Here I go along with the majority and stick with the Olt—a nice tone, easy to tune and easy to work. You'd be surprised at the goose callers who don't know the little feeding noise, though; it helps a lot when they're just on the edge and can't make up their mind. (Here I'm always glad to demonstrate as it often changes the direction of the conversation to something other than gunning.)

Q: *Does your wife agree with you on all this?*

A: For the most part, yes. But we still have a problem with the sandwiches. She tends—I guess most women do for some reason—to put tomatoes on the rolls which makes them too soggy for my taste. And now and then she'll get my stuff mixed up with the school lunches and I end up with peanut butter and jelly which does a number on my calling. She also will forget and shrinks my good long underwear every so often. But she can dry-pick a mallard with the best of them and I'll match her roast black duck with anything in the world.

Q: *Does she like all those guns around the house?*

A: She doesn't basically mind, but I object to your use of the word all, especially when she might overhear you.

Q: *She doesn't think they're horrid?*

A: She *knows* one is horrid. That's the one with about 4 inches of drop and kicks like a hammer. I really don't know whether to get it restocked and hang on to it or trade it off for something else. The problem is that it's bored just right for an ounce and a half of heavy 2's—just the ticket for long passing shots. But she's after me to get one of those new Ruger 20-bores with a 3-inch chamber so she can use it over the decoys. All in all it's a problem, but we've worked these things out before and no doubt we can get some sort of agreement.

Q: *She must lead a dog's life.*

A: She says she wishes she did. Just joking, of course. But she's been known to remark that I think more of Rocky than I do of her. That's ridiculous, obviously. But, then again, Rocky is one in a million. She's probably still a little upset that I took one of the old chairs from the living room and put it in the kennel because he always likes to sit in it and we had plenty of stuff in the house anyway.

Q: *Don't you think we need better gun control?*

A: I certainly do. One of the biggest problems is that too many think it's in the left hand—if they're a right-handed shooter. Actually, the best shots use their right hand; the one that really holds the stock. That's was Fred Etchen's whole purpose in inventing the Etchen Grip. It gives you better trigger control, cuts down on flinching and helps keep the comb up where it belongs. You'll find a lot of argument on this particular point, but that's my belief and I'll stick to it.

Q: *What about the criminal use of guns?*

A: I've certainly seen a lot of that. One of the worst examples is a friend of mine from Texas who hunts ducks with a fully engraved, side-lock Woodward. He's going to ruin it and it'll serve him right. Some others that come to mind are putting swivels in the stock and shortening the barrels where they lose all the choke. I've seen a lot of bad engraving too, but I'll admit that's often a matter of taste.

Q: *Don't you ever feel sorry or have any regrets?*

A: Constantly. There was a Model 21 Winchester bored improved-modified and full, ventilated rib and factory engraving, that I could have picked up for less than a thousand. Gorgeous piece of wood, too. And a Lem Ward pintail drake comes to mind a lot.

Q: *I mean about the shooting.*

A: You have to be philosophical. Some days you're on and some days it's all pick and shovel. I know I don't shoot enough trap, for instance; last year I didn't register more than 2,000 16-yard targets. My skeet isn't all it ought to be either. Station 3 high house has me about licked. But on the whole I'd say I'm doing better than average.

Q: *What about all the blood?*

A: I'm not a medical man, but offhand I'd say that a beef steer has more of it than a teal or a widgeon. If you're talking about personal taste I prefer the well done side.

Q: *You're not very broad-minded, are you?*

A: Not at all. Like most of my hunting friends I'm happily married.

Q: *Don't you ever think that what you're doing is basically wrong?*

A: It often is. But mostly it's raising my head off the stock. Late at night I often consider going to a 1¼-inch Monte Carlo with about a ¼-inch more pull.

Q: *You and I will never see eye to eye, will we?*

A: I've been noticing that, and I think your problem is that you have a dominant left eye, whereas my right eye is the master. That's fine, if you're left-handed, otherwise you'll tend to cross-fire a lot.

Q: *You think I'm one of those "do-gooders," don't you?*

A: Definitely not. Unless I'm grossly mistaken you've never bought a duck stamp, spent a minute working for conservation, or even given a thought to where all the dollars for wildlife come from. You know nothing about nor care for nesting areas, habitat, or food sources. You spend two dollars for a bumper sticker about braking for animals, while I spend hundreds and am nearly broke...

As you can see this is general, but we do get a look at the most common remarks suffered by waterfowlers in non-segregated groups. I offer the answers as guidelines only, personal attitudes and special conditions will always require specific remedies. I only ask, as I've tried to show you here, that you be patient, helpful, and courteous. If they're true animal lovers and you have a 90-pound retriever who likes to jump up on people, you're lucky; introduce them.

Above all, have a good time. Remember that you're right and they're wrong. And if you've been married as long as I have there's a corner of the ring that you haven't been in for a long, long time. Enjoy yourself—it's still four months or so until opening day.

THE UNSEEN EGG

I started mulling over the old saying that "A chicken is an egg's method of reproducing more eggs." This sort of semi-distorted philosophy has always had a great appeal for me because of its splendid blend of truth and humor. It follows then that we can see the bite in an observation I overheard at a huge trapshoot a year or so ago to the effect that, "The biggest reason a lot of these people shoot trap is to collect the empties." We have to agree, being honest with ourselves, that a lot of people we see plugging and spinning are doing so to give themselves a decent interval until they can run up the big 50 and throw a roostertail and a heavy wave over their lesser brethren with only 25's or just plain oars.

There are hordes of fly fishermen who prefer to collect fine rods but never risk one of them to dampness, some who collect flies, and some who just like to tie them. Others are so deep into streamside entomology that they spend little time casting because they can't decide *exactly* what to use. We can't say that none of them are fine fishermen, but neither can we say that all of them are fishermen in the sense of really catching fish.

I admit to the possibility of embarassing myself in having to give you an honest inventory of the stuff I lugged along to a three-day trapshoot. And I further admit that I'm not getting any better with experience. My Great Solution to the whole problem was to buy a van; not exactly the practical, "beware the man with one gun" attitude, but when you're not very good you at least try to look as if you might be.

We all know those duck hunters who only get deeply involved with the decoys; others who hit the deck at 3 A.M. so they can fool around with a retriever. An ever growing crowd are the calling experts, and there's still the hard core of boat nuts who have a harder time settling down to just one than a skeet shooter does in picking out a hat.

And how about the legion of gun dog owners who hardly ever gun? All they want to do is handle the dogs—which is just fine by me as long as I get to do the shooting…and they're not all that fussy about my not being related to Annie Oakley in any way whatsoever.

Still, I'm always a little surprised, but not critical, of the trapshooters and skeet shooters who don't hunt, the fly collectors who don't fish, the decoy merchants who have never set foot in a blind, and the field trial people who have never really gunned in the wild. The list could be longer and potentially embarrassing to some perfectly fine people, and that would be pointless. All of us have decoys that we won't use, guns we won't shoot, plugs we won't cast, and so on.

I'm probably wrong again, but I don't know of a passion for collecting old tennis rackets, or old skis (no doubt there's even a magazine devoted to such pursuits). The field sports have a deeper hold on us when it comes to memorabilia or finding a corner where one can still be "sporting" and yet be doing something different than most of the crowd.

Being a low-average in most of my own endeavors, I'd be laughed at, rightly, if I was suspected of collecting goose calls, trout and salmon flies, and bamboo rods. But in fact, I do—to a small extent. The real collector might say, with some heavy justification, "Hell, he's not a collector, he's just a guy who never throws anything away."

I'd rather, by a lot, have an old Herb Parsons call that I could blow, but I'd rather have one and not be able to blow it than not have one at all. I'm sentimental where I'd rather be competent, and appreciative where I long to be skilled.

Could be that some of this is part superstition—believing, yet knowing better, that by having something that's a work of art, I might rise above myself, even for an instant, and be equal to my instrument. Who among us hasn't thought, at least for a fleeting moment, that Dan Bonillas' trap gun would improve his scores? Or that a Gillum or Garrison rod would have strangers on the stream watching his casting with awe?

It's human nature, if hunters and fishermen can be called human, to admire the tool, not the artist, to a disproportionate degree. You attend a fishing gathering where Lefty Kreh is throwing 90 feet of fly line with a cocktail stirrer and we all gather around to admire the stirrer. We watch Chip Youngblood run 10 million straight wearing a hat with a hole in it and we all go out and cut holes in our hats. The advertising people know this, you and I know this—but they get rich on it and we foot the bill.

The point of this is that we are all a little bit odd, compared to the followers of lawn bowling, curling, horseshoes, badminton, or the like.

I don't, offhand, know of any sports that have such a volume of literature—adventure stories, how-to, diaries, and so on—as hunting and fishing. And, thank goodness, it's growing all the time—both in quantity and quality.

Why? Are there that many hunters and fishermen? No, there aren't. A rough estimate would be about 16 million licensed hunters and about four times that many fishermen. I think the reason is that we who hunt and fish have an involvement, a passion, an anthropological twitch that won't let us rest unless we can dust a decoy, clean a gun, play with a dog, sort flies, tune reels, read stories, or look at pictures that involve us in some way with the out-of-doors.

I half-suspect that some smoldering instinct left over from an Asian or African cave-dwelling cousin is the reason. No matter how unnecessary such skills and knowledge are for our modern survival, some chromosome or gene is making sure that, if the need ever be, we could make some sort of attempt for food and shelter...keeping us "in touch," as it were.

I think that all of us have certain days when we actually feel as wild as an animal ourselves. The cold northern winds of early winter can peel away centuries of civilization from my mind and, at time, I experience an eerie physical energy, a sharpening of senses I didn't realize I ever had—I believe that I can actually smell game, or sense a flavoring in the air that's pungent with the promise of something about to happen—the strike of a fish or the coming of a flight of birds. I know that for a little while I can walk like an animal, think like an animal, because some ghost in me has awakened and brought the animal in me alive.

I think this is the same ghost that so subtly haunts the gun collector who doesn't shoot, fly collectors who don't fish, and our other gatherers of odds and ends who appreciate function, design, and ingenuity beyond the intent of the maker. For example, who would float a Ward brothers black duck in his working stool, stick a Mason curlew in the sand, or throw a Childers tied by Megan Boyd to a salmon? Yet that's precisely what they were made for.

As things—artifacts—surpass function, we realize that we are living in a time of indulgence; we can afford not to use them and move on to the level of pure appreciation. Civilization has given us that option. Yet we know what these things were created for—to lure the bird so that we might take it; to entice the salmon to our plate.

Still we surround ourselves with our custom knives, flintlocks, paintings, wooden reels, whittled plugs, derringers, and libraries about an Africa that will never be again. Why? Something inside us keeps reproducing itself—some instinct keeps some tiny spark alive against the day when we might need that very special kind of fire.

Is the hunter the way this unknown "urge" chooses to keep itself alive? Are we the chicken to this unseen egg?

I WISH I HAD

As a forgetful, careless, negligent, disorderly, and slovenly daydreamer (your average irresponsible adult male sportsman) one of my living codes has become *I wish I had:* not forgotten to bring my wader patching kit…not been so stubborn as to have refused to try what the guide said was a sure-killing fly…checked the screws on my scope mount…remembered that where I was going was about 40 degrees even though the room I was packing in was about 94 degrees…called ahead to find out if 28-gauge 9's were sold in the area where I was going to hunt woodcock…checked to see if I had set the alarm clock…bothered to tie on a new tippet after landing two fish on the old one…looked behind me to see where my backcast was going…checked the fly after I heard it tick on a rock…not tried to get one more weekend out of my old rain parka when I had a perfectly good one I could have taken…checked the batteries in my flashlight…bought handwarmer fluid the day before…remembered what Texas chili does to my insides…only had "one for the road"…not counted on Jim to bring Rolaids…

Listened to Marcia when she said "It might get colder than you think"...listened to Marcia when she said "It wouldn't hurt to bring a necktie"...listened to Marcia when she said "That road doesn't look like it really goes anywhere"...remembered to bring an extra goose call in case one froze...the vaguest idea where I put my takedown Heddon plug rod...bothered to mark what line size is on my System 8 reel...not bragged the night before about what a helluva trap shot I used to be...not bragged the night before about what a helluva duck shot I was...not bragged the night before about my retriever...not insisted I could wade back when the guide offered to bring the canoe over to get me...paid a lot more attention to where the guide said he'd meet me at noon...paid a lot more attention to where the tent was when I left in the morning...gone to the dentist before going on my trip to Labrador...

Remembered that the last time I tried to jump a barbed wire fence I was 20 years younger...marked my .270 cartridges so I'd know which were 150-grain and which were not...used some restraint when it came to mail order catalogs...bought trap loads by the case when they were half what they are now...bought that 20-gauge hammer gun for $250...not sold my Winchester 21 for $450...not traded off all my Model 12's but one...some vague idea where I put two dozen No. 1½ traps...listened to Marcia when she said "Why don't you stop here and ask where the road is?"...listened to Marcia when she said "An extra sweater won't take up that much room"...remembered to let Josephine run a little longer before I locked her up in the car...enough sense to make reservations before the absolutely last minute...not insisted on always saying "Oh, don't worry about a map, I'll find it"...remembered that a lot of places don't carry nonresident licenses...remembered that guides won't test a landing net until it breaks with a fish in it...not been so stubborn about using a wading staff...called ahead to find out what the water was like before I drove 600 miles...remembered to sharpen my hooks and test the leader knots...checked to see if I had really put film in the camera...remembered that Canadian beer bottles don't have twist-off caps...

Listened when they said "When you see something you really like, buy two, because when you want another one they'll have quit making it"...kept a list of who I lend books to...learned to tie flies...learned to write down telephone numbers...asked the farmer about bulls in the pasture...asked the guide about where was the best place to cross the river...remembered to turn the light on before I tried to walk around three Labradors in the dark...remembered that there are four different hands that can beat a full house...bought more decoys when they were asking $5 for "old ones"...learned how to really sharpen a knife...taped an extra set of car keys behind the license plate...never bragged about what a helluva dove shot I am...bought more bamboo rods when they were less than the price of a good used car...not traded my 28-gauge Model 12 for something I'm still too ashamed to mention...enough sense to tie my fly boxes to my fishing vest...the brains to stick with one trap gun...not traded my 3-inch magnum 1100...bought more good wildlife art...

THE COMMON sense to stick with one method of shooting skeet instead of fooling around with three or four...not told the guide that poling a canoe didn't look all that hard...the ability to wear a cowboy hat and not feel silly...the knack of handling a horse...some idea that someday I'll have the ideal trap gun and never, ever, want to change again...my old bamboo casting rod and my box of wooden plugs...some way to make the little brook that I grew up in seem as mysterious and sweet as it used to long ago...a picture of a brown dog that was once as important to me as life itself...some way of recalling exactly how my grandfather sounded when he laughed...some idea of why the myrtle and violets don't smell the way they used to...an Indian moccassin growing in my yard...about one tenth the excitement I used to have at just the very idea of going fishing through the ice for pickerel...the eye for identifying more than two or three wildflowers...the ear for picking out bird songs that go beyond *bob-white*, *quack*, or *honk*...the trick to the feeding chuckle on a mallard call...a good Model 97 Winchester with a 30-inch barrel bored full—like the one my father used to shoot...the 3-inch magnum Model 12 I traded...two months to just putter around in Texas...a stomach that could handle raw onions...the concentration or whatever to shoot just one clay target at a time...more conviction about identifying ducks in an early morning mist...some way to keep my feet warm on a deer stand...the sixth sense that you need to be a really good tracker...

Well, given time and a very flexible threshold of boredom the list could go on and on. No doubt yours and mine are pretty much the same—substituting pintails or prairie chickens for birds or crappie and walleyes for fish, or whatever. No doubt whatsoever that you've got the names of a dog or two that you'd like to have over right on the tip of your tongue—and how about taking back a gun trade or two!

THE THING about the list that strikes me is that it shows a childlike faith in someone else coming along at the right time (and thankfully that almost always happens), an inability in certain areas of our lives to get past the mental age of twelve, and a fair share of "It's easier to wish for it than to work hard at it" when it comes to certain skills.

Some might think that this attitude is somewhat moronic—and they could put up a fair talk on their point. But the truth, to my way of seeing it, is that those who love the bits and pieces of being there—the sweetness of a singing lark, the way one whitetail can suddenly fill up a clearing, the fearsomeness of a sudden storm and the almost unbelievable sense of relief when we've gotten out of a very sticky situation—have to have a sense of the magic of it all, a belief in the intangible and unknowable, and no small degree of unquestioning wonder. For example, we are very likely to put the same faith in a carelessly tied knot that we had when we waded across a river that was better than fifty-fifty to at least give us a fast free ride—if not worse. The fact that we got lucky on a bad right angle from Post Five gives us (unfortunately) the idea that we can do that with regularity. We tend to edge skill in long before the place where luck leaves off.

And there are a lot of our "...wish I had's..." that would be sentimental and almost maudlin. But I'll trade you one of your private ones for one of mine: I wish I had Mr. Ralf and Tippy with me one more day. But on the other hand, they may be better off where they are, and somehow it doesn't take too much imagination to see them sitting somewhere watching me and scratching for one decent excuse between them as to why I haven't learned a thing in all these years.

TIME...AND THIS PLACE

It is the year 1938. A young man decides to take up the sport of hunting. But there are problems. He has no gun of his own, no shells, no money. However, there is a simple solution: chop wood and mow neighbors' lawns for 25 or 50 cents for a couple of hours work. In time he accumulates enough money to buy half a dozen No. 1½ Blake and Lamb traps and sets up a little trap line for the less wary. Several opossums, a few muskrats, and some skunks later he has accumulated the handsome sum of $10 and learned several important and interesting things about living off the land. The .22 rifle he used on his trapline to dispatch skunks quickly and humanely was kept in the kitchen closet with the other common tools. His ax was in the woodpile, and a box of .22 shorts required an outlay of around ten cents. So, for a minimum investment of money and a little effort and ingenuity, he's ready. Being fourteen years old he is entitled to be treated as an adult in the woods, so he purchases a license permitting him to hunt and fish for $1. He is issued a pin in the appropriate year's color and proudly fastens it on his new brown canvas cap. The hardware store has been delighted to save a 20-gauge single shot for him: $6. A box of No. 6 shot shells: 50 cents; the new cap: another 50 cents. The rest of his field outfit is his blue denim work coat and his everyday work boots. The season opens, and he simply goes hunting. His family and the neighbors are pleased with his initiative and welcome him as a sportsman. He is a hunter; one of them. They know that if he finds a fence down, he will put it back up. If he finds that the bull has gotten out of the pasture, he will stop and tell Mr. Jeffers, likely leaving a rabbit or squirrel for Mrs. Jeffers in the process.

When the deer season opens he will be excused from school for a few days with most of his friends. The grown men will welcome him along and will fairly let him in on the venison, as well as the camaraderie, the lore, the privilege, and the responsibility that come with being a hunter. He has arrived at one of the most important rituals of manhood, he knows—and will treasure this beginning and it's warm memories all the rest of his life.

IT IS THE YEAR 1980: A young man decides to take up the sport of hunting. But there are problems. He has no gun of his own, no shells, no money. And there are no simple solutions. He is unskilled. Jobs are few and far between; not too many neighbors want to pay $5 or more to have someone mow their lawn. In order to take a skunk or muskrat from his local marsh he must first attend a state trapping school and then buy a license for at least $10. He is forbidden by law to use a simple, inexpensive leg-hold trap. If he wants a .22 to dispatch skunks quickly and humanely, he has to apply to the police for a permit; since he is only fourteen, he can't even apply. A box of shorts would cost over $1.50 anyway. But his family knows of his love for the outdoors and decides to sponsor his gun and some shells.

But before that can happen he has to attend a Hunter's Safety Course, and someone has to drive him back and forth for his sessions. He passes with highest marks. But he cannot buy a shotgun either since he is too young to apply for that permit as well. He has to find someone who will sponsor him—and to accompany him every time he hunts because the state assumes that he is irresponsible or dangerous or both. His father finds a friend who would be delighted to take the boy hunting and help him out in the choosing of a first gun. At the gun dealer he discovers that virtually every new gun—even the cheapest of pumps or autos—is pushing $200. They decide on a used single-shot 20-gauge with the legally required case, and his father is handed a bill for $55. Shells? Another $7 a box. Fine? Not quite. His state insists on so many inches of blaze orange as an outer garment, which comes to another $15 for the least expensive vest. His hunting license is another $10. If he later wants to fish, that will be another $10 on top. Since he must display his new license on the back of his new jacket, he has to spend another $1.50 for a plastic holder.

Well, here we are. Fourteen years old with a house full of outdoor magazine and books that have been telling him how wonderful the hunting experience is, filling his imagination with visions of delicious adventures and tales of the laughs and handshakes and stories hunters exchange. He is ready with his new gun, a box of shells, a license and holder for it, a blaze-orange jacket to pin it on, and a man who has kindly consented to take him out. All set? Not quite yet. A long survey of the county finds that, except for a few state areas, everything else is posted NO HUNTING or is leased by private gun clubs. So be it, we'll start out on state-owned land and see if we can run up a rabbit flush a pheasant or quail. Does he have the special stamp for $5 that the state requires of him to use public land? No, he doesn't. But his friend helps him take care of that little detail. On their return the area warden checks his licenses, stamps, and Hunter's Safety Certificate, adding the warning not to shoot a woodcock without a special stamp for that ($3) or a duck ($7.50 for the Federal Stamp) and if he has the duck stamp, he is cautioned that he is now in a steel-shot zone—his regular rabbit and pheasant loads are illegal here for waterfowl. He had been thinking about the glories of swinging on mallards so he asks "How much is a box of steel shot?" He is crestfallen to find that it isn't made for 20-gauge guns and for 12-gauge it runs about $12 a box. And should he decide to go out for a duck or so, his boat must be licensed by the state, inspected for flotation gear and safety. "Even on the edge of the lake?" he asks, getting more and more discouraged. "Even on the edge of the lake," he is warned.

His attitude about even the least tinge of "wilderness" experience has been deeply dampened, but the worst seems to be over, so licensed and stamped and glowing of coat he and his companion return to the state gunning area. The control officer there shows them a vacant parking space, reminds them to lock the car and leave nothing of value in it. The older chaperone's dog tugs at his leash and they all set out. At last, he thinks, inhaling the pungent airs of early fall, carefully carrying his single shot broken over his arm and fingering the $7 worth of shells that comfortably tug at the pocket of his new hunting vest.

As they approach the area suggested they see four glowing-orange coats working ahead of them behind a pair of dogs; the edge of the road is littered with spent shells, candy wrappers, and empty shotshell boxes. The older companion looks at all this and at the boy and shrugs his shoulders in distaste. He thinks of all that the young man has been through and feels that somehow he deserves a better first day than this. He suggests that they go back to the car and try a farm he knows about. As they drive, the boy is silent. He no longer holds his cased gun with the pride and expectancy he had an hour ago. The lurid jacket is on the back seat—pushed aside by the dog.

As they drive the older man remembers his first outing. He went alone—the way he wanted it. His mother had made him a sandwich and put it in the pocket of his farm coat, kissed his cheek, and told him how much she wanted a couple of rabbits to fry up for supper and was this very minute going back to the kitchen to make up his favorite kind of cornbread to go with them. As he walked off the porch he whistled for Tom Mix (part Collie, part mixed) to come along, and they left on an adventure that was still so vividly pleasant and exciting that it nearly made him reach up and pretend something had gotten in his eye.

At the farm he told the boy to wait in the car while he went and talked to the owner. The boy watched his companion and the farmer, and although he couldn't hear what they said he saw the farmer point to a broken window in the chickencoop and then to a riddled old horse weathervane on the barn. He slumped lower in his seat at the obviously heated discussion, knowing full well what the argument was about. He thought of all the hours he'd spent taking the Hunter's Safety Course, the books he'd read, the money his father had spent, the time his companion had offered, the tales he remembered about the thrill of a dog on point, what he had planned to say when he missed—as he was sure he would at first—and how he would feel when he had taken his first game. It was all a jumble of contradictions: pleasure and shame; fear and excitement. But what was worst of all was that the things he wanted most, the sense of cleanliness, the strength that comes from personal achievement and discovery, weren't there at all. He had long dreamed of the sounds and the smells, hungered for the feeling of revelation at what it was all really like—and this is what it was really like: fine print, high prices, unwelcome attitudes, and now even the orange coat made him feel another uneasiness about the whole adventure. Where was all the good talk and the handshaking and the kind jokes? He turned to pet the dog and was a little reassured at the worn gun case of his companion and their lunch boxes and cooler for the game. He rubbed the sole of one of his new boots against the toe of the other to dull the shine of just bought. He had wondered why so few of his friends were interested in hunting and now he thought he knew; they were right, and he was a fool for even giving it a try. Just when his companion came back he was wondering how he'd explain to his father that he wanted to sell his gun.

On the way to where the boy was waiting, the man debated about whether or not to tell him about how he had to leave $20 as a deposit against damages and that he had promised to come back and fix the windows that someone else had shotgunned out. The farmer was really a decent sort, and he couldn't blame him for the way he felt. He even had a feeling that the farmer would let him and the boy come back again and he knew that the place had some interesting covers. No—he thought—I will tell the boy about fixing the windows and bring him back to help me. It would be a good lesson, and he was sure he'd enjoy the companionship; after all, land rights don't come with a hunting license, and he felt that this boy would like to earn as much of his way as he could.

As they started out through the farmer's orchard he went back in his mind again to his own fourteen-year-old days and wondered if he'd have gone to all the trouble and aggravation that this fourteen-year-old had...and decided that he might have, at least now, knowing what immeasurable joys his years of hunting had brought him along the way. Out of the corner of his eye he noticed and was reassured, but not surprised, at the careful way the boy handled his gun; he could sense the feeling of joy in every new-booted step. He was about to remark that they could do without that little bit of whistling, but then he remembered Tom Mix and a mother's kiss and began to whistle a little bit himself.

OBSERVATIONS
AND INSIGHTS

About this time of the year when there is little to do except wring our hands over our trap and skeet scores, I often reflect on the almost incredible amount of know-how that it's possible to cram into an already bulging brain. Some of these are near-brilliant insights off a pace or so from Sir Isaac Newton's revelations stirred by the fall of an apple; others are observations ranging from mere or casual to probable interglobal significance. I ask that you be the judge of their magnitude, finding, as you no doubt will, that some will make you a better person, others will lead to insights and observations of your own, while a few must wait until a more penetrating philosophical mind than yours or mine can relegate them into their most deserving place in our human scheme. I place them in no particular order, since most of us are more comfortable in the familiar atmosphere that consists in equal parts of disorder, chaos, and "I'm sure I have it here somewhere."

The worst shots at the gun club are those most free with instruction, criticism, and advice to the beginner.

A gun dog's behavior is inversely proportional to the amount of praise and bragging prior to the hunt. Same with trap and skeet scores prior to shooting.

Your best shooting was done with a gun you no longer own.

They no longer make your favorite waders, hunting coat, or shirt, or if they do the quality is diluted by the multiple of the price increase.

A guide or camp owner has never told you "Thank God you weren't here last week!"

The guide or outfitter will say "That's the first time I ever had that happen," when you are bucked off by Old Maude, his pointer flushes three big coveys in a row, you cast his "secret" plug all day in his favorite bass cover, he arrives a little after dark where the camp should be and there's no camp, his Chesapeake tears a big hole in your hip boots, and the needle on the spare gas can is stuck on "E."

The biggest rising trout is always farther than you can cast. The water is always too deep and too fast for you to be able to wade closer.

The difficulty of finding a dropped part (outboard, gun, engine, etc.) is directly proportional to its absolute necessity.

"Guaranteed not to shrink" should carry a prison sentence; "Guaranteed waterproof" calls for torture.

You are the only person in the camp who likes black coffee in your thermos.

When you miss an easy shot in the open you will have a minimum of four witnesses. How many will you have if you make one most of us wouldn't even try?

If you run out of tobacco or matches, how many other pipe smokers will there be in the camp?

Your guide tells you to walk about an hour until you come to an old well. In an hour you find four old wells or none.

The distance back to camp increases in direct proportion to darkness, sleet storms, or the nearness of lightning strikes.

If there are three vegetables you just can't stand, how many of them will the cook serve at every meal?

How does the zipper on your sleeping bag know you forget to bring pliers? Same with loose scope screws/screwdrivers, reels/oil, boats/bailers, waders/patches.

How does the airline know to lose your gun, rod, or boots on the way *to* an outing and never on the way home?

A covey of quail or flock of ducks will always fly closest to the man having his best shooting day ever.

A covey of quail or a flock of ducks will flush or fly at a distance in an inverse relationship to the choke of your shotgun.

The biggest fish will be caught by the cook making a couple of casts from the dock.

You save for months to buy an expensive down jacket. It will be reduced 50 percent the following week.

The only defective factory ammunition you will discover all year will occur in a shootoff. You will also draw the most right angles from station 5 and left angles from station 1.

You catch and release a truly remarkable trout; if you remembered to bring a camera (unlikely), the drugstore will lose the film.

The guide apologizes for dropping the brown bag. Will it contain your extra socks or your only bottle of whiskey?

Your skeet squad brings in a score of 121. Who has dropped the four birds?

The density and persistence of a sudden fog is always coincidental to how much you talked about knowing this part of the country "like the palm of your hand."

The good-looking guy with the Mercedes and the highly engraved Perazzi's will turn out to have an average of 98 in singles, 96 in doubles, and a 27 yard handicap.

Your dog will only fight with dogs whose owners are bigger than you.

A buddy opens your lunch bag by mistake; in it he finds a note from your wife. Will the note be of a very intimate nature or merely a reminder to bring home milk?

No doubt you have many of your own as poignant or more so, funnier or more able to draw tears of sympathy. I have only dwelt on the more common ones—the everyday version of splinters in trigger fingers or motes in the master eye.

Those who think that the life of the outdoorsman is a bed of roses don't realize how many of use are allergic to roses. If I am praised for a column and several can quote from it, it often turns out to have been written by Trueblood, Tarrant, or Zern. But this is the sort of everyday reversal of form that those of us who gun and fish have come to expect as a matter of course. Far from being surprised when I run one of my rare 25 straights, I immediately look on the board to see who has broken the 50. If in gunning in a point system area for ducks

I make one of my infrequent sensational shots, I assume that the dog will return with a 90-point hen. Who among us is immune to this stuff of fate that balances (and a lot more for good measure) every stroke of luck or occasional showing of skill?

The veteran sportsman has long since learned to keep his mouth shut and his ears open for the voice that, now and then, will shout, "Look out behind you!" Most of our wives have learned the fact that we do have more flat tires than normal people, that camp telephones rarely work, and gas stations close down before us like dominoes. On the other hand, not all of these things come on us all the time.

There are even the uncommon days of glory, when we are "the other guy." Alert on our deer stand, following through on crossing birds like an Etchen, with coffee untainted by sugar or cream, our chair-worn dogs performed like prodigies, and not a leak or a tear in our raiment.

But we know better than to count on them. Like fine steel—or valorous soldiers—we need a bit of tempering in the fire. I've always liked the remark of the old sailor to the young seaman as they were rounding Cape Horn, homeward bound in a violent storm "That's the way it is, young man. You have to smell Hell before you see Boston."

Observations and remarks are chips off the old block of Truth. They confirm our minor attempts at being too big for our britches, let us laugh at ourselves, spice the memory, and give us a tiny peek at what might, now and then, pass for wisdom. And before I leave, two more: "Nobody but a bachelor knows how to manage a wife," and "Too soon old, too late smart."

LOSING THINGS

Every so often I get what might be loosely termed "lost," where I'm really only exploring a touch beyond my known territory. This sort of thing has happened often enough that I come to expect it. (You may read *dread* for expect, if you want to.) But what I never really prepared myself for is the time of life, if that's what it is, where I've started to lose a lot more than just myself. I'm not counting the thousands of pencils and lone socks of a pair that disappear; that's to be expected—not totally understood by any of our prominent scientists, but expected just because it happens as mysteriously as it is predictable.

What is happening now—and it's frightening—is the fact that I can be alone in a room, not counting three or four dogs, and be cleaning a gun. I put the oiled rag down to put a gun back in the rack, and when I turn around with another gun the oil rag has moved itself, and I have to spend five minutes looking for it. It's damn near eerie. I feel silly walking around with an oiled rag in my hand for hours, but I don't dare turn it loose anymore. And it's really tempting fate to let go of a hammer, rule, or screwdriver; some overwhelming magnetic force moves them from exactly where I left them on the sawhorse and puts them under a board or behind a chair cushion.

I began to understand losing tools because I wasn't cut out by my Creator to use tools except in the most basic of circumstances. I can saw a piece of lumber so long as you're not fussy about it being true or use a nail if you don't care about it being crooked with half the nail and the head bent deep into the wood. If you don't care about destroying the groove, you can let me use a screwdriver. If you want me to hang a picture—stand by with a patch or a can of spackle. But if it's anything that requires more intelligence or a defter touch than you get from an ax, maul, or sledge, don't look to me.

At the moment I have a spare trigger assembly that's creeping from the drawer where I know I left it to one obscure place or another and taunting me to guess where. My favorite Orvis hunting chaps, coiled like a snake, are lying somewhere for the winter and won't appear until trout season, and then they'll have slid themselves under a pair of waders and pretend that's where they've been all along. I know better! I can understand my cowboy hat hiding somewhere because of ill treatment, but why would my box of 00's sneak off the shelf where I put it just before deer season and spend two weeks hiding in the trunk of my wife's car?

Or why is it that the meat saw Howard Symonds gave me can only be located in June or July, and I have to do my December venison with a rusty crosscut? The season phenomenon is about to drive me crazy. All winter long the reel with the WF5F line is lying around on my desk dripping a drop of oil on a book or a magazine now and then, but when I need it desperately, it's gone off and crawled in the pocket of a fly vest I *know* I haven't worn for months. I mean this whole thing is frightening. Anybody with any brains knows that things like guncase keys, pipes, lighters, and gloves constantly move in response to moon phases and gravitational tides like the planets— but so far I haven't gotten any good answers I can live with as to why my felt-lined Bean boots will turn up in the garden tool shed in May when I can produce witnesses to verify that I put them in my duck-hunting bag in September.

We all know that anyone who buys only *one* ivory front sight, or ejector spring, or 12-pound-test leader material just because he only needs *one* is either naïve, a fool, or a consistent lottery winner. He probably doesn't have to remind his wife that he likes his eggs boiled for seven minutes, not four, every single morning, either.

Of course, I do have help in certain areas that require me to buy more than one of something. Did you ever see that bumper sticker that reads "Do you know where your children are?" Well, I know where they are: they're under my favorite tweed fishing hat, covered with my good camouflage duck hunting parka and warming their grubby little hands in my good sheepskin mittens. I used to sit back and smoke my pipe and smile at my friends who went on raving mad about their kids swiping their stuff; why, after all, I just squeeze into an XXL or 46 R, and the fruit of my loins happens to be a pair of petite little girls. I actually felt superior to this common twist of fate. There was a time when I could open up a package from L. L. Bean, prance around in a new chamois shirt (17 × 36), and have my daughters admire the rugged look of No. 1. No more, never, under no circumstances do I commit myself to such chancy vanity. I have discovered, to my dismay, that a young lady who is barely getting a C − in chemistry is more familiar with shrinking process of a variety of fabrics than duPont de Nemours.

Maybe you've noticed it too, that some things tend to get lost more often than others. Eyeglasses have a category of elusiveness that rivals the Bongo, so we won't even count those. Given a full hour from a standing start I'd be willing to bet you several fingers of Jack Daniel's (black) that you can't find a single pair of spare bootlaces, the extra reed for your duck call, the right-hand glove for the pair you like to shoot in, a flashlight that works, or lighter flints. I know you have this stuff, everybody does, but why are most of these the things you see first when you go into a store? Why are they right there up front? Simple. These are among the living creatures that cannot exist by themselves, out in the open in a dresser drawer or in a fishing or gunning bag; they have to exist *under* something else that is rarely moved: chairs, bureaus, desks, car seats, filing cabinets, etc.

One important rule is not to show affection publicly for something that has an adverse affect on its behavior. You'd think that a slow-witted object like a hat would appreciate your saying "This old Stetson is the best hat I've ever owned—wouldn't dream of ever fishing without it!" Wrong again. If you ever see it hence, it will have spent the past six months under the spare tire or on a nail behind a ladder that is only used once a year to clean gutters. Praise a pair of boots, and they'll immediately tease the puppy into chewing them into scraps too small to use even to straighten a leader. Brag about buying the last pair of cashmere longjohns that ever might be available, and next time you try to get them on you'll discover that not only are they now a 28-inch waist, but they're hiding in your wife's dresser.

But like Newton's Law of Opposites and that sort of thing, for every thing you like that you'll unquestionably misplace, there are certain things that you loathe that will end up as part of your estate. Cheap pipes, purple scarves, dog whistles that won't, boots that blister, eternally fishless plugs shaped like a frog, poorly tied flies, locks with no keys and vice versa, hats that give you a headache, and off-key goose calls. Vacuum bottles that won't keep hot things hot or cold things cold, out-of-focus photographs, decoys that list to port, gun cases with broken zippers, clips for guns you no longer own…the list is endless, and unfortunately the reasons I don't fully understand, these things cannot be thrown away. I had a friend drive 45 miles to bring me a pipe I'd thrown under the front seat of a duck boat after gagging on it all morning. But leave one of my good ones in his car's ashtray, and I can forget it.

I had a very funny line about the Nobel peace prize waiting for the guy that invents a sock magnet, and I know it's around here somewhere…

THE DREAMER

The Dreamer has long ceased to think of the Atlantic salmon as a fish. He has followed it as a religious might journey to shrines, devoted to mystery and much taken with signs, portents, and myth. He is foolish, wasteful, superstitious, unrealistic, stubborn, and passionate.

His idea of a day well spent might be one where he has idled away hours pretending he is with Charlie Phair—greasing a line to weave a Silver Doctor through the pools at Brandy Brook. The pages are smudged with Butcher's wax from when he last groomed his crooked 12-foot Payne, and here and there an errant drop of oil from his Bogden is left to mark a place. So it is with his copies of Kelson, Sage and Wood and Bates and Lamb and Weeks and Wulff and Schwiebert. He believes they would feel uncomfortable if he kept their books pristine. In these volumes you will find a variety of broken flies (he is an indifferent caster), faded, out-of-focus snapshots, and a variety of notes—things to remember, insights and revelations that were, once, profound. He notes the rivers he has fished, the camps he likes the best; rarely a mention of what he caught. One such note reads "Salmon fishing is a dangerous sport, too much of it can destroy the mind." There are no records of expenditures, no lists of rods and reels, beyond a slip or so that indicates a need for "a dozen No. 10 doubles," or "order 5/0's from Jorgenson."

The Dreamer will, in January, prepare a box of flies to use in June. He holds a 2/0 Dusty Miller up against a drift of snow and fluffs its feathers like a jeweler rolling gems. This is his traditional first fly, regardless of the guide's advice. He sharpens hooks on two of them and places them in their clips. He debates about retiring a tattered Rogers Fancy that took a 32-pound hen last year and thriftily decides to keep it in the working box.

Cork grips are scrubbed, a loose guide gets a wrap, and a tailer, kept close at hand for just such use, prods a sleeping Lab to wakeful play.

He will change lines, carefully coating meticulous nail knots with a secret glue, off and on until a day or so before he leaves for fishing. Debating, as usual, between the degrees of tip-sink and ending up, as usual, convinced he's made a grave mistake. Second and third choices and spares are wound on extra reels. Few things fill him with quite the satisfaction as his array of Bogdens, Vom Hofe's, and Zwargs, and he looks forward to doing the same with his Hardy's that wait in reserve for late summer dry fly assemblage.

His rods are no less witness to his extravagance and self-indulgence. He is ready with a technical and philosophical justification of each. A more discerning eye might discover where a fly has ticked the varnish here and there, but all in all he is a spendthrift too with loving care, and the bamboo gleams with polish as he slides the rods home in sturdy cases for the waiting season.

The Dreamer's walls—beyond rod racks and the hanging tackle bags and hats, the vests that clink with jars, the tools and raincoats, nets and priests, and just plain stuff, all refreshing to his single-minded inclinations—are hung as well with favorite scenes. Tartan-kilted gillies gaffing silver monsters from the Spey and Brora. Sleet-pelted anglers bowing to the weather on the George, tall and fierce-scowling polemen watching their sport play a Moise giant, mist-shrouded runs on the Grand Cascapedia, a smoke-wreathed cabin on the Restigouche, sketches of fly boxes, mounted flies, and an angry-eyed, cracked of skin, spear-kyped mounted cockfish with someone else's name on the brass plate. A fine place for the worshipful, all in all.

The Dreamer is happy here, comforted by his regalia, impedimenta, essentials, and memorabilia. *This is a good room*, he thinks, inhaling smoke from a faulty fireplace, stumbling over a line-winder, and rummaging through his collection of wading staffs, looking for one to carry along on his evening walk with the dog....

The Dreamer is a man who thinks of little else than this strange thing—this wild swimming soul, this chimera, this sometime visitor from foreign seas. He has long since ceased to see it as an entity—a thing itself—but part of a cycle of creation that still exists beyond all the depredations that have afflicted it. He sees in it a miracle beyond his understanding but embraces it fully in his heart. He sees it as a microscopic seed cast in a wild river to become, God willing, an egg lodged beneath gravel that was once a rock—now ground down by uncounted time just to shelter this fragile gel. And then a thread of flesh and blood that will, God willing, grow into a tiny speckled silver parr and grow until some strange compulsion drives it out to spend a year or more to course the seas. And then some corkscrew chromosomed directive sends it back to pass beneath the shadow of his Rusty Rat and then, intrigued by Lord knows what—it catches him...God willing.

The rod bends and throbs as the salmon runs and shakes its head. The Dreamer, all the disciplines of Phair and Wulff *et al.* abandoned now, both wants and does not want this fish. He has been there with this salmon in his life and knows just what it's like to have so few choices to be free. So at the net, should that be the end result, he unhooks the fly and strokes the fish in thanks and bids it well. A gift of life; he has allowed himself to play a part in what he sees as Good. He knows that by giving this he gives himself a gift not all too different from the one he gave the fish. This is the essence of it all, he knows; the ultimate privilege, the quintessential grace. Such as warriors in more chivalrous times would do—one offering the life, one accepting, and both deserving and grateful for such an end to such a test.

So the Dreamer and his kind will stand, wadered or borne by a long canoe, attached to something of themselves as circumstance and chance permit and watch it arc against the sky, and send it on with thanks and hopes of meeting it again—*Deus Volante*.

THE IDLER

I could guess where you'll be this November. If you're like me, you're probably finishing up chores that you ought to have done in September. I figure that on the average I run about two months late every year, just like a cheap watch.

But nothing prevents the Idler from pausing over his lawn rake, looking up into the sky at travelers heading toward Chesapeake Bay, and wishing he were on his way as well…somewhere…almost anywhere.

The Idler lights his pipe and begins to dream. If only he were rich. He can see himself in a tailored tweed gunning jacket, his favorite side-by-side resting lightly in his arms waiting for driven grouse from a peat sod shooting butt high up in the heather-covered hills of Scotland. His gillie is astounded by his casual expertise. All morning long he has taken a pair of birds coming in, reloaded, turned, and taken another pair going away. At the noontime luncheon break the Idler sips a glass of sherry and admits that in the States he occasionally enjoys a round of skeet or trap, graciously allows some of the other shooters to admire his hammer Hussey, and modestly admits to being lucky. In the afternoon the whole shooting line watches him twice accomplish the incredible four dead in the air, and in the evening the loveliest of ladies fuss over him. His champagne glass is constantly refilled and the conversation is filled with references to Lord Ripon and deGray, with his name frequently linked with theirs. Tomorrow will be driven pheasant, the Idler muses at the edge of sleep. Perhaps he ought to take the Purdey, and wear his doeskin vest and Loden jacket with side vents. A knock at the door interrupts his wardrobe selection, but before he can answer it, the door swings open as if by itself and a jeweled hand carrying a bottle of champagne appears and switches off the light.

The Chairman has noticed the Idler dozing and has arrived to prod him on with his lawn work. Rake in hand he once again copes with oak leaves, their musty odor sharpening his senses and reminding him of the aspen stands that fringe the black timber in elk country. Now the Idler is alone, leading his favorite trail horse, Hurricane, toward the grassy meadow where the stallion will remain hobbled while the Idler stalks the one bull he wants among them all.

Like an Indian, the Idler travels light and feels confident of his ability to live off the land—come what may. An ancient but beautifully cared-for .270, a handful of shells, a knife, and some matches are all he needs. This may be a primeval wilderness frightening and fearsome to others, but to the Idler it's home. Among the tracks of the huge herd he finds the ones he has been searching for. The slight nick in the right front hoof that he has so often seen in his mind's eye is right there where he knew it would be. The hunt is on. Late that afternoon the snow accumulation from a sudden storm slows his pace to a mild jog, just slightly faster than the wandering speed of the great elk he is coursing. Like two warriors seeking battle, they are alone, the bull having long left the confines of the herd, and the Idler, his senses as finely tuned as a wolf's, more a creature of the forest than the average man could imagine, begins to know the thinking of the forest giant.

With his uncanny instinct the Idler now knows exactly where the elk is heading; he has less than half-an-hour to cover the three miles. He grins to himself at the deliciousness of the challenge and vows that should the elk beat him to the heavy timber he will wait a year before challenging the animal again. With the deceptive lope of a born athlete he lengthens his stride. Twenty minutes later, without even breathing hard from the thin air of the timberline, he chooses his place of rendezvous. His hearing as acute as a whitetail's, his eyes as perceptive as an eagle's—he waits. Suddenly, as if the curtain were rising for the last act, the elk appears, his massive antlers rivaling the forest itself. The crosshairs come to rest. The Idler takes in a long, silent breath, when suddenly the elk steps back into the cover of a shadow and he sees instead the glowering form of the Chairman and hears her tell him that to the best of her knowledge nothing is as good for casting muscles as the vigorous use of a leaf rake.

Without looking, the Idler deftly ties on a new 8X tippet and clinches the knot to a 22 jassid. He stares at the ripple—one that most anglers of lesser perception would miss entirely—made by a smutting brown trout that rivals any he has seen in this section of Argentina. In a half-crouch he makes two false casts to test the wind and then drops the tiny fly precisely 2½ feet ahead of where the last dimpling was seen. A soft voice floats up to him in the gathering dusk: "That was the most skillful casting I've ever seen!" He turns and sees one of the most beautiful women he has ever encountered, wearing waders and carrying what looks like a Garrison or Gillum rod. Quickly he adjusts his silk scarf and returns his eyes to the water just in time to see the giant trout sipping in the fly. His strike is perfect, measuring instinctively to the last gram of strength the force he can apply to the gossamer tippet and plunge the tiny hook into the mighty jaw well past the barb. In less than an hour the huge trout, far larger than he had first imagined, lies nearly exhausted at his knees. The lady, who has been watching his every move, applauds, but he waves her quiet. "I dedicate this trout to you," the Idler says, handing her the scissors from his fishing vest. "I accept with pleasure and gratitude," she replies, cutting the leader just at the eye of the hook. Then lightly touching the flanks of the great fish, she places his head in the river current and they watch him swim away into the darkness.

As the trout disappears a pair of headlights suddenly flood the scene. "My car," she says, "may I offer you a ride back to your inn?" "Thank you," replies the Idler, "I am a bit tired and would love to get back in time for cocktails." "No need to hurry," she smiles, and in the headlights he sees that she is lovelier than he had first guessed. She walks over to the car and has a few words with the chauffeur. The chauffeur steps out and begins striding down the road toward the village. "I sent him back with word that you would be late and not to hold dinner for you." As the Idler lights his pipe she steps to the rear of the classic Rolls touring car and opens the trunk. "Would you like your martini with vodka or gin and with a twist or an olive?" "Gin," replies the Idler, "and just a drop of vermouth, no olives but a touch of lemon if you please." She sings in a sweet and soft voice as she mixes the drinks and when they touch glasses she makes a short toast in Spanish. When the Idler asks her for a translation she smiles again in a most unusually captivating manner and promises that she will explain later, for it is not a fishing toast, but one between a man and woman.

The fishing rod he had placed against the Rolls as he reached for his martini is caught in a soft breeze and falls across his foot. As he picks it up he is amazed to find that it is suddenly heavy and cumbersome—it's a rake handle to be exact. Instead of the dulcet-voiced mystery lady he hears the Chairman reminding him that supper will be ready by the time he finishes and if he wants a martini he had better hurry up and then go mix it himself.

The Idler's black Labrador, who has been dragging sticks from somewhere and leaving them on his just-raked lawn, suddenly pauses and sits staring at the sky. The Idler hears the noise before he makes out a long wedge of birds framed just above the sunset. Off to one side, just above the horizon, he can see the Evening Star. He calls Maggie and she runs to his side, carrying a small limb. The Idler scratches that certain spot behind Maggie's ears and, for the first time since he was a child begins reciting "Star bright, star light, first star I have seen tonight, I wish I may, I wish I might, have the wish I wish tonight" and turns toward the house, tugging playfully at Maggie's stick. He can see himself at Bombay Hook in the final test of the National Amateur Retriever Field Trial with Maggie tight at heel. The gallery is breathless in anticipation. He reaches down, takes the stick, and throws it as far as he can into the gathering darkness. As Maggie returns with the stick in her mouth the Idler hears the first beginnings of a tremendous wave of applause.

THE GENTLE GIANT
OF TIME

There is a small wandering brook in my backyard and along its edges here and there are seven sycamores. Each of them is just what a fine specimen ought to be—ponderous of trunk, huge of limb, and (the way they seem to me) graced with the charming, awkward gentleness of a giant.

One of them is very special. Little kids come around early every spring to see "the owl tree." (I asked one boy why he called it that and he said, "because it grows owls.") This particular tree measures about 24 feet in circumference at breast height. I have no doubt it sheltered Delaware and Leni-Lenapi Indians, or that George Washington, who marched through what is now my yard, saw it—or at least it saw him. Throughout the years its strength has withstood the storms and floods, and luck has spared it from the ax and saw—until just the other day. A sudden summer cyclone, no more than a couple of minutes of violent wind, somehow caught one of its giant topmost limbs and wrenched it from the trunk.

My good neighbors, Howard and Jess Symonds, who knew I had a ton or so of tree down to clean up, came over the other day with their chain saws and we set to work. As the saws ripped through the big limb, hollow for who knew how long, a variety of nests, leaves, straw, and sticks tumbled down. We had the feeling (and spoke about it) that we were tearing down an old cherished house. We began wondering, in awe, of how many thousands of creatures had been born and raised in just this single tree.

Way up near the top is a hole that I know has produced somewhere in the area of sixty or so great horned owls, at least since I've lived here. I've peered up at them with curiosity and pleasure as they've peered down coldly and imperially at me as though I had overlooked some very visible NO TRESPASSING sign and they were annoyed at my lack of manners.

At the base of the tree I've found over the years countless mice and mole skulls in the owl casts, and now and then the remnants of a pheasant or a duck and once—to my thorough amazement—the head and feathers of an osprey.

Below the castle of the owls are smaller digs taken in turn by squirrels, wood ducks, and a variety of brave or indifferent neighbors. At the far end of one limb a family of Baltimore orioles have suspended their basket nest for the past five or so years.

I see this tree as some sort of miniature city. During the summer it must respire a thousand gallons of water a day, and I don't have the wisdom to even guess how many tons of ice and snow its great limbs have carried in our winter storms. My mind cannot begin to comprehend the engineering that supports, from a base of about two feet in diameter, a limb that is 50 or 60 feet long. Nor can I hazard how much the whole tree must weigh or how many millions of gallons of water it has used to run its vital functions. Or how many tons of fallen limbs, wind and weather pruned, I have carried away in the past fifteen years. Or what total leaf surface, each one a third larger than my hand, it uses to absorb energy from the sun.

My children have swung from it with confident joy in its massive strength. I have, on many occasions, just stood there and looked at it, feeling the same awe and wonderment that others might draw from contemplating the spiring architecture of a cathedral. How easy it is for me to understand the ancient Druids and their worship of trees. How simple it would be to do as they did and talk to the tree, expecting in some strange way that it hears me and some day might deign to answer if I could ever think of anything important enough to say.

In some odd way I am deeply upset by the loss of this giant limb. It may be the twisted stem jutting brokenly in a grotesque and disfiguring way is a mute reminder of a fragility that even giants must endure; or that I shouldn't trust anything to endure forever without harm, and that one day, in some unforeseen future, this incredible being will lean against the ground and return to the earth.

I find myself going out and looking at my tree from an angle where the lost limb doesn't show, as if to hide from the truth of mortality. Or perhaps it's just an extension of my own vanity—another great pretense that nothing has happened, that everything is the same and will stay that way…"forever beautiful…forever young."

I don't know why it never occurred to me before to talk to people about my tree, but now I've discovered almost everyone has a special tree somewhere. An apple tree on the farm they grew up on, the oak or ash or beech where they took their first deer. A peach or pear tree where a loving mother gathered fruit for homemade jam. A tree to climb and watch the clouds and think. A tree to shinny up and look down on ponds and pools and see the world turned upside down, the sun shining at your feet, and fish swimming on its face. One old man once told me that the reason he kept a fireplace was so he could hear the wood speak to him. I wish I had asked him what he heard it say, but now I'm close to guessing what he heard.

Somehow the simple form of the ax and crosscut saw seem more right to use in cutting wood than the loud, growling motor-driven chains we use today. The quiet back and forth between the chunking of the ax is soothing. It lets you contemplate time and strength—both your own and that of the tree. And I enjoy the polishing of what used to be a famous skill, seeing how neat a cut my ax can make or how easily the saw can work guided by a careful hand. I like the smells the ax releases, the pungent mix of mysterious elements that make the acrid smell of oak or the slightly sweet odor of cherry. It's mystery after mystery to tease the mind. I can lay the log over and count the rings; this is the year I was born, this was the year twelve thousand men died in the battle of Somme. I can turn the pages of the book with my ax and saw, smell the storms and summer drought, the pond water sucked up and cast out to cool the wind. I can almost see the infinitely careful probing of the earth with tiny tendrils the size of a human hair coursing nitrogen, iron, copper, and zinc up through the web of cells to change a winged teardrop of a seed into this giant maple.

"How does a tree grow?" was the one question on a three-hour botany exam I once took. I knew and yet didn't know the answer. The subtle differences between the how and why still haunt when the philosopher's ax becomes heavy and he takes a rest.

In the long nights of the coming months the owls will return to my old sycamore and make another home. Perhaps in the new hole where the wind wrenched out the limb that lays across my lawn I will see soft-feathered owlets in the spring. Herons will rest on it, bass will cool themselves in its shadow, and I will stand under it, look up, and ask the questions that have no answers.

I thought it would be a good idea to go out and take another look at the sycamore before I finished my writing—it seems that I'm constantly finding new aspects even after all these years. This evening the moon is coming full and a west wind is pushing the leaves into the night light. The tree seems to be brooding, sitting heavily on the earth under the weight of the great owls and moon.

I had forgotten how frightening a tree can be at night when the light is just so and the keening wind has a song that you'd just as soon not hear. No doubt all this is a comfort to the owls who are awake and of no matter to the rest who sleep. But to me, now rather restive and edgy, the short journey to the brook edge of the yard ended with a touch of sorrow, for I had wanted a bit of reassurance and instead found a note of somberness. It was almost frightening to discover how much I did not want to think of nighttime things, haunting tricks of light and shadow, now-you-see-it, now-you-don't. But it was only the old sycamore answering a question that I didn't realize I'd asked until it was too late, with an answer that I'd have rather done without.

WHAT MAKES A HUNTER?

Two hunters return from a trip together. Let's say that they have been in some upland covers for grouse and woodcock and that each has taken a few birds. One is delighted with his few days; the other is not. Why the difference? Who is the one with the better perspective?

A hunter, in my personal definition, is a man who has a special feeling about the "wilderness." He can become part of it with ease. He has some knowledge of what is about to happen and why—either consciously or subconsciously. He is the one who knows where and when to look for his particular quarry; some sixth sense tells him that this cutover is more likely to hold grouse than another, and he's alert to the fact. He feels a shift of wind, notices partridge berry, the beech mast, the quality of aspen, the presence of grit, and he puts these pieces of the puzzle together and says to himself, *This is good bird cover.* Let's assume that he's right—birds move and he misses a couple. A less experienced hunter takes the misses at face value and is unhappy; the more experienced hunter is delighted that he has put it all together—

found the birdy spots by know-how—which was his ultimate objective; the shooting success is almost anti-climactic.

Again, in my mind—you can disagree and some of you will—the truly skilled bird hunter goes afield with a decent dog. He doesn't wander aimlessly, hoping to stumble across something in his six-hour walk, and he may actually hunt for only two hours or so. But he carefully picks covers that by their nature ought to produce game; naturally he is not always right, but the odds make this hunter the superior one.

We have a distressing tendency in this country to keep score. And I'm dead against it in the fishing and hunting area. Our successful grouse hunter had a better day than the man who might have stumbled over and bagged a brace or so of birds; even though his shooting might not have been what he had hoped, or he found his birds in cover that was too heavy to do very well in. It didn't matter—that was not the game he was playing.

Now take your average deer hunter. He knows little about what deer feed on, where they rest, when and why they move. He heads for the deep woods, provided he doesn't have to walk too far from the car, and says to himself, *This is the spot.* Of course it isn't. It might have been once, and it even might be in certain areas still, but the majority of whitetails are farm-country animals—to be found on the edge of pastures, feeding before dawn and at dusk, commuting back and forth from patches of cover that look most unlikely to the unobservant and un-woods-wise hunter. The woodsman knows that covers change from year to year. A patch of sumac or cedar that didn't hold deer last season may be just perfect this year. He knows that deer are not great travelers. He knows that deer will as often hide as run, and he knows that they'll find concealment in places that eight out of ten hunters will cross off as unlikely. But the real hunter doesn't just think like a hunter—he also knows how to think like a deer. The real hunter doesn't slam car doors and clank off into the woods. He pays attention to breezes, he notices rubbings, he sees a variety of distances from food to resting areas and watering spots. He puts all this information together and uses it at the right time of day, quietly and with that special alertness, that sixth sense, and he sees deer. If he chooses to shoot or not, if he wants a trophy or roast venison, that is his final option, but he has derived his basic satisfaction from solving the problem.

The frontier Indian had a game he played called "counting coup."

In its non-lethal version (and there were both) it was to touch an enemy and let him go, ride up to a running bison and slap his flank with his hand or touch him with a spear and be satisfied that had he wanted to take it, he could have.

One of our most famous oldtime American trophy hunters used to do that in his own way. One year he spent a considerable amount of time and money finding out where he could find a true trophy whitetail rack; about the most difficult task you can pick if you have an eye on Boone and Crockett listings. But, knowing where to start his search and how to go about it, he finally located an area and made his plans to hunt it when the season came around.

Opening day he was there, and by all the signs he was right: the tracks were plentiful and huge, the cover was ideal, and he knew that he and the giant buck would meet. But this particular man has a special rule of his own when it comes to whitetail deer; a step beyond the constraints of what we—most of us—would consider abiding by the concept of "fair chase." He allowed himself but one shot; if he missed the chance, the hunt was over and the deer had won until another year had passed. His favorite rifle, the one he had used for record after record, was an old sporterized Springfield .30/06 that was as much a part of him as his right arm. He was modestly and rightfully proud of what he knew he could do with it, and I can remember his smile as he told me of seeing the rack of a lifetime picking its way through the blowdowns and he tracking it with the trusty 06…and splintering an unseen sapling that stood between him and the animal. I asked if he'd ever gone back again. He smiled once more and said, "Just about every night in that minute or so before I fall asleep."

Every so often we ought to sit back and think about what we want and need from the hunting experience and what we are bringing to it. By that I mean skills beyond the pointing of a rifle or shotgun. Lately I find that calling (or trying to call) geese gives me as much pleasure or more than filling a limit. I'm trying to be better at general bird identification and paying more attention to the historical and geological points of interest when I travel to someplace new. I listen more than I used to and try to see beyond what lies over the sights of my gun. I am trying to find out something about myself, trying to understand the part of me that would desperately like to know what it is that the geese are saying, why the coyote calls, trying more and more to "count coup" in the too few hours I can spend outside.

Around me at this minute is a small selection of simple treasures. Some shotguns, some rifles, some fishing rods. A couple of Labradors asleep in front of the wood stove, and some empty places that once held Tippy and Ben and Judy and Josephine, to mention a few. Hunting coats and duck calls and fly boxes and boots and hats are scattered around amidst boxes of shells, decoys, nets, and odds and ends of this and that. You might call them the tools of pursuit if you weren't a real hunter or fisherman. Or you might look at them in another way—as you see your own similar collection of virtually identical things. Underneath any coat or hat, carrying any gun or rod, dangling lures or calls or whistles is someone who is trying to find the trail that leads him to a place where he is a part of an elk or grouse or goose or whatever. A place where he feels that incomprehensible tingling which tells him that at this moment he is completely alive and part of the wild as no one but a true hunter can ever be.

No doubt this is but another inadequate way of expressing the unexpressible. But no doubt you know what I mean. On the one hand we can't put it into words, and on the other we don't have to. There is almost always that hour of the winter day when we can hear the pheasants call goodnight, or the geese or owls...sometimes just the barking of a distant dog...familiar and comforting notes that suspend the coming of darkness for a moment and let us stand in the last of the light and almost understand the un-understandable.

OUR WORLD WITHOUT SHOTGUNS

As a man unfortunate enough to have to plod shamefully through life without a nice side-by-side 28 gauge, or even a decent boxlock 12 (28-inch barrels, straight grip, bored improved cylinder and modified), I have long periods of time when I feel a little sorry for myself. It was in one of these low periods when I was wishing I had a little more money or a little more common sense (asking for both would be too much) that I began wondering what our world would be like if there weren't any shotguns at all.

I doubt if we'd have any Labradors, goldens, Brittanies, springers, setters, pointers, shorthairs, or beagles if there were no shotguns.

We wouldn't have field trials, duck clubs, or all those nifty-looking pins for our hats. We wouldn't collect shooting sticks, shell bags, tweed hats, leather boots, duck calls, or flasks if there weren't shotguns.

Without shotguns, there wouldn't be any skeet (I wouldn't miss high 5, though), trap, quail walks, wipe-your-eye, high tower, or pasture afternoons with a hand trap.

We'd never know the joy of fried rabbit, honey-glazed mallard, fricasseed squirrel with dumplings, roast goose, fried quail, broiled dove, or pheasant with sauerkraut and sausage if it weren't for the shotgun.

There wouldn't be any Hennessey duck marshes, Reneson grouse covers, Maass canvasbacks, or Ripley woodcock if they didn't have shotguns.

Would we have L.L. Bean, Orvis, Gokey, Eddie Bauer, or Woolrich? I doubt it. We wouldn't have the neighborhood sports shop to hang around in and gab, much less Wild Wings, Crossroads of Sport, Collectors Covey, Sportsman's Edge, and the others who have the carvings and the sculpture and the art that all came about just because of the shotgun.

There wouldn't be any thick coffee cups with wood ducks or puppies on them. No camouflage neckties, red flannel shirts, shooting vests, or heavy parkas. Easton, Maryland; Grand Junction, Tennessee; Vandalia, Ohio; or Stuttgart, Arkansas, would each be just another small American town.

None of these names would mean anything to you either: Nash Buckingham, Burton Spiller, Corey Ford, Havilah Babcock, Ed Zern, Robert Ruark, Archibald Rutledge, Eugene Connett, Dave Newell, or John Alden Knight. And Samson, Reiger, McManus, Trueblood, Barrett, and Brister would likely be names on a factory time-card.

Whose pulse would quicken at the morning call of *bob white, bob white*, or the evening song of geese or the chatter of mallards? The pheasant, chukkar, wild turkey, and a host of others would just be pictures in dusty books.

There wouldn't be any reason to get up and have a diner breakfast with your buddies at 4 A.M. Or learn to make sandwiches two inches thick, or carry an extra candy bar. We wouldn't dream about sink boxes, Barnegat Bay scullers, or layout blinds. Or find any delight in a November northeast wind. I know I'd miss the arguments about 3-inch magnums, 2's versus 4's, and the virtues of copper over lead. I wouldn't own six pairs of long-johns, wouldn't care about not being able to find my hand-warmers or whatever happened to my sheepskin mittens. I'd probably have a car in my garage instead of piles of decoys and an olive-drab boat. And I wouldn't have a hole in my rug, a chewed-up chair, and three ruined pairs of shoes either, because I wouldn't have Maggie.

I'd never have spent any time looking for abandoned farm orchards, alder swamps, or spring-run pastures. There wouldn't be any old collars and dog bells in the barn, and I'd have no reason to turn my head and blow my nose if someone started to talk about Little Ben, Daisy, Belle, Rocky, or Tip. My suits wouldn't be all covered with dog hair, my car seats wouldn't be muddy and torn, and there wouldn't be a special stone or tree here and there in my lawn. I'd never have had the sun in my eyes, my pants hung up on barbed wire, or the safety on. Sixes, 7½'s, and 8's might only mean hat sizes.

Who would have thought of building a hollow-cedar Canada, making a root-head swan, or a sleeping black duck? Why bother with carving a dainty, slender wooden yellowlegs or turnstone? How much poorer we would have been without the likes of the Wards, Elmer Crowell, Shang Wheeler, or Ira Jester. What would be magic about the Susquahanna Flats or Merrymeeting Bay or Tule Lake?

Fred Kimble, Doc Carver, Adam Bogardus, Annie Oakley, or Rudy Etchen might have taken up golf.

A hundred thousand Englishmen and Scots would be playing cricket, or worse, tennis, on the twelfth of August.

Opening day wouldn't have any special meaning except for worm fishermen and baseball fans. Oliver Winchester would be famous for sewing machines, Remington for the typewriter, and the brothers Parker for coffee grinders. I might have a car less than seven years old if it weren't for Lefever, Baker, Smith, Greener, Hussey, etc., etc., and just possibly a savings account.

I wouldn't have a dozen coats that are fit only for duck blinds or briars and only a couple for weddings and funerals. I wouldn't have eight pairs of boots and only two pairs of good shoes—one brown, one black. Ninety-five percent of my neckties wouldn't have birds or dogs (or chili) on them. And most of my vests, hats, and raingear wouldn't be camouflage.

The Chairman wouldn't know how to dust a stuffed duck, patch a wader, worm a dog, pick a goose, clean an 1100, mow a lawn, paint a house, shingle a roof, or use several words she didn't learn in some girls' school…if it weren't for shotguns.

No shotguns, no poetry. No shotguns, no exuberant competition. No shotguns, no silent days alone, or with a dog, to merely walk and think. Take the shotguns from my life and take the books that go with them. Take the paintings and the etchings and bronzed pointing setters and Labs with a proudly carried duck. Take my decoys and my marsh boat and my string of calls. Take my old photographs of friends at gun clubs and duck camps and at the simple farms. Take my faded coats and briared boots and old soft hats. Take my whistles and dog bells and the red and yellow field trial ribbons from their frames.

What friends I have, what days I treasure most, what places that I think about and smile...they are because shotguns are. Without them I would have been empty. They have made my life full.

Nothing that I have is worth a lot, and yet nothing that I have is so priceless. The treasures are not the guns themselves, but behind the doors that they open.

As I write this I'm thinking about tomorrow. Toward late afternoon I'll take a gun and a dog and walk an hour, not caring all that much about the chances for a pheasant or an evening duck, but satisfied to have the heft of half a dozen shells and to watch the puppy lark around a little. Behind the yellow lights of home are the voices from the pictures and books that never ask, "Did you get anything?" But always ask, "Did you have a good time?" And as I put the shotgun back in its corner I can always answer, "Yes."

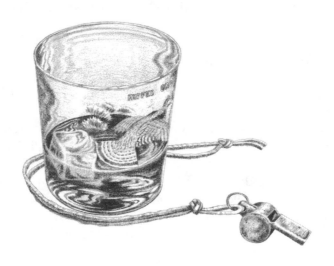

SOME THINGS NEVER CHANGE

I'd be willing to bet, since you're a hunter, that your favorite necktie has ducks or pheasants or quail or some kind of big game head on it. And that you've got a print or two hanging in your house or office that's some kind of hunting scene. Further—that your favorite shotgun or rifle, or both, has some kind of relevant engraving on it, or you wish it had. Same with the glasses you use to hold your favorite version of spirits. Most of you are members of D.U., or the Wild Turkey Federation or one devoted to preserving more quail, or wild sheep or deer.

In one corner of my own office is an old spear and in another is a 375 H&H Magnum—with the usual variety of similar odds and ends scattered out in between. It's an odd obsession, this deep and tight hold that we and our animals have on each other, and it's as old as anything we know about the history of man. The walls of the ancient cave dwellers were covered with drawings of mammoths, saber-toothed tigers, deer, antelope and men hunting them. In fact, all of the hunting peoples down to the relatively modern American Indian, found the presence of animals, real or in art form, somewhat of a philosophical and emotional necessity.

There isn't any essential difference between your prints and a cave drawing or the engraving on the floorplate of your 30-06 and the scrimshaw on an ivory or flint spear point, or your cocktail glass and a pre-historic gourd or horn covered with rude antler-like scratchings.

I don't know for sure why we do this, but it's surely an interesting thing to speculate on. I suspect that the ancients felt their art encouraged bravery; knowing that someone before you has speared or hamstrung a lion or elephant is reassurance that such a thing is at least possible. No doubt some of the artwork was intended as a lesson or to commemorate an event. But, I suspect that most were close to our own reasons; a form of honor, a display of affection and some attempt to understand the independence and freedom that animals in the wild have always represented.

Some of the more primitive things I've done have always held some strangely strong appeal beyond the simple act of capture—if and when that actually happened. Using a fish spear is one of them; me with my flashlight, and some time-lost relative with a burning torch, staring into the mystery of water, leaning on exactly the same instinct. Setting a trap for a mink or a muskrat is another where the basics, if not the tools, haven't changed much over the past millenium.

I seem to find more and more hunters who are feeling the same way. Look at the incredible numbers of primitive-weapon hunters— the flintlock and cap-and-ball riflemen and shotgunners. The painted-face bow hunters and the handful of "Indians" who have taken to trying to run down a deer and end the hunt with a stroke of a sheath knife.

One way or another we are tied, each in our own fashion, about as tightly to our game as ever.

Those of us who still hunt with the latest models of hardware find variations according to our personal ideal as well. There are a growing number of deer hunters who are purely trophy hunters— hunters who will go from season to season without taking a shot until they find that particular animal that will, in their estimation, justify the chase. Others will take the first halfway decent head that comes by and some, with more than half an eye on the freezer, are delighted with a chance at some tender yearling.

Some live for the essence of the stalk—a particular animal under particular circumstances. Most take whatever comes along and is legal. Some are still hunters who like the odds and the mood of staying put in one place, while some can't stand still for a minute and others must have the convivialty and excitement of the old-fashioned gang drive.

The way we hunt is, of course, tied to the reason why we hunt. Some of us hunt to enter into things, others to get away from them. Some are lugging battered 30-30s that would look at home propping open a cabin door, others swear by the wildcat calibers that are the brainchildren of fear-naught technicians; all separated by a couple of million plain-vanilla 30-06s and 270s.

But we're all brothers under the skin; what we carry in our hands may vary a bit; what we carry in our heads and heart hasn't changed too much. The high road and the low road will both come out at the hunting camp—and the evening stories and the morning hopes will differ only in language from the plans and dreams that most surely once lived in a cave where on the walls some ancient artist scratched a set of horns—and no doubt debated whether or not to add an inch or two here, and a point or so there. Some things never change!

Most of us have a trophy or two on a wall somewhere or a set of antlers stuck on a shelf. Some of my non-hunting visitors seem to feel that this is a little barbaric or some sort of ego display. My hunting friends know better. First off, my "trophies" are of such mediocre proportions that anyone with any ego about such things certainly wouldn't put them out on display. I would admit to this being the wall of my "cave," and admit here that my moose horns will forever recall a near-dark evening in northern Ontario and a cold and thrilling stalk by canoe; a deep friendship made with an Indian for whom I have the greatest respect and admiration...and a week away from the world in the wilderness with the night sounds of the north country stirring through my ancient dreams. A small deer antler—just one, to remind me of an 11-year-old who was admitted to the society of men he deeply admired and a father who told him that he was a hunter and let him prove it. Our trophies are not there so much for the impression they might make on another as much as they are there for ourselves...like the engraving on our favorite rifle or the print of canvasbacks swinging through a sleet storm.

Each of us honors our "hunts" in our own way, knowing that these experiences enrich us and that without them there would be a restlessness and feeling of being incomplete. We may not need them to survive in the physical sense or for food, but spiritually they are essential. I believe that hunting is a link in a brotherhood: it gives us a bond with each other, it is part of our deep involvement and understanding of animals—and the wilderness and the part of us that belongs there.

You and I and the game need each other; without one the other would lose a definition and meaning and purpose. As long as we are here, the wild things will be honored for what they really are: a symbol of our real evolution.

It was the hunter that evolved the rifle from the spear. It was the hunter that made art from rude etchings on stone walls. It was the hunter that formed civilization by letting others be dependent on him so that they might be free to do other things.

The songs that we hear carried on the wind are in different voices. But the meaning is clear to the one listening in the wilderness. It is about life at its most basic. It is about being strong and wise and successful. It is telling us who we are and why we are there. We learn again that without us there would have been no need for fire...there would be no need for anything.

TAKE A GROWNUP
FISHING

We've got a celebration day called "Take a Kid Fishing." Not a bad idea, but to my way of thinking, not nearly as good as a day set aside for "Take a Grownup Fishing." Kids have enough as it is: ten-speed bikes, motorcycles, their own rooms, understanding parents, designer jeans, sugarless gum, and their own hair dryers.

Grownups need someone to talk to besides people their own age so they can learn about the real world. They ought to have someone to row the boat or run the motor, younger hands to tie knots and younger eyes to read the fine print.

I think it would be an unforgettable day for a kid to take some semi-forgotten man or woman out for a day every so often. The kid would get a thrill from listening to someone who didn't say "you know" every other word. He might even learn something about ancient history—listen enthralled to stories about the dark ages when you had to learn how to thumb a bait casting reel, use real worms that didn't

106

(for all I know) taste and smell like anise or vanilla or strawberry. What kid wouldn't thrill to reminiscences of wood boats and oars, or be charmed to use a rod made of bamboo or steel, just to see what hardships some of us used to endure?

Youngsters need someone to look after, to give them a purpose as well as a good glimpse into the future. I don't see any harm in discovering or at least giving some thought to the fact that you won't be young forever. Kids ought to appreciate that we've had to learn to whistle two or three times. The first time was with a scattering of teeth, the second was with a full set of nature's own, and then, due to the ravages of time and chewing tobacco, back to a scattering again.

Kids today spend a lot of time in school learning "arts and crafts." They could teach us what they've learned about whittling. Nobody taught me how not to cut myself—I learned the hard and bloody way.

I seem to remember a time before every town in the country had pedestrian lights, when a good Scout tied a knot in his kerchief if he had the luck to be able to help someone across the street. I, for one, know plenty of streams where I'd welcome a little help getting across. In turn I'd be delighted to teach a strapping youngster how to chew tobacco; it's a lot more involved than sugarless gum and it would be something useful to aggravate his parents beside playing his stereo at peak volume.

There is a lot of opportunity here for a kid to sort of adopt an older person. Perhaps even a parent, if there's no one else handy. You can ask anyone why he should take a kid fishing and he'll give you a dozen good reasons—probably none of which include really teaching someone how to fish. You ask him if it wouldn't be a good idea for a kid to go out of his way and take someone else fishing, and you'd be lucky if you get more than a blank stare.

I'm not an anthropologist but I'd bet that there are ten cultures or peoples that are devoted to their children for every one where the middle-aged and older are cared for with more than a desultory attitude. As the politicians are fond of saying, maybe "it's time for a change."

Of course you realize by now that I'm not being very serious. But I am a *little* sincere. I know a lot of parents who would give a great deal to have one of the sprouts off the family tree really want to spend a day outdoors with the people who bore and raised him. I know we have to wait until the children pass the age where they're convinced that their parents are ignorant and uncultured, but that will eventually happen; having children of their own does a lot to hasten the process.

The people of the age usually associated with grandparentage or older are the ones that need youngsters around most of all. I'm being absolutely sincere when I suggest that it might be a wonderful thing if more to the "scouting" groups and the like made a point of visiting retirement homes and taking some of the folks there out for a day of fishing once in a while.

I've been lucky enough to have had a guide who was close to eighty on two or three occasions and I class those times as some of the most pleasant and informative I've ever had. Men with this kind of seasoning are almost always patient, knowledgeable, kind, and understanding. They are living encyclopedias and usually pretty witty and wise to boot. Being with a man of this depth and character is as good a reason to spend a day out fishing as any that I know.

I believe it was Shaw who said something to the effect that "Youth is such a wonderful thing, it is a crime to waste it on children." Well, a lot if it isn't wasted on children, since a lot of us believe that youth can be a glorious state of mind that has little or nothing to do with calendar years. Wouldn't it be a nice thing if some of the worried "young" might come to learn that?

High among my personal regrets are the times when I should have and could have gone a little bit out of my way and taken an old, old friend along for a day of fishing—and high among the things that make me feel good about myself are the times when I've done just that. Not in the idea of "Christian charity" either, but just plain good and enjoyable company, with more than the usual laughs and "reasons for just being there."

A good friend of mine in Texas started a movement a good many years ago, called Operation Orphan. And it's just what it sounds like. A group of men and women take children from the local orphanages on hunting and fishing outings. I know that they all have a marvelous time; it was a wonderful idea and it has done a lot of good for everyone involved. I don't know what the reverse term would be for older and neglected people, but they're "orphans" too in a very real sense. This is perhaps even more tragic in a way because they knew and gave what they could and now when they need it most, they have no one who remembers what they so much loved to do.

I KNOW it's considered "corny," but I am often touched by the common illustration of what seems to be a grandfather and his grandson together. It's usually some common pastime they're sharing and as often as not, it's fishing. But how seldom we wonder who is taking whom along? I'd like to think that it's the youngster, remembering all the good things that came his way from the old folks who live alone, who decided that he'd go dig some worms or catch some shiners and get Grandpa to come along for company.

I like few things better than fishing with a youngster, but I know that I'm a little selfish, because I'm the one who is usually having the most fun. Unfortunately it isn't typical, but I remember a man, who happened to run one of our biggest tackle companies, trout fishing along one of the better Eastern streams. He'd done fairly well and at noon was sitting watching for any activity on the water, enjoying his lunch and just taking things easy when a boy of about ten or so came along and started fishing. The man watched him struggle with his cheap and heavy telescoping rod for a while and then called him over for a chat. The kid's eyes went immediately to the man's tackle—a fine bamboo rod, Hardy reel, the works—as any kid might say. The two chatted about fishing until the company president had a brilliant idea. He asked the young man if he'd ever used a fine rod. The boy said that he hadn't, but some day he sure would like to. The man said to take his for a while since he was tired and wanted to rest. The boy was the picture of delight as he waded out into the stream and started to cast. The president watched him for a while, remembering another boy from another time, then wrote a note and placed it on his fly box where the boy would find it, and very quietly walked out to the road, got in his car and drove away.

Come warm weather, I'm going to take a kid fishing; I hope you do too. But nothing would make me happier than to look across the cove or down the stream and see a young one help an old one remember what it was like to be young in Springtime.

THE HUNTER:
REAL AND RARE

There ain't anybody up in this high country but me and some elk and some muleys, each of us a little bit wild from the time of the year and the sense of being full of ourselves.

The elk and the muleys are thinking about finding a lady to dance with, mostly, but I'm here, mostly, just to think. I listen to the whispered gossip of the popples as I climb up searching for the quiet of the black timber. I want a place to mull about some big and little things. Like where did most of my life go when I wasn't paying close attention, and what am I going to do with the little bit that's left; you know, the same things you think about, give an inch or a day here and there.

I'm taking some time to empty the wastebasket in my head and turn a little animal, primitive, basic; lean a little harder on my senses— instinct instead of logic. Try to find out if the mountains that are real and underfoot are as steep as the ones that we have to climb, back home, in our imagination, everyday. Time to see what's real and what isn't. Time to work out what's worthwhile and what isn't. Time to find out what I am and what I'm not. Time to go it all alone.

Up here, well away from manmade things, you can get a sense of what it must have been like when Jim Bridger and his like cruised this country. And if the day is soft enough and you're feeling good enough, you can believe that this might be exactly what you were made for—running a few traps, learning a little Indian talk—just seeing if you could make it, man against come-what-may.

You sit there and strip everything down. You see yourself with everything you own rolled up in something you can carry on your horse, a rifle across the saddle and your wits and know-how taking the place of money in the bank. At first you've got to cope with the fears that come with being what passes for civilized. You wonder "what if," and go down the list: "what if I get sick, break a leg, get lost, run out of food," and all the rest of the little everyday nightmares. And after a while, you figure you can handle the few that are real, you feel that growing sense of strength that breeds freedom to go where you want, when you please.

You find you can walk a little softer and a lot stronger. You're becoming *part* of the high country—another animal that can make it about as well as the elk. You take note that you can see better, your hearing is sharper, and the shifting winds have a smell of their own. That it takes a little time to make the slide from being just a man carrying a rifle to being a hunter.

I've always leaned toward the idea that most of the important things happened when the man they happened to was sitting still. Really sitting still, when your body seems to go away and all that's left is reason and instinct. I have no doubt that it was a time like this when Galileo came to grips with the stars and Newton with gravity. This is when you can see farther than your eyes will let you and hear things imperceptible to the ear. This is when the moment of discovery will come, this is when the answers to the questions will arrive.

What the hunter hunts is complex indeed. He is there because the elk is there, but this is not all he seeks. He is looking for that essential freedom, that moment of revelation of who he is in relation to his society. He is testing himself and finding the answers to the mysterious questions.

To the non-hunter, all this seems overly complex and often un-believable—an excuse or a rationale. To the real hunter it may be unspoken, but all this is as much a part of why he's there as any quest for food or trophy. Wherever wild game has existed, hunting has been a major part of the ritual of growth from child to man. The ability to provide for others, to not only exist but thrive, physically and emotionally, has marked the quality that man looked for in leadership. There can be no denying that the hunter, then and now, understands such things and finds both motivation and personal satisfaction in them.

If most of us were to sell our hunting rifles, more than likely we could afford to buy enough meat for our needs. But economics, or any one-on-one food/hunting relationship, misses the point completely. Such arguments from the non-hunter are listened to in disbelief by the woodsman. To really understand, you have to experience the secret things that only the hunter has felt.

The non-hunter asks us, "Why don't you race cars, fly planes, or some other excitement?" The real hunter can only answer that his challenges and thrills are more basic, more private and personal; we go to escape the machine-worship and the outside world, not to perform in front of it.

I picked the mountains for my place to be as a hunter, not out of any effort to extend a masculine image, but because I have always separated my great loves of big-game hunting and shotgunning into a personal equation of hunting and shooting. A small point perhaps, and one that you don't necessarily have to agree with, but I approach them with a different philosophy myself and find the challenges and rewards to be different as well.

A hunter uses different skills, much more so than a shotgunner/bird hunter. He has to be skilled in tracking. He must learn to think like his quarry and know its routes and lifestyle. He is coping with an animal capable of some reason, with complex instincts and physical resources. We do not look for a specific quail or pheasant or duck. But more often than not, we have an ideal in mind when we are in sheep country, a certain personal standard of satisfaction when it comes to taking a deer, elk, or moose. No small part of the personal challenge is this factor of selectivity, a personal standard of self-imposed difficulty. Perhaps we seldom achieve it for one or more reasons, but I've yet to meet a hunter whose idea of the perfect hunt didn't incorporate a difficult or idealistic trophy to bring home.

The competent hunter is a complex of skills. He knows how to build a fire, make a camp, and be comfortable under all kinds of conditions. He has a sense of geography and an instinct for weather. He understands his equipment, its limitations, and how to fix what needs fixing. He is self-reliant in an advanced yet basic way that no non-hunter would ever understand. He is challenging himself and the environment and knows very well all the odds, be he on his home ground, on the ice pack, or in the desert. His coming and going is as natural and unobtrusive as that of any wild creature. His presence is minimized by his carefulness not to intrude. He takes nothing he does not need and uses everything completely. He is as innocent of harm to his world as the wind,

Am I idealizing? Of course I am. But a hunter ought to set increasing levels of accomplishments for himself as well as set his levels of desire for what he takes from the wilderness. Perhaps the time will come when most of what we have left to lure us to the hills will be the exercise of these timeless skills.

No, we don't have to bring all the skills of a Green or Bridger to our few days of high-country adventure. But we can bring more than most, or more than we had in the past. It's not always enough in today's world of 7mm magnums and 300 Weatherbys to roll over a deer at 300 yards; not enough of the satisfaction that hunting can offer or the kind of experience we ought to look for and find in our sport. I know this is more than a little idealized, but the pulling of a trigger ought, in its finest tradition, to be the ultimate result of what has been a true hunt—a chase in the classic sense. One animal singled out, tracked, and stalked, come what may. I don't think many of us will do it; some will never consider it and others would never consider anything else. But it's some sort of adventure worth thinking about, when you weigh all that it will mean and prove to you. After all if the only thing important about hunting is what we can nail up on the wall, then we're not really hunters and we will bring little honor to ourselves or to what we hunt, or why.

JAKE

I can never drive by an alder cover without checking the wind and putting down the ghost bird dog I once served under. Ideally the ground will be liberally spotted with telltale splashes of whitewash and a recent rain will have made the earth just right—not so soft as to be really squishy under our feet, but perfectly moist and slightly soft.

The morning sun will be at our back and the uphill slope feels the first warmth of day. We just know how a woodcock ought to feel right now. He's had a good breakfast, the sun has warmed him up, and the light breeze has just enough promise of the coming frosts to make him think of moving on. He thinks of packing up a little extra for lunch and taking a nap and moving on a little just before dusk.

My old pointer, Jake, has it figured out right from the start. He scuffles his feet in the leaves, sneezes a few times to clear out the pipesmoke he's been breathing in the car, and then fills his nose with the bittersweet smells of October. He dances around like a fighter in his corner while I rummage in my vest, sorting the light 8's into the left-hand pocket and the 9's in the right one. I wipe the tobacco crumbs off my shooting glasses, tug my cap down a little tighter, and slip the bell collar over Jake's impatient head. I swing the 20-gauge through the flight of an imaginary woodcock just to loosen the muscles. Jake checks the wind and then decides on a little quartering jog, so that the wind pulls on his right-side whiskers, making him look slightly lopsided.

Jake was always a very serious dog. He was never one for a lot of horseplay or funny stories. The way he always looked at me verged on some sort of reprimand, and every so often he paused and looked back over his shoulder to make sure I wasn't fooling around with my pipe, or poking for arrowheads, or generally skylarking. Jake was always reminding me that time is money, or some such homily. He should have been a Methodist minister, or a regular army sergeant, or a schoolmaster.

As Jake instructs, we weave our way across the hillside, leaving an invisible pattern of footprints on the tapestry of fallen yellow leaves. Jake has figured out some sort of grid—thorough and mathematical—and I plod along like a slow schoolboy being drilled in the multiplication tables. Jake stops, and I can see him about 40 yards ahead looking over his shoulder at me. Then, knowing I'm under orders, he straightens up, holds his head high in the air, and waits a little less than patiently for me to come up and walk in past him.

Jake always expected no less of me than perfection, and it always made me nervous. But this time, the bird curls up to the left through a small clearing where the 9's are waiting for him. Jake carefully works his way over, knowing full well that there might be another bird on the way to the fallen one. I stay put as instructed—he doesn't like me bashing around and messing up his bird field unless it is absolutely necessary.

For some reason, Jake always showed off a little when he retrieved a bird. Some pointers like to hold the whole bird in their mouth and sort of spit it out when they bring it in. Not Jake. He held as little of a woodcock as necessary, as if to display it in a neat and elegant fashion. He would actually prance back, sit in front of me, and wait until I rubbed him under his chin before he would roll the bird down into my open hand and watch as I held it for a moment before carefully sliding it into my game pocket. Only when he was satisfied that I had it put away would he turn around and issue his marching orders.

Actually, Jake was a little pompous, and I was often tempted to laugh at him and tell him to take life a bit easier, but it just wasn't his style to kid around. Once, at home in my study, he was sitting and looking so seriously at the book I was reading that I reached down and slid my glasses over his nose. It was the perfect touch, and to this day I'm sorry I never took a picture of him that way. He wouldn't have liked it, of course, but I would have always treasured it—in private. I can still see him sitting there, not cracking a smile, the glasses magnifying his small brown eyes. He seemed to be waiting for me to say that seven times two was fourteen.

Jake never made a remark when I missed a bird. After two shots were fired and the gun was reloaded, he would watch the bird for another second or so, if he could.

Then, satisfied that there was nothing to be done except try again, he would lope off without so much as dignifying my performance in any way. It was as if nothing at all had happened. I had come up with the wrong answer and he would patiently try again. When he was younger, he would sometimes shrug his shoulders at being with such a partner, as if to say, "Well, that's life." But eventually he quit that little gesture and just went back to his blackboard to try again.

Jake was always physically on the small side for a pointer, and I think that had a lot to do with his attitude. The other puppies in his litter were the usual madmen—knocking each other witless, standing in the food pan, trying to chew each others' ears and legs off. Not Jake. He would always be off to one side waiting patiently for the fracas to calm down. He was the last kid picked for the team. That's why I chose him; I knew exactly how he must have felt. When he was first home with me, I'd bring him in the house and offer him squeaky toys and bones, and roll around on the floor trying to make him play. He gave all this foolishness an honest effort, but it really wasn't his style. He'd take the bones and toys back into his kennel to please me, and sometimes I'd think I heard a tiny whistle from the rubber mouse, but when I cleaned out his house, there they would all be, as good as new, pushed back into one corner.

But he loved the hunting and all that went with it. At the sight of a gunning coat or a shotgun, he'd prance around as if he couldn't help himself, and as if to prove how much he appreciated me taking him out, he insisted on always riding in the front seat of the car. If I had someone with me, Jake would squeeze over in the middle, and if he was very tired after a long day, he'd sometimes slide his head very quietly into my lap and fall asleep. I think he took my love completely for granted and did his best to show me that he didn't need any presents or playing of games to prove our relationship. I was the hunter and he was the hunting dog. That was enough.

When you tell a story about your dog, it has to have an ending. None of those endings are pleasant and they always leave you with the feeling of emptiness. You're saying one thing or another out loud but in your mind, you're thinking something else. You're remembering the little toys pushed into one corner of the kennel, or his way of falling asleep standing up, as if pretending he wasn't tired at all. Or the times he knew you'd hit a bird and insisted on looking until he found it, taking some small satisfaction in proving you wrong, or better than you thought you were.

I really don't exactly know what happened. It was late summer and Jake and I had been out for our usual walk—just checking things out in the evening, watching some ducks circle into the pond, hoping to see a dusking woodcock or hear a pheasant call goodnight. Jake liked walking around the pond. He would permit himself the indulgence of rousting out a bullfrog or chasing a firefly, but in the main he had a strong feeling of property and was along to see that things were running smoothly before we went to bed.

The next morning Jake didn't seem to be feeling too well and I left him in the kennel while I did some chores around the lawn. Later that afternoon when I visited him again, he was gone to wherever our bird dogs go. It was the way he would have wanted it. He left his life as he lived it, by himself, with dignity and calm.

Jake always seemed fond of his little hunting bell, so I put that with him, along with a couple of empty shells, because he always seemed to like the way they smelled. In the fresh earth I stuck a small white pine. I like to think that Jake would have approved of the tree. It is a more natural reminder than a stone would be. Now that the tree has grown a bit, I sometimes see the wind lift one side of its branches and I think of how Jake often looked, with his head tilted into the breeze, his whiskers lifted up a little cockeyed, and his eyes rolling back at me to make sure I was there.

In the beginning of this story I called Jake a "ghost dog." I don't really mean that because there isn't any such thing. As long as we live and remember, so do our dogs still live. I still hunt with Jake; he still has the same hold over me and always will.

I've been thinking about Jake a lot lately; you tend to do that with a dog who isn't here and left before he told you all that he wanted you to know. Maybe I was wrong about him. Maybe Jake saw himself as being droll rather than professorish. Maybe he thought that he'd set an example for me, and when I came around a little, he could afford to relax a bit—you never really know about these things. Now I've become concerned about the white pine. There's a ridiculous game kids play about "if you were a tree, what kind of a tree would you like to be?" Well, it's too late to do much about the tree now. But I'm beginning to lean toward putting a small stone under the pine— nothing to it, just a plain stone. Jake would understand a formal touch and what I meant by it. Just because he wasn't sentimental doesn't mean I can't be.

A LISTENING WALK

I think, now, that the thing my father liked best about bird hunting was the listening. The sounds you made through the crisp orange of the covers, so sharply punctuated by the abrupt quiet when you stopped. The straining to hear the tinkling of the dog bell, the sorting out of all the little noises until what you wished for came through the rest. Past the rustling of the trees, under the wind, over and around the calling of the crows and the barking of distant farm dogs, the threadlike tingle of the little five-cent bell would call us off to some new and exciting direction.

Now and then we'd stop, trying to catch the waxing and waning, trading disappointment for eagerness, the bafflement of silence leaving the next steps to our woodsmen's judgment until one of us could see the dog standing there on point, her head turned to our footsteps until she was sure we'd seen her. One off to each side we walked, and then, at the sound of the shot, we'd stand dead still, putting the rolling boom away in our memory against the instant silence that suddenly seemed almost a rebuke to the violent sound of the shot. Sometimes one of us would speak, sometimes not. The ritual then was not to talk just for the sake of talking. Idle chatter wasn't the way of country people. We were as thrifty with our emotions as we were with our little money. Chattering was looked on as impolite or worse, empty-headedness. Bird hunting was a private delight.

The woods are where I go when I'm starved for quiet. But, of course, the quiet is only relative. Few things in nature have idle tongues. The chattering of a squirrel will alert those of its kind that are listening—as it's meant to do. The scolding of the jay precedes my presence like a siren. These are important sounds to creatures that live by listening. As a small boy I used to practice walking, as careful as a warring Iroquois not to snap a twig or rattle a rock, and few things filled me with more pride than to walk up on a browsing deer and be able to stand so still that I could pass for a tow-headed, slightly ragged, runny-nosed tree. And I still take a certain amount of joy in my quiet ways, helped along by some dulling deafness, absorbing the small, now-and-then bits and pieces of quiet like a tonic. I take to the woods alone a lot more than I used to in younger days.

You stand there and the scratching of a match to light your pipe sounds like a tearing of canvas. But you don't dare stand still too long or the silence forbids the idea of moving. You begin, after a while, to shed a few of the layers of man and you understand, however so insignificantly, the demand for quiet that is instinctive in an animal in the wild—the ghost fears that have existed for a hundred thousand years.

So we follow the old dog, shuffling along well inside the need for a whistle, knowing that any chance for a bird is slim and knowing that's not really why we are here. We are not really here to shoot birds this time. We are after something else. We are looking for that layer inside us, that subconscious antenna, that feeling that here, in these woods, we are washing something away in the quiet.

We come to watch the beaver and understand his hurry to get things done. We note the rubbings of the buck and the heavy nests of the squirrels. Most of the songbirds have left, and you stop and imagine, or try to, that the lady jay is two thousand miles away and in four or five months will find her way back to just where her bold and cheeky mate is perched, telling you that you haven't spoofed him for a minute. Some crows are worrying an unseen owl who couldn't care less. The old dog comes back and asks us a question, and to humor her sense of industry we move on.

They ask me, "What do you think about in the woods?" I tell
them all sorts of things, but actually I'm trying not to think of
anything special at all. This is the country of few second chances for
the unwary, and you might think about that. Or you might wonder
about the certain odd shape of a stone and turn it over with your foot
and think about it trying that side up for another few hundred years.
Just idle ruminations of the mind. Animal curiosity.

My father especially liked the sound of snow falling. He used to
say "listen...," and I couldn't hear anything but the softness. It took
me years to understand what he heard in the sounds of snow and rain
and that it was possible to understand something and never be able
to explain it—that some sounds you absorbed deeper than in the
labyrinths of the ear. What does the bark of a fox sound like to the
mouse? Or the croak of the heron to the frog? I tell the old dog that
none of these are the voices of poets and she, to humor me, agrees.

The work shift changes with the coming of twilight and the voices
wane. There is a chorus of good nights as the pheasants pull the
covers up over their heads. The fox barks to let them know he is there,
but I think they know already. If you're a pheasant, the fox is always
there. An owl orders silence and gets it. Some odd night birds call,
forever mysteries to me; others have voices I can put faces on. The
old dog has heard the pheasants too and looks over her shoulder to see
if I'm following. I am, but unwillingly. Ordinarily I leave the roosting
covers alone in my theory that a man's house is his castle and that
goes for the pheasants as well, but the old dog is sort of twisting my
arm and reminding me that there is some time to go before dark. I
try to argue with her but it's no use. She reminds me that we took a
bird or two there when she was a puppy and I tell her that was
training and she says that she's old and can't see or hear too well
anymore and has to make do. We head toward the little swamp, she
at a trot, looking back to make sure I'm there.

The quiet is palpable now. All I can hear is the dog splashing
back with the cock bird. I turn away and head back toward the car
and she follows along with her prize.

I feel guilty at having broken a promise I long ago made to myself.
But I have given the old dog her way and now it's too late for remorse.
How often we have to reflect on the price of satisfaction—the toss of
a coin, so to speak, that often seems as willful and arbitrary as the
Roman judges in the Coliseum.

I take the bird and carry it myself, and I can hear the delighted snuffling of the old dog as she shuffles along, poking her nose into the feathers to reassure herself that the bird is still there. We stop and take a last minute to look at the ruby eyebrow of the setting sun and listen to nothing. I unload the gun and slip the shells into my pocket. What I want, right now, is to hear another cock bird calling from the swamp, a voice that will echo through the evening mist with a wild bravado to reassure me that this little corner of my world is still quick with life. I know it is, for we heard half a dozen crowings just before the old dog had her way, and I want someone to tell me now that the incident has already been forgotten. But nothing happens.

I, who had wanted only a quiet walk, have become the owl *and* the fox. I, who had gone only to listen, have become the one who was listened to.

Sitting by the car I dress and pick the pheasant. The old dog stretches herself out for a little nap and the feathers drift over her dull, black coat. I take a handful and slide them under her nose and she thumps her tail without opening her eyes. I think that I ought to tell her the story of Eden, but being a woman, I'm sure she understands it far better than I do. I tell her that I'm just a pushover for a pretty face, but she knows that too. She climbs into the front seat with me, ignoring her kennel in the back, puts her head on my lap, and sleeps.

DOG HAIR
IN YOUR DRINK

The bird hunter's wife had been too long neglected. I can't understand why the Post Office hasn't put out a stamp depicting a lady picking pheasants, or mending britches, or reloading No. 8's, or feeding a setter, but then there are lots of things I don't understand about the P.O.

Lacking government recognition, I feel that someone ought to pay tribute. And since I have a good model to work from (B+ to A−), there's no harm in being the one to get the thing rolling.

First off, a bird hunter's wife doesn't have to know much about the actual process of bird hunting. Chances are she's been subjected to enough hours of conversation, monologues, soliloquies, and group discussions to get a Ph.D. in the subject without ever having laced up a pair of boots or screamed herself hoarse trying to track down Lady, or Ben, or Rip.

To find her house you turn in at the mailbox with the pheasant on it, use the setter-head door knocker, and wipe your feet on the mat covered with images of quail. Knock very loudly—you have to be heard through the barking of dogs inside and outside. She will be wearing an apron decorated with birds, dogs, or a recipe for braised partridge and, of course, covered with dog hair. She will hand you a drink in a glass decorated with shotguns, or shells, or dogs, or birds. There will be dog hair in the drink. This is not a matter of careless housekeeping. She doesn't see dog hair anymore. It's just *there*—part of the very air she breathes.

The aroma coming from the kitchen is tantalizing; it seems she's discovered a new recipe for quail. She knows at least forty-three ways to prepare any gamebird and this one is a French recipe that the wife of another bird hunter has passed along with high recommendations. Bird hunters' wives also know how to cook fish during the summer months, and if pressured, at least six out of ten can do a marvelous job on a rabbit, especially if the bird hunter is running a puppy or two.

Her home is pretty much as you'd expect. Lampshades, pictures, curtains, and the usual decorative items feature scenes from the upland life. The table is set with salt and pepper shakers in the shape of shotgun shells. Plates feature paintings by A.B. Frost or some similar motif. The gravy pitcher is in the shape of a pointing dog's head. All in all, the atmosphere is one of great comfort to the eye and body of the bird hunter.

As we mentioned, the bird hunter's wife is almost always a fine cook. We safely assume a most deft touch with feathered game, but the details of other repasts make her outstanding. Her sandwiches are never soggy, because she abjures the use of tomatoes and is judicious with lettuce. The bread is an honest inch thick and, being homemade, reeks of health and love. Her breakfast biscuits hold a decent portion of ham, if desired, and are topped with her homemade jelly or jam— enough to give an ordinary man (not a bird hunter) second thoughts about ever leaving her home alone. Her way with cakes and pies deserves public acclamation, and several bird hunter friends of her husband have fallen deeply in love with her, merely on the basis of a shared lunch in the field.

She is never surprised or displeased to find that her bird hunter will be late in arriving home or that he is bringing several companions in for dinner. She truly delights in their company and has known to ask several of them to repeat just exactly how they made that difficult double on quail. She almost never forgets to ask about their dogs, and always by name.

A bird hunter's wife is an astute detective. For example, she can tell by the footprints on the kitchen floor a lot about the day. If the prints are mucky, she knows they've been in the swamps after pheasant. If they're just muddy, she is prepared to listen to tales of woodcock and alder bottoms. If they're just dusty, she braces herself for stories of busted coveys and wild singles. If they're clean and unsteady, she just braces herself.

She is a competent amateur veterinarian and attends to the worming and heartworm schedules. If need be, she can handle a check cord or blank cartridges, and she can grass a thrown pigeon. She has no objection to using a station wagon whose windows are smeared with nose prints and whose cargo area is usually filled with cages and sundry impedimenta. Her wardrobe is what might be called "utilitarian chic"—chosen with the ever-present dog hairs in mind and the likelihood of being summoned from a dinner party or social function to look for a lost dog or assist in a whelping.

In the brief off-season that the bird hunter enjoys, she is ever willing to extend her cheerful expertise to cover fishing contingencies as well as the various activities of the local trap and skeet club.

Time was, when a bird hunter sought a mate, he concentrated on the offspring of older bird hunters. If he was not invited to dinner at certain houses, he made excuses to visit and look over the young ladies. A woman raised in a house where bird dogs reign is an obvious gem, accustomed to apple pie at breakfast, hot toddies just before bedtime, and all the other niceties in between.

In times past there were a lot of bird hunters' daughters to select from, and a very selfish young man might add onto his personal requirements that the father be the possessor of small-gauge Parkers or L.C. Smiths, own the right amount of the right kind of acreage, kennels, walking horses, and so on. No doubt the father often did own these things, probably with the intention of seeing Patty or Jennifer use them to their best advantage in selecting bird hunters who came up to their father's standards.

Alas, times have changed, and the number of young ladies who aspire to become the wives of bird hunters has either diminished or, in their cagey, feminine way, these precious jewels are being very quiet about their matrimonial ambitions in order to have the field to themselves. Today such a woman is often found gracing well-attended trap and skeet tournaments or setting out glorious lunches at field trials. When none of these are handy, you're likely to find her fishing. I might add, with pleasure, that a woman can participate in all these activities with equal skill.

The bird hunter's wife quickly becomes a woman possessing an almost unbelievable variety of skills. Along with the basics of being able to patch boots, reload shotshells, tie flies, make shirts, etc., one of her most desirable roles is that of the devoted listener. One only has to see the dreamy look in the eyes of a lady listening to a conversation about the pros and cons of various theories of choke boring to know that here is a "One of One Thousand" of a fair sex. Who could help but treasure a woman who can recall, including the weather and wind direction, your classic double on woodcock? Or your first 50 straight at trap? Or someone who longs for the evenings in front of the fire as you read your favorite passages from Nash Buckingham or Burton Spiller?

Such a woman is more than likely to insist that she can get along another year or so with the old stove, since you so obviously need a new Ruger 20-bore or an 870 trap gun. She understands the critical priorities and sees that they are accomplished. You never have to look all over the house for your red handkerchiefs or your heavy socks. She knows where you left your duck call and your shooting glasses. She remembers to buy pipe tobacco and lighter fluid. She even sees to it that the alarm is set early enough and the gas tank is full!

That such a woman is a rarity is obvious, but I firmly believe the many I know are doing their best to insure the survival of the species. I also believe that the subconscious dissatisfaction many young women have with their golf, tennis, weightlifting, crew, marathons, and the like, is because, as yet, no bird hunter has come along to show them where this energy and skill is best deployed.

I once asked a bird hunter's wife what her husband's favorite perfume was. She thought for a few seconds or so and with a very sweet and knowing smile said, "I'm sure it's a blend of sourdough biscuit mix and cinnamon!" Anyone who doesn't fall in love a little with a woman like that doesn't deserve to have dog hair in his drink.

"JUST AFTER
YOU LEFT..."

It's obvious to those few of you who have followed my writing while waiting for the dentist or barber, that I take an uncommon interest in the pursuit of woodcock. I use the word *pursuit* as opposed to *gunning* or *hunting*, since it's much more apt. The word *gunning* has always implied to me the enviable expenditure of more than two or three boxes of shells a season, while to *hunt* carries an image of some rugged and demonic individual tirelessly trudging through bird covers with his shotgun constantly at port arms and his senses ever alert to even the most obscure sign. I *pursue:* an ambling wander through alders and abandoned orchards, encouraged by wishful thinking that has relatively little basis in fact, probability, or past performance.

Typical of my adventures is that for years I have eagerly trekked to the Canadian province of New Brunswick to spend some time with my old friend and outfitter, Fred Webb. Flanking the Tobique River, Fred's hillside covers are classic—stand after stand of alders, birches, and spruce hard by slightly damp grazing meadows. It's impossible for any bird pursuer to drive by and not remark to himself that these hillsides just have to be stiff with woodcock in flight time. And he'd be absolutely correct, providing he arrived during that one perfect week—the one just after I left. The week just after I left is generally a good time to be anywhere if you're a sportsman, but especially during woodcock season in New Brunswick. It so happens that the Tobique Valley is one of my absolute favorite places and since I fully intend to spend some time there every season, I shall, no doubt, one of these years, hit a week when the woodcock are confused due to Leap Year, or a shift in the lunar tides, or something equally unexplainable, and they'll be there in the numbers usually reserved for "just after you left...."

But don't feel sorry for me. Just a couple of years ago I ran into ruffed grouse in unbelievable numbers on a trip to Manitoba. In fact I actually got a true, simultaneous rise, double with my full-and-full, 32-inch barrelled duck gun—no witnesses, of course! Why go after grouse with a F&F? Because I was there just to gun ducks and geese, that's why. I honestly hadn't given a thought to grouse; I did the next year and brought my Cylinder & Improved Cylinder, and you can guess what stage the grouse cycle was in!

Another such incident: It had long been one of my fondest dreams to pursue woodcock in Great Britain, and not too long ago it came true. I was fortunate enough to be in Wales, hard by the Irish Sea, where fine flights of woodcock are not uncommon. I was even luckier on the trip to have had two reasonable shots at European woodcock (about twice as big as ours) and to bring one down. My elation lasted until the inevitable "just after you left..." letter telling me that from one cover they had flushed over 100 birds and a party of eight guns took forty-three. Not that my lifetime plan includes a great bag of woodcock, but how sweet it would have been to be able to say "a few" when asked if I've ever taken the bird in England or thereabouts, instead of giving the obviously evasive and inadequate answer, "yes."

I don't even have to be there to get my expected "just after you left..." letter. There have been plenty of trips planned to Michigan, Pennsylvania, Vermont, Maine, North and South Carolina, Louisiana, and even Texas that I've had to cancel. Needless to say, it seems that I always missed the week of weeks. The letters frequently use the phrase "never in the memory of man have we seen...." Even taken with the necessary grains of salt and allowing for forked tongues, I am forced to assume that they at least flew as many birds as they usually do.

What I'd really like is to set up some sort of scientific experiment: one week when I'm supposed to be there but can't; one week when I'm actually there; and the celebrated "week after you left...." I don't for one minute really believe that a small brown bird with such important things on its mind as a heavy travel schedule, visiting friends, going back to old restaurants and discovering new ones, etc., etc., really has more than a suspicion of where I really am at any given time in the fall. Yet, the strange feeling continues to grow.

Of course, the odd straggler or uninformed bird does cross my path now and then, often enough to keep my dedication to nicely grained walnut stocks and a touch of engraving on the receiver. To dwell on that for a bit, I'll admit that I have coveted a 20-bore with 28-inch barrels both bored improved cylinder, with a straight-hand English stock and a weight in the neighborhood of 6½ pounds. I still do, but lately I have had a yearning for the same general statistics but in a 28 gauge. To take it all a step further (and why not, since it's my usual wishful thinking?), I'd enjoy a pair of outside hammers, double triggers, and perhaps a setter and a bird or two nicely done on the locks.

If you ever see me in the upland covers and ask, "Where's that little 28 gauge you were so high on?" I will resist the urge to ask that you kick me and admit I have owned two and sold them both for reasons I don't remember and could not explain if I did. Suffice it to say that I'm sick over doing it, and while I'm not asking for, nor do I deserve, any sympathy, you must know how quickly and tragically stupidity can strike any of us when it comes to fooling with shotguns. Not that either gun was anything resembling my imaginary side-by-side, but even so, I wish mightily I had them still. (If any of you has had a 28-gauge double, please for sanity's sake don't write me saying "just last week....")

I also confess that I know it's irrational for me to spend as much time and give as much thought as I do to messing around with woodcock, woodcock guns, woodcock this, and woodcock that. But here we have an irrational bird and we have to meet him, or try to, on equal terms. What other creature do you know of that was a shore bird not too long ago and decided to hell with that and left the shorelines and seaside marshes for perpendicular hillsides and impenetrable thickets? It's just another segment of the mystery of a bird that is said to occasionally carry its young between its legs and has had scores of learned ornithologists arguing for years about whether its sweet peenting whistle is done vocally or is actually a sound made by its wings. What other bird amuses its mate by aerial dancing in the spring moonlight or, as far as I know, has never been seen perched in a tree? Why won't an otherwise superb retriever pick one up without looking like he wants to spit or use mouthwash? All of this for the same obscure and irrational reasons that make us willing and eager to part with the mortgage and egg money for a 28 gauge, spend an embarrassing amount of time and trouble driving all over the countryside to fritter away six or eight shells, and have about half our library stocked with titles that start with "W."

When opportunities present themselves, I can turn into a dedicated waterfowler, a devotee of pheasant and quail, and can hardly wait for September so I can embarrass myself on flighting doves. But when you think about it for a minute, you'll agree that these are, given this or that little oddity, fairly reliable birds. They are, for the most part, where they should be, when they should be. They are as rational and as well behaved as a banker; you know their hours and places of business. When you itch for one of these, you can reach where you want to scratch.

But your woodcock is at best a blind date. He promises to meet you at the corner by the best worm restaurant in town and when you get there right on time, where is he? It seems he just forgot, or got lost, or found someplace he likes better; no messages, no forwarding address. He's fickle, untrustworthy, unpunctual, selfish, and forgetful. He takes the money I've saved to buy my wife a new washing machine and makes me toss it away on a new stock with a quarter-inch less drop.

Well, I've learned my lesson. No more listening to promises about the next full moon in October in Canada, or the one after that in Cape May, New Jersey. No more hanging around in the hillside birches by the spring run. Okay, just one more time, come the right winds and a light fall rain, there is *one* section of a secret cover that I just have to visit. But if I do and there's a letter in a week or so that says "just after you left...," and I find an alder leaf with a spot of whitewash on it enclosed, I quit.

IT'S BETTER
NOT TO KNOW

You've spent an hour of incredibly careful stalking, and as you top the last ridge, the big buck is just where you expected him to be. But suddenly, he raises his head, stiffens, and in one magnificent leap disappears into the tall timber. What happened? It's better that we don't know.

The brown trout of a lifetime has responded to your perfect presentation. For half an hour you play him superbly, giving and taking line, avoiding any sudden stress on the 4X leader, steering him past snags, keeping him out of the deep holes where he could lay and sulk. Suddenly the line is slack. You reel in and everything is fine—no straightened hook, no broken leader. What happened? It's better that we don't know.

The times are endless. The covey of quail that both dogs swore was right there on the edge of the broom grass field has suddenly vanished. The dogs mess around a little and come back waiting for you to cast them off again. The half dozen Canadas work nicely to your call until, at about a hundred yards or so, the leader suddenly turns and takes the flock away. The gobbling tom that the forest just swallowed up, the rolling largemouth by the stump, the woodcock you so carefully marked down from a wild flush... all gone. Why? It's better that we don't know.

I remember a goose hunt in Maryland that was over about 9 A.M. We laid our dozen honkers out in four rows of three and went back to the farm house for the pickup truck. When we got back to the blind, about 15 or 20 minutes later at the most, there were just eleven geese. Eddy Boyd and I have wondered about that one bird ever since. How about the giant oryx that I stalked to well within a hundred yards? I laid my rifle on a fallen tree and very calmly put a 130-grain .270 right behind the shoulder. My hunter, David Ommanney, standing just a bit behind me saw the dust fly where the bullet hit. "Perfect!" he said. We ran to where the animal had to be, but there was no oryx, no tracks, no blood. No explanation. Unless you easily believe in ghost oryx. And later that day we were ready to do just that.

Why does your dog suddenly get up and growl at nothing in the night? What was it that suddenly made your blood run cold and the hair stiffen on the back of your neck? Ghosts? It's better that we don't know.

I wish that where Atlantic salmon live at sea was still a mystery and I rejoice that where the tarpon go and why is still unknown. No doubt it's hypocritical of me to rejoice in scientific know-how and still deplore the loss of mystery, but that's the way I am. I'm curious, to a point, but the thrill of speculation, the pleasure of being able to wonder, to guess, or even hope is still some atavistic part of me. I don't really want to *know* what makes the coyote howl or my setters bay at the moon. Nor why the ducks have suddenly decided not to fly or why the trout settle down to the bottom. I used to dream about being able to know just what was lying in the deep green-black of the pool I ran my streamers through, or if there were any birds in the next cover and how many. But no more. Some of us have to seek and others have to hide—in more ways than one. I'm afraid my days are numbered, but the number is, in fact, not a question that I want the answer to right now, or even when I hear the ticking of the eternal clock. I shall be gladly ignorant and just wait my turn. It's better that we don't know.

There are even things that I know better about that I still like to believe in because of the tinge of mystery. It was with reluctance that I abandoned the idea that horsehairs would turn into baby eels or that a snake sought the killer of its mate. I don't believe that lightning will strike a beech or sycamore because I just don't want to. I do believe that finding a penny is good luck and that if someone gives you a knife and you don't give him something in return, you'll cut yourself with it. And what's the harm in believing in falling stars, making wishes, and four-leaf clovers?

Why do we have *those* days—days where we can't do anything wrong, and days where we can't do anything right? Why do our dogs and our shotguns have them? Why is it that a retriever who delights in lugging a splintery stick around, or chewing a tin can, or browsing on an expensive shrub refuse to pick up a woodcock or more than a few doves? Why will a shotgun, which has heard itself praised beyond all reason, suddenly turn malicious? The same gun that has given you twenty doves from a box of shells, a triple on mallards in front of witnesses, and even a couple of straights at skeet suddenly take it into its mind to quit hitting quail or grouse? It's better that we don't know!

All of us have little mysteries that continue to intrigue us. Some of my favorites are how and why a flock of feeding geese can suddenly get up, seemingly all at exactly the same time, and all fly in the same direction. Who says GO!? Who says fly directly northeast after you reach the right altitude? What in the world possesses a bass to make a savage strike at a spinnerbait that looks and sounds like a runaway Cessna? A lot of real hen mallards sound worse than I do with my duck call. How come they get results and I don't? If "in-line" breeding can result in stupid and badly conformed dogs, why doesn't the same thing happen with deer, or bear, or elk, or what-have-you? Does an animal know who its father or mother or sister is? Does it give a hoot?

How do geese and mallards find their way back to the island in my pond—a piece of ground not quite big enough to bury a horse? Why does an Atlantic salmon hit a fly? Why does one species of fish jump and another not jump when they're hooked? Why are wild animals so spooked by human scent? Does a trout really see a hook and say to himself, "can't fool me"? Does a woodcock really carry its young between its legs? How can an ant lift ten times its own weight when I can't? Is it fair that so many creatures can grow a new tooth when they lose one when I can't?

What does a dog dream about? Do all animals dream? How does a horse know its way home in the dark down a mountain where it has never been before? Why is it that Ed Zern can imitate animals—bull alligators, Cape buffalo, even a hissing snake when he's asleep but never when he's awake? It's better that we don't know.

Someone said something to the effect that "ignorance is bliss," and I have to agree that in these meanderings, it, blissfully, is. There's a sweetness to the surprises of traveling down a path that isn't scientifically labeled, charted, or marked "no left turn" or "dead end." I like being lost a little, whether it's in reality or just idle conjecture—dreaming a bit, making up my own imaginary conclusions, seeing things the way I'd like them to be—truth, logic, and scientific know-how be damned.

I most fervently hope that the simple, everyday happenings never lose their magic powers to awe us. How much poorer we would be if we didn't have those moments when we could, in our imagination, put the words we'd like to the evening song of the quail or the bugling of an elk. Just another humble reason why it's better that we don't know.

A MATTER OF GRAVITY

Among the many talents I don't get recognition for are my powers of pure scientific observation and my mathematical genius. The fact that I can't balance a checkbook or make change has nothing to do with it; no doubt you recall that Albert Einstein had the same failings.

I certainly don't want to cause any sort of general panic, but I'll just state the facts, as I see them, and let the professionals take over from there. My premise is simply that the force of gravity has become noticeably stronger—and here follow some random notes to back up, reinforce, and prove that statement.

Late last summer I noticed that those big bags of dog food started sticking to the floor of my van. Not the sort of problem that immediately causes a scientific investigation, but just enough of a warning to the scholarly mind to make a mental note and see if similar phenomena were evident. Well, I didn't have to wait very long. Still troubled by the dog food incident, I began to be positive that my fly line wasn't carrying the distance it used to. It doesn't take an IQ of three big numbers to get right to the source of the problem. It was gravity—again!

Of course, two incidents don't constitute a body of proof, and I know that as well as anyone. But when my gun club opened in the fall, a couple of painfully obvious facts—almost frightening, really—were added to the list. First, my trap gun was notably heavier and decidedly slower to swing. And remarkably, even the clay targets were falling sooner than they ever had. I struggled to keep the evidence to myself for a lot of reasons, not the least of which is the old legalism that you don't shout *"Fire!"* in a crowded theatre.

With the opening of duck hunting season came another series of hard-to-fault proofs. The duck boat was much more difficult to row. I'm not sure of the exact difference, but let's say it took at least thirty minutes to row the same distance that last year took only twenty. And a dozen or so decoys were clearly harder to move and pick up after gunning. And if that wasn't enough to seal the case, the way the shells performed removed any doubt that might have lingered. My old lead of three feet or so on a crossing broadbill had to go way out to four or five or six feet. I'm sure the ammunition companies are keeping this quiet until they come up with an answer, but you ought to bear it in mind if you've got any late-season shooting planned. Since facts are facts, universally, this ought to go a long way toward explaining why *you* didn't do as well last year as you usually do.

Sound waves, as everyone knows, are affected by gravity as surely as No. 5 duck loads or a WF8F fly line or 50 pounds of Purina. So if you're not hearing as well as you used to, take what I've told you into consideration. There's no doubt that the government and the scientific community will completely ignore what ought to be staring them in the face. And if they have come up with the same truths I have, they may have already been told by some computer that there's nothing to be done. I expect that's the case, and no doubt I'll be getting stronger as I adjust to the change. In the meantime I think I've answered some of the questions a lot of you have been puzzling over.

I suspect it has something to do either with the state of economic affairs or the leaning to the metric system, but a lot of things like clay targets, hook eyes, and belts have gotten a little smaller. Gradual changes are bound to occur for a variety of reasons, and we all have to learn to adjust. We've all noticed that the opening day of trout season is colder than it was just a couple of years ago and that the same thing is true on deer stands. Nature has altered the ways of the weather and evolution; natural selection has changed the habits of a lot of things. Doves, for an obvious example, fly a lot faster and more erratically than they used to. Geese are higher and teal have learned to fly only downwind. Deer have gotten harder to see because the color of their coats has obviously changed a little. No doubt acid rain has been a factor, but streams are a lot more slippery to wade and a good drag-free float is no longer as easy to come by.

Maybe the skeptic would say that I'm not shooting as well as I used to or that my technique with the fly rod leaves more than a little to be desired. Or maybe I'm looking at things in a different way than I used to. To be honest, I won't argue the points—maybe it is me that's changed after all.

It's possible that deer are getting harder to see because I'm looking for other things, where once I was most intent on the animal. Maybe doves are smaller because the other things in bird country have become more important. Maybe the time has come when taking a limit of broadbills or Canadas isn't quite that crucial. Maybe the balance, or some personal measuring stick, has changed.

If you sat, for lack of much better to do, and analyzed the "maybes," you might find that the pride of throwing a perfect cast or making a double on those downwind teal has shifted a little. Not that it isn't pleasing to do these things, because it is, but maybe we've come to know that it's better if we don't care as much about them anymore. It's not that they're not important, it's that they're not *that* important.

I'll admit that there was a time when I counted the shells and the birds and let the score dictate whether or not I had a good day. But I think I like the present better because I honestly don't measure things that way. It's not that I've given up admiring such skills, but that I've found some other things I think are just as important.

If it happens that I have a good day in the dove fields—which, to me, is taking around three birds with five shells—I'm delighted. But if I don't, it no longer is that important. Call it a matter of intensity, if you will. One of my friends will make a hundred or so more casts a day than I will and, of course, he'll take more fish. But I find that I like to walk the riverbanks a bit and take some time to watch the birds. I'm still as intent as he is, when I get serious; it's just that I'm no longer as serious for as long a time. And I'm still a fair shot in the field; it's just that I'm satisfied now with fewer empty shells at my feet.

Maybe it's just that the personal gravity has changed. Some things have gotten too heavy for me to carry very far and others have gotten too heavy to carry at all. I used to forget, too often, that the whole purpose of being outdoors with a rod or a gun and a dog is to come back a bit refreshed, sometimes a bit wiser, and, hopefully, a little more relaxed and happier. But it didn't always happen that way. It wasn't the outdoors that had gone wrong, it was me.

For a little while I almost stopped going out at all. I wanted to find a different perspective, to think about it, to discover why my attitude had changed. Why was I caring more about the part that didn't matter than about the part that did? In a way I was selfish and demanding. Ego and skills got themselves all mixed around.

But in time, things began to sort themselves out. I discovered some very simple truths, one being that I really didn't have to do things that I didn't want to do just because a lot of other people were doing them. And no one who really mattered really cared. Not a great or weighty insight, I'll be the first to admit, but it was important to me.

You can learn not to be so disappointed when the things you thought you wanted didn't quite work out if you give a little thought to why you wanted them. There's a lot of personal satisfaction in knowing that. Maybe that's what people used to mean when they talked about "growing up." And that's probably what I've been talking about all along—a little maturity and a little commonsense.

I know that this has been old and rather personal stuff for some of you. But perhaps a few of you will find some reassurance here that you are not alone when a certain wind seems to ask a question and you don't know the answer, or even if you ought to answer at all.

MENDING HARNESS

I'm a great believer in almanacs, "signs," and other country truths largely known to outsiders as superstitions. There is, no doubt, a right time to do things, as we've all learned from Ecclesiastes and other sources, but I really can't say much for the things to do in early March. In times before mine, March was a good month to mend harness, sharpen the plow, and attend to other chores of the kind we all tend to put off until there is absolutely nothing better to do. But here where I live—the way I live—the only tools of the trade I have to fool with are fly rods and shotguns and the stuff that goes along with them.

There's a pair of waders that have defied about twenty man-hours of searching for a leak that lives somewhere just below the left knee. I'll probably end up with a patch that looks like a grafting wrap, but that's what March is for. Time to get out the bamboo rods and give them a good looking over. Those that need new wrappings go over to Jim Foran, whose skills include such work; and those that don't will get two or three good coats of wax from me, whose skills can barely cope with chores on this level.

All the reels will get a little cleaning and a drop or so of oil, and a major attempt will be made to find the extra spools and do a little match-making. As usual I'll find that the extra spool for the WF7F also carries a WF7F, which will lead into trying to find what I've done with the WF7Wet Tip, which will lead in turn to at least two days of putting such things back in some sort of order than will be as short-lived as usual.

Clean the cork grips. Wipe out the ferrules. Maybe go outside and make a practice cast or two with this rod or that if the pond isn't all frozen over. Clean out the fly vest, put flies back where they came from, make lists of new salmon flies to ask friends to tie—never have enough Rogers Fancy's, Bombers, or Dusty Millers; always have too many Rusty Rats and Orange Blossoms. Dismiss idea of learning to tie my own…easier and more in character to bum…get much better flies.

Clean and oil bait-casting reels. Start to rummage through tackle box and give up. Plugs and spoons always a mess no matter what. Clean and wax the one bamboo casting rod…sorry to see them all disappear. Put old reel on bamboo rod—the kind you have to thumb yourself…wonder if the old skill is still there. Go out to the pond and try a few casts…spend half an hour picking out backlash. Skill still there, but very rusty.

Put all the rods away except for three or four in case a nice day comes along so I can go out to practice. Always need practice. Always cast better in the yard than on the stream…mystery to me.

Start to sort shells. There's a separate shelf in shell closet for each gauge, but find that does not work out in real life—just in March and a few months after. Find great variety of shells in old gunning coats and gun-club bag. Some so old and worn have no idea of shot size—put those to one side. Need 16- and 20-gauge 8's. Need 12-gauge trap loads—always need 12-gauge trap loads. Find ten 270's…no idea of bullet weight. Put those to one side. Find box of 12-gauge snipe loads—so marked on crimp; put those to one side. One-side pile growing to ominous proportions.

Clean out duck hunting packbasket and find lost handwarmer; half pint blackberry brandy. Put that to one side.

Certain digressions have taken place. The pond has, in turn, become the Snake River, Fishing Creek, and a certain beat on the

Restigouche that I live for from year to year. Casts are made to specific fish…and improved on, I may add. I do not step on my lines as I did in a canoe in Quebec just after watching a 30-pounder roll. I did not place the fly in a tree as I did in Wyoming—just a few inches above a sipping 5-pound brown. The line I strip from my Bogden here in the calmness of my room has not twisted itself into a locked position as it did once on the Matapedia; but then again it never does…at home.

Duck and goose calls blown now don't go sour as they did not long ago in Maryland and Louisiana at a very crucial moment. No doubt even my handwarmers would stay lit here before the red-tinted Franklin stove. Digressions prove the fact that things never go wrong if they aren't important. The pup gets excited at the calling; the old dog merely waits 'til it's over and goes back to sleep.

The shotguns are looked over. My gunsmith, Mr. Schielke, has forbidden me to do more than clean and oil the outside. This I do, and as long as the wax is out, I do a touch of polishing on the stocks. The digressions here are painful. A low house six that I should have smoked; an incoming pintail that has retired in Central America to enjoy his old age; and so many one-bird trap incidents I can barely bring myself to think of them. Ordinarily it bothers me little or none at all to miss in the field every so often or even just plain often, but like most of us, there are certain shots that we "specialize" in, as in trap and skeet there are certain shots that are our nemesis, and when we get by, say, a high five or a succession of doubles from three at trap, we consider ourselves to be fortunate. My so-called favorite shot in the field is a high incomer—a fair amount of dove and waterfowl gunning shows here—and to miss one of these ruins my whole day; so much so that late in the winter I stand here in front of a pair of Labs—both of whom have been mute witnesses to a couple of missed birds, to say the least—and swing a shotgun or two until I think it has all come back. Such a digression might even include leafing through a couple of books on shooting, and a period of wanderlust and daydreaming about the few times and places where I did truly well, often with a gun that has long been traded or sold with the idea, rarely fulfilled, of going up a grade in the never-to-be resolved quest for a really fine English double…the will-o'-the-wisp "Best London gun." "Sharpening my plow," as the old almanac suggests.

Call these days of rummaging with odds and ends of guns and rods and reels and what-have-you "nothing days" and you'd be absolutely right. Nothing really has been attempted and nothing has been gained. Nothing done is work that really needed to be done or at the worst couldn't have waited weeks or months.

These are the kind of days that make up most of our lives, days just like any other, sort of cold and gray days where wasting time seems the very best we can bring to them. Days that just fall out of our unknown calendar and lie on the floor of our existence totally forgotten, and justly so. Just those days that help us remember other days—mending harness, as it were, for more important times.

One more digression, if you will. Why bother? Why not just sit and read or take a winter walk and give the dogs a little air? Because sometimes you have to get the feel of things like rods and guns that someone made by hand. You have to sit and think that this rod once was just a slender foreign tree, and the craft and skill of a man made it something else. This shotgun was the work of many hands, all trained to do a certain thing as well or better than any other man on earth. You'd like to talk to them about the things they did and why...did they think that a day spent fiddling over where the guides should go or setting the barrels of the side-by-side just exactly right was just another day? Or did one of the men, by some chance, think *Today I made a rod that will delight someone, I hope, as much as it delighted me to make it the absolutely best I could.*

Every so often I sort of sit and shake the hand of a man I never knew and appreciate the work he's done...not that he will ever know or care...but I believe that this kind of craft and pride had that thought in mind. And then I take one last look at such a gun or rod as he who made it so must have had one fleeting hope that for years and years to come someone, every now and then, would muss with it with equal pride and understanding.

IT'S ALL RELATIVE

I'm sort of in the middle of packing for a late-season quail hunt and I find that the tingle of excitement that comes with getting ready to go someplace new is as strong as ever. I always take some sort of atavistic pleasure in the thought of *going*—even it it's just for a day or so. I'll be meeting new people, seeing an old friend or so, usually trying out a different gun or a new fly rod, then inevitably coming back to one of my favorites.

Heading out in my old van, pleasantly lulled by the familiar creeks and rattles, never fails to make me wish that I hadn't missed the old days when it was somewhere called "West" that you could head for—guided by rumor, gossip, heresay, and what was kindly refered to as a map. You know, back when the unknown was really just that, and you literally took your life in your hands once you crossed the first of the great rivers. It must have been an adventure that can only be imagined in today's world.

It's almost impossible to really feel what it must have been like being on that unfamiliar ground, wondering as much about "why" as "where." Some went because they needed a change of name and the hoped-for luck that went with it. "Nothing to lose" was a prevalent philosophy that covered farmers and faro players, trappers and those who just felt trapped.

From time to time, a lot of us feel exactly the same way, but we don't have any place to go or any reason that we could voice that would convince most of our families, or even ourselves. Yet the urge can be strongly compelling, however indistinct and confusing the logic behind it.

So we find that our little voyages and expeditions take some of the sting out of being tied down, locked in by circumstances, or fear, or indifference, or boredom, or whatever. So we go, pushed by some reasons and drawn by others, and find, hopefully, that however small the adventure, it's always better than no adventure at all.

Where we now see a sparrowhawk or a redtail, the old trappers might have spent a few minutes pondering the gyrations of an eagle or a condor. Where we see a flash of whitetail, there could once have been a congregation of buffalo that took days to pass. I often smile about my pleasure in taking a pair or so of grouse or woodcock as I think about a little girl who would someday be Annie Oakley helping to support her family as a market gunner. As we often have to remind ourselves, it's all relative.

I remember a one-time commercial duck shooter handing me an old Remington automatic. I noted that the magazine extension was as long as the barrel. The checkering was worn smooth, and saltwater and a bayman's calloused hands had left only the faintest traces of blueing. As anyone would do, I threw the butt to my shoulder and swung through a ghost flock of canvasbacks and handed the gun to the old man. "It's not likely you'll take as many ducks as the old gun has," he said with a reflective smile. "How many?" I asked. "I'll say— and I don't mean to brag, but we didn't know any better in those days—about eight thousand."

Now think about that for a minute or two. If you laid out that many ducks in a line, how far would they stretch? How many dawns? How many fog-bound hours searching for a familiar creek channel? How many hours breaking ice? How many decoys picked up and carefully wrapped with your fingers frozen and your arms numb up to the shoulder? How many hours of rowing into a three-foot chop?

I didn't have to ask *why* because I can recall more than one time when I was on the bay myself and the cans and redheads stretched as far back into the sky as I could see. My empty gun was taking a pair here and a triple there, and my imaginary pickup man was running three barrel-chested retrievers.

I wanted to chat a bit more about those bygone days but he slid the gun back into an old canvas slipcase and wandered off. That evening I overheard another hunter bragging about taking four ducks with six shells on his morning hunt and I wondered what my old market man would have had to say about that....

I don't think it's the plenty that we miss the most. I can look up at the Tetons or the Wind River Range knowing that many a trapper on his way to the rendezvous would fill his stomach with fresh-killed sheep or elk with no more emotion than we would display unwrapping a store-bought ham. It's the sense of loss we miss. Without the elk and sheep, and the redheads and cans, the places just aren't the same. The old house is empty and the kitchen garden has gone to weeds.

Well, we've all learned to live with and enjoy what we have. After all, it isn't realistic to become bitter about losing something that we personally never really had. While I would have enjoyed the times of plenty, I wouldn't have known that they they were "the good old days." So, like most of us, I've sort of adopted the philosophy of many a football coach that yesterday is past and future is tomorrow. And my adventures, although "little" and brief, are all that I have and I must cherish them.

I will still take as much enjoyment from my few quail hunts, in all likelihood, as did the old sports with their bags of game numbered in dozens. In some ways, restraint—playing under new rules—can put a fine edge of pleasure on a day afield. Among other things, I honestly believe that I'm contributing more to the wildlife than I'll ever take away. I am less of a threat to a covey of quail than the hawk or the fox (for more reasons than one!), and that's just the way I've come to like it. In the duck blind, the constraint of waiting to be sure that the incoming mallard is a drake and not a hen has bought a new flavor or husbandmanship for wild creatures that I am pleased with. If I am a predator, at least I am a careful one—as selective as the wolf culling the weak, the old, and the infirm. Admittedly it is for different reasons, but it's something I can believe in. It's as close as a gunner can get to a fisherman taking a hard-battling trout and then releasing it.

I often wonder what would happen if we were stripped of the

laws. I like to think that most of us would stay with two or three shells in our magazine firearms and that we would only take what we could quickly use, and give constant and serious thought to tomorrow. I believe we all can imagine how hollow life would be without the evening song of the bobwhite from somewhere off behind the barn, or how forlorn the field of stubble would be without the red and gold of a pheasant gleaming in it. Too many of us have known how close we came and how worried we were that things had gone too far.

But things are pretty good right now. I see a lot more retrievers afield than I used to, and more good pointing dogs. That means, to me, a change in what we all look for in getting out—a widening of the experience that more than compensates for the shrinking of the take.

So come tomorrow morning, when the broom grass is brittle with frost and we all pile into some sort of wagon to head for the bird covers, my bets are on the same sort of jokes and hope and eagerness that delighted our great-grandfathers. The pointers will be just as wild and to the same degree good, bad, or indifferent as they always were. The guns are about the same and the arguments about 8's and 9's, and light and heavy loads, continue. And sure as hell someone will be dropping a dime down a barrel in the firm, but still mistaken belief that he's checking the choke. And you can bet that you're not the first gunner in the world to offer a little prayer that your first flush won't be a hard single heading dead left and out in the open where everyone will see it and, to a man, swear that they'd have made the shot and never dirtied the second barrel.

The cornbread might come out of a packaged mix and the buttermilk out of a carton instead of a springhouse churn, but you'll have to admit that the ladies seated around the table were never prettier than now.

If you're still grumbling about how it was, take another minute to think about not having to crank the car to get it started, not having to milk a couple of dozen cows by lantern light, or split wood for the kitchen stove and thaw the outside pump to draw enough water to wash with.

As for me, I'll settle for Johnny Cash or Tom T. Hall on the tape deck with the car heater turned up pretty good. Except for that first quail hooking left, and the ladies forgetting that real cornbread needs a touch of sugar, it ain't all bad.

A QUIETER TIME

It seems that right now most people think the largemouth bass was invented so it could be chased in high-powered bass boats, spied on in its bedroom with sonar, and scared into defending itself against plugs that resemble a World War II fighter plane.

While I have nothing against technology or spending a ridiculous amount of money on fishing tackle, proper hats, polarized glasses, beer coolers, et al, I have the uneasy feeling that things have gotten a bit out of hand. No way do I think that we ought to stop the clock of progress or pretend that this is a softer and more gentle time, but there's no harm in taking a moment or two to reconsider a few things about fishing.

It's no doubt symptomatic of the time that everybody wants to catch fish; all well and good. But it also seems that we want to catch the most fish in the least amount of time while covering the greatest distances. I doubt that the Creator had that in mind when he so kindly designed the largemouth.

Time was when the bass was the end piece in a long chain of events. No small part of the fun of fishing was getting bait. I remember a tiny spring-fed brook that tumbled through a cathedral of spruce. Everything was cool and green and somehow magical. Small leopard frogs were sprinkled here and there, and we splashed around together getting equally wet until a dozen or so were collected in an old milk pail filled with moss and ferns. It was always a delightful adventure, spiced with the pleasure of the farm dog barking instructions and the stalking of water snakes with the Red Ryder carbine BB gun to deal with the ones that considered the frogs their private property.

Another evening, after the chores were done, would find us in scratchy wool bathing suits seining the tiny coves of a nearby lake for minnows and the occasional perch or bluegill. Whatever we caught ended up in a washtub that we invariably filled with too much water, and this added to the already swampy smell in the back seat of our Model A Ford.

Nights after a summer rain were spent barefoot on the lawn catching nightwalkers with flashlight and swift but gentle hands. We spent other afternoons in one brook or another for hellgrammites and crayfish, which pinched our fingers and had the habit of disappearing from the boxes and buckets we kept in the coolest part of the cellar. Braver souls than this one also added a small mouse or so to the arsenal, which they would swim over the holes where only the biggest bass were thought to lurk.

I know I can never recapture that incredible excitement I used to feel as we pulled away from the dock in our boat (watched by a pair of tiny barn owls that were almost always there), and tried to row as silently as we could so as not to break the spell. I liked the dead calm mornings best. Behind the boat was a silver path dotted with the little whirlpools of the oars; it was a matter of pride to have that soft wake as straight as a plumb line. If you were good at rowing, it was not small source of satisfaction, and perhaps one day you might overhear a grownup, none of whom were noted for lavishing praise on small boys, mention that "Hilly's boy knows how to handle a boat."

While we rowed, keeping a certain distance from the giant lily pads, as silent as dawn, my father would be casting his favorite topwater plug: a homemade contraption shaped like a wedge that sort of popped when you jerked it. He called it a "vacuum bait." Like all his favorite plugs, it was red-headed with a white body, and had three huge single hooks that, only in theory, made it weedless. My rod trolled one of my precious frogs or a four-inch shiner or a bluegill about the size of a silver dollar.

Needless to say I felt that I was a far more sophisticated fisherman than my father. A devoted reader of all the outdoor magazines we could afford, at ten or fifteen cents a copy, and a constant student of all the catalogs, I absolutely ached for stuff I couldn't afford. My dream fishing tackle box was one with two or three trays filled with Creek Chub Darters, Pikie Minnows, Heddon's Go-Deeper River Runts, Pflueger Chums, Johnson's Silver Minnows, and Hawaiian Wigglers. In the bottom compartment would be pork rind, pickeled killies, and a bottle of luminous paint used for topwater plugs, which were made to glow by shining a flashlight on them for a little while!

My tackle box in reality was something else. A cedar cigar box with some odds and ends of hooks, bobbers, a one-bladed pocketknife, and a few spoons I had salvaged from a shallow rock ledge that snagged the unknowing trollers. In time, however, I did manage to garner a couple of the plugs I most coveted, but the one thing I never owned that I think I wanted most of all was casting rod made by True Temper and, if memory serves, called the American Boy model. It was four-sided and looked like a fencing foil five or five and a half feet long. One of the summer guests at the lakeside hotel had one, and as I rowed him around the lake for fifty cents a day I could hardly take my eyes off of it or the Pflueger Supreme reel he used with it.

The rods we used were bamboo, five feet long, and stiff enough to throw a bait pail. I had some nameless free-spool casting reel, while my father pleasured himself with a South Bend that sported "ruby" end bearings and a level wind. They say that adversity always has some compensations, and one of mine was that I became a past master of picking out backlashes in the dark. We used a button hook, by the way; shoe stores still gave them away out of habit as an advertisement although an eccentric old maid great-aunt of mine was the only person I remember who wore shoes that buttoned.

Back to the fishing. In contrast to the modern outboard and the wave-slapping, stepped-V hull, one of the absolute musts of our outings was quiet. Country folks weren't much on talking in the first place; it was "showy." So we didn't chatter and above all we didn't bang around in the boat. You didn't scratch an itchy bare foot on the anchor cleat, you didn't slide the bait pail over where you could reach it, you didn't squeak an oar in its lock, you didn't thrash around the boat trying to recatch a loose frog. You were as quiet here, or more so, than you were in church—since my father didn't have the same constraints on him as did our Methodist minister. We fished a lot on cloudy days that either threatened rain or really did, since most of those days gave us time off from working out of doors. When the boat needed a little drying out we used a sponge—and when you wrung it out you did that quietly and gently too!

Between the worms and the frogs and the shiners and the plugs and spoons and a little luck we almost always seemed to catch fish— sometimes bass, pickerel more often, and catfish and perch almost always. Now and then there was an eel, which we loved to eat as we did everything else. I don't remember ever throwing anything back unless it was illegal, out of season, or too small. My father took as much pride, almost, in his ability to clean a fish as he did in catching one. I was only allowed to scale them for a lot of reasons, chiefly my careless attitude about sharp knives and the remoteness of medical help. I was always cutting myself with something, not out of any incredible clumsiness but more because of a very short attention span for any given task.

I said before that I couldn't recapture the excitement of those early mornings I so looked forward to—and I'm sorry, because I still believe that this is the reason, the essential *why*, that we go fishing. But I think you know just what I mean.

I still have a few of those old plugs and spoons—even Pop's "vacuum bait." And once or twice every summer along the shores of a local bass pond you could see a middle-aged man chunking a plug about half the size of a shingle along the edge of the lotus lilies. When the light is just right and he can see his reflection in the water, a certain magic that only fishermen know about takes place. He sees the shadow of an old wooden rowboat and the silhouette of two fishermen. One is a young man of about thirty who seems to be smoking a cigar; the other, rowing, is a tow-headed boy about ten or so. The quiet is accented by the rhythmic plop of a huge wooden plug and the distant murmur of barn owls. He wonders for a moment why the man and boy never speak, and then he realizes that they don't have to—they are fishing together, and that is all that matters.

THE BEST AND THE
WORST OF IT

There are some random thoughts that I ought to tell someone about, just so they won't bother me so much anymore.

I was watching a man at one of the local gun clubs struggling to put together a new side-by-side. I came over to see if I could help and noted that it was a brand new Purdey 20 gauge. We got it together and in way of explanation he told me that although he'd had the gun for several years, he'd never shot it before. I knew he did a fair amount of bird hunting so I asked him what he used. "Oh, either the Boss or the Holland and Holland," he answered. He turned out to be a terrible skeet shot. Things like that can make you a little religious.

The best fly caster I ever saw (except for Lefty Kreh, maybe) was a French lumberjack who very rarely fished, but did a little guiding now and then for a salmon camp. I had a new graphite rod and I got the feeling that he was anxious to try it out, since he'd heard about graphite rods but had never seen one. We came to a pool that held one or two very dark salmon and I let him try the rod. He was casting left handed because the pool fished best that way, and every cast was absolutely perfect. I was so impressed that I let him fish the next pool and he fished it right handed. Again, every cast was perfect, right out to where he was single-hauling about 90 feet of line. His English was very halting but the meat of his conversation was: "I never seen nothing hard about it but some don't do it very good." I asked him if it made any difference whether he did it with his right or left hand. He said: "I chop trees the same way and it don't make no difference to the ax."

I very rarely let my guides fish anymore. And I still wonder if French woodsmen have strange senses of humor.

One of the best shots I ever heard a lot about (except for Rudy Etchen and Joe Devers) was a Georgia farmer who shot a hammer pump—the old Winchester Model 97. Take my word for it, he almost always took three quail on a covey rise. But then he only put three shells in the gun. Also take my word that the three shots sounded like one rather drawn out shot.

Someone once asked him if he ever practiced and Red said, honestly: "What for? Just to hit quail?" That reminds me of the supposed conversation between the legendary Fred Kimble and another self-fancied duck shot. The self-fancier asked Fred if he ever had trouble with downwind teal. Fred was a little astonished at the question, then finally answered, honestly: "If I can hit mallards in the head all day, why in the world would I have any trouble hitting a *whole* teal?"

As someone wisely remarked: "Some men are more equal than others."

The best retriever I ever saw was a sheep dog in Wales. I won't even tell you what that dog would do; I still don't believe it and I've spent a few years on the retriever field trial circuit. I thanked the dog's owner for letting me watch her work and when I tried, inadequately, to praise the dog, he quieted me down and told me that if I ever wanted to see a really first-rate retriever, maybe Mr. Jones, from a farm down the way, might be persuaded to work his bitch. But only if he was through using it on his sheep, he added, as retrieving tended to make it frivolous.

One of the best trap guns I ever owned, and I've owned several, was an experimental one of a forgotten Japanese make. I hated the look and feel of it. It was always hard to open or close, the wood looked like sub-grade flooring, and the so-called engraving was beyond the charity of the word ugly. I shot it for a couple of months only because it was all I had at the time and I couldn't find a buyer any sooner. I shot it in the cold winter months we have in the Northeast— in the sleet, in the snow, and in all sorts of wind. I had an average of about 94 when I began using it and when I sold it I was a bit over 98—for the last time, I hasten to add. The only redeeming virtue it had was an uncanny ability to break targets. If you're a trapshooter, you know exactly why I sold it; if you're not, you'll never understand.

There's a line about "not being able to stand prosperity" that seems more than apt.

One of the best fly rods I've ever owned was one that a well-to-do neighbor was throwing out and I rescued. He didn't like the rod because it was a cheap one to start with and both tips were as wavy as a chorus girl's profile. I, feeling charitable, was going to give it to my wife so she could us it for bluegills in the pond. It wasn't marked for any particular line weight so I gambled and put a WF6F on it. It's an old bamboo Heddon, and I have never let it out of my hands since, as hard as that is for both of us to believe.

Another "best" is an old gunning vest made, I'd guess, in the 1940's, by the Masland Company. It has straps like suspenders, an ingenious belt, more than enough pockets, and you can wear it with anything from a T-shirt to a down vest. I've never seen one quite like it and don't expect to. It's one of the few decent things I've ever had that is still part of my net worth. Somebody gave it to me, too, because they wanted something fancier. I'll bet they don't have the one they thought was "better."

Looks are too deceiving; otherwise, I'd still be using the old Ford Model A as my shooting vehicle. (Just in passing, I would like to thank whoever it is that has refrained from improving such classics as the rubber-bottomed Bean boot, the Thermos bottle, and the Zippo lighter.)

One of my most delightful days was spent gunning quail with a world-class skeet shooter. He has forgotten how many 200 straights he's had. I had it fresh in my mind that the week before I'd missed more birds in *one round* of 25 than he'd missed all the past year. How's that for a feeling of confidence going in? But for once, all those twice-a-day sessions of Sunday school paid off, because he was just not there. Oh, he took a few birds, but brother, I was something else. I don't claim to understand it because, believe me, it's not my normal average, but when I shot, something fell. But, champion that he is, he never made one excuse for himself and never missed a chance to say "nice going" about my shooting. On the way home he did, however, offer to take me over to the local skeet field for a couple of rounds. Needless to say, this was an offer I found very, very easy to refuse. The sun doesn't shine on this old dog's rear end that often or that warmly.

Of course, for every day like that you have to pay, and pay heavily. I recall a duck camp when rather late at night my sometime friend Jack Daniels was speaking for me and I heard myself remark that I considered myself a rather more than fair man when it came to waterfowl; not a Kimble or Bogardus, perhaps, but not exactly shabby. I had my favorite duck gun, an old side-by-side that I'd used for years, I had my favorite loads—heavy 5's—but what I did not have was what is known as "the touch." It was dreadful. It was humiliating, and even worse, it was remembered. Long into every evening after someone would say something and then, add "...while not a Kimble or a Bogardus...," the room would rock with laughter—not a unanimous laughter, but very, very close.

And one of the best comments I ever heard about dove shooting came from an old Texas friend. Someone asked him how he had fared in the morning and he said; "Well, I took five doves with only one box of shells and then,—I really can't understand it—I seemed to lose the hang of it."

The best and the worst of it and all the inbetweens. The hard times and the jokes, the sweet times and the memories. I guess that The Best and the Worst of It isn't a very apt title at that. It's the "Ordinary of It," salted and peppered with a little wit, sharpened by a cutting phrase or just a picture hung up in our memory where we can see it when we want to.

By most standards there isn't any best or worst of it to most of us hanging around somewhere waiting for the fish to bite or a bird to fly. And that's the way a lot of others see us. I don't suppose you could call standing in a river up to your armpits "hanging around," anymore than you can say the same of picking your way through deadfalls, or watching your hands turn blue in a North Country duck blind. A lot of folks wouldn't call it fun either, the way we do. Sometimes I wonder why I spend so much time either being there or wishing I was. But when I wonder a little more, I always get the same answer: "Why not?"

I think all of us go looking for a lot of things—not the least of which is an experience, an excuse to try an old story or a new one, to peer into the other side of our friends and ourselves. I think we like to laugh, inwardly or outwardly, at the worst of it and along with the best of it. Again, "Why not?"

I've forgotten now how the duck shooting really was for those few days in that Cajun duck camp, and I suspect that the rest of the men have too, by now. But I'll bet none of them have forgotten the long and frequent laughter inspired by the free and careless soul who was rash enough to sort of think a dream out loud where he saw himself "...while not a Kimble or Boardus...." Things like that are so much a part of why we hunt and fish that I could almost weep for those who will never understand or be a part of such small, but so important, human delights.

NEW TOYS

If you follow hunting and fishing for trends, as I do, you'll find that some tend to be functional, others pure fads that come and go for no apparent reason, and a few that, at least to me, lean toward the whimsical if not the purely funny.

When I started fly fishing, the big craze was for the so-called "midge" rod. If you didn't have one of these 6-footers, you just about had to go fishing by yourself; not owning one was admitting you were a non-sportsman, a man cruelly indifferent to the ultra niceties of the sport. One friend went so far as to make a whole rod out of what had been just the tip section of another. For a time, I fooled around with an old Leonard that weighed about 2 ounces, but it made me so nervous that I didn't enjoy my fishing. I never did use it without the almost certain feeling that it was going to snap off right above the grip, but I wasn't going to be one of those know-nothings thrashing around with an 8-footer.

I guess we all looked good standing around the station wagons in our waders, handing those tiny rods back and forth and talking about half and quarter ounces in terms of life and death. Now, of course, that's all changed. The absolute only rod to fling a no-hackle or parachute with has to be made of some space-age material and be a minimum of eight feet long; nine is a lot better. The old midge rods are eagerly sought by sophisticates who consider it a heinous crime to *use* anything that falls under that current catchword, *collectible*.

Another great move that appears to have lost some of its momentum, at least in my circle, is the knife thing. Not so long ago, guys were laying out more for a handmade knife in a sheath than they'd spent on their honeymoon. You'd see them sitting around the stove in a deer camp shaving the hair off their arms with their knives and arguing about Rockwell numbers as if they had some idea of what they were talking about. I don't know what would have happened if I'd joined in one of those religious sessions with my old Marble, but I'll be honest and say I didn't dare. One of my buddies overdid it, and when his wife got wind of the kind of money he was laying out, he gave me a knife with a famous maker's name on it. The sheath never fit and the knife weighed about a pound, and I finally gave it away after the craze had calmed down. I recall that I never saw anyone actually *use* one of these treasures, not even to sharpen the gin rummy pencil. All they did was slice paper and shave their arms, then get out some twenty dollars' worth of stone and put the edge back on with everyone else telling them they were doing it wrong. You know, the stone was too hard, or too soft, or too something. Now everybody's back to some kind of folding belt knife, and the jewels made by Andy or Ralph or Prescott with their handcheckered or scrimshawed handles have joined that great beyond of *collectibles*. I sort of coveted the one or two that I remember being small enough to use and light enough to carry. Maybe I can make a deal or a swap for one of my 5½-foot fly rods.

I have also had my share of the magnums, both shotguns and rifles, until I no longer knew what it was not to have my ears ring or my head ache. I recall one of my buddies with some mach 5 number hitting a running mule deer in the rump and bragging all night and most of the next day about what the bullet did. Well, what the bullet really did was shred up about half the deer, all the good parts anyway, and leave shoulder meat for a one-man stew, and the rack. I wasted a few minutes of my time and his my remarking that my old .270 wouldn't do that and he agreed, firmly believing that I was admitting to being criminally undergunned. Maybe he didn't hear me right; the crack that rifle made was something else! Two or three rounds of sighting in and you didn't need a seashell to hear the ocean; a chunk of chaparral or an ax head would have done just as well. Now, as far as I know, most of those six-digit calibers with supersonic names are in the hands of the few true believers who treat them as if they were relics of the true Cross.

Of course, there have always been magic words for the true outdoorsman, and for the past couple of years, the *in* word has been "lightweight." If you're shopping for a 17-foot canoe and your pre-teen daughter can't swing it up and over her shoulders, it's no sale. I always thought that a canoe ought to spend most of its time carrying you, not the other way around. When I was a *kinder* we all wanted good heavy boots. Now if boots are all leather you can't be seen in them outside of your vegetable garden. In fact, it seems like the less leather in a boot, the more it costs. (I'm just not very smart. If I was, I'd find out some way of selling a column with 500 words for more than one with 1,500.) The same with packing stuff—get rid of the weight. Cut the toothbrush handle in half and go for another pint of Jack Daniels, that's what I say. You've got lightweight decoys, lightweight portable blinds, lightweight motors, lightweight long underwear, etc. The only things that aren't lightweight are retrievers and duck hunters.

But right now the biggest thing, the absolute, sure-fire, must-have, can't-go-without, is camouflage. I saw a gun in a Texas hunting camp last year with camo underwear! He wasn't a real Texan, I'll admit, but he knew he'd get by down there wearing an outfit like that. If what you want doesn't come in camo, you can spray it with camo paint, or wrap it in camo tape. Just looking through any of the latest catalogs makes you feel like the whole world is military issue or all the storekeeps are ex-Quartermasters. I even saw an ad for a ladies nightie in camo. (I never saw a camo sheet, but that might be the next, and as far as I'm concerned, the last step.)

I haven't been famous for resisting anything so far, so I'm up to my neck in the stuff along with everybody else—I've been known to wear a camouflage necktie occasionally when the festivities demanded a very special touch. Being a very practical person, I also have camouflage suspenders, bandanna, a belt that looks like leaves, two insulated camo beverage coolers, a camo sun visor for dove shooting, and camo parkas and hats for duck hunting. What I have long coveted is a camo vest for skeet and trap. I almost had a camo umbrella and a camo wallet but decided I ought to show a little restraint. However, a couple of my gun cases are camo, plus one Thermos and a rifle sling. Like any famous collector I have discovered jealous rivals, and two of them have challenged me to a camo "wear-off." I really don't stand a chance since one of them is on a first-name basis with every major surplus store in the country, and the other has spent a little time as a mercenary and can call on desert or jungle motifs from a couple of wars. Maybe I should have gotten the umbrella....

None of this means very much, nor is it meant to, except to re-prove the obvious, which is that when we're not actually hunting or fishing, we're wishing we were, or at least we're getting ready. Most of use have long since learned that you can't really buy skill, but we've also learned that we don't mind kidding ourselves a little and maybe letting a touch of wishful thinking creep in every so often. A new rod or knife or rifle and the anticipation of the magic that new things bring with them proves at least one thing to me—the average American sportsman has a ten-year-old living very happily inside him, a ten-year-old who looks forward as eagerly and as hopefully to opening day as he does Christmas or the arrival of a new puppy.

It was a very wise man (or more likely a woman) who remarked that the only difference between a man and a boy is the price of his toys. Not too many of us really *need* a new whatever that's better than the old one, because not too many of us are that short on worldly things. But every so often something new and shiny doesn't hurt. It's one way to guarantee a smile or a sparkle in one's eyes.

EVERYCAMP

There used to be (in fact there still is) a character in English literature called *Everyman*. Everyman is just what you'd expect—an attempt to describe the human condition through the experiences of one person, who is a composite of society. I've always thought it was a marvelous idea, however impossible it is to make it work. Still, I feel the urge to try my hand at it, and though doing a sketch of *Everyhunter* is beyond my modest talents, experience and imagination tempt me to translate the idea to *Everycamp*.

We open the scene in the interior of a tent, or a log cabin or an old motor home. The time is very early in the morning, before sunup. While we cannot show, to our sorrow, an odor, we must create one in our imagination, for odors, good and bad, are a large part of the atmosphere of Everycamp. This early morning odor has the consistency of something from a forbidden place; were this odor visible, it would be an ominous yellow. The source of a goodly amount of this odor is a number of bodies encased like sausages in their sleeping bags, limbs and head at odd angles. Low moans and groans are heard, and the viewer could be forgiven if he remarked that the whole reminded him strongly of the hospital scene in *Gone With The Wind*.

As the men dress, a large bottle of what seems to be some sort of antacid is being passed around and what conversation there is seems centered around the theme of "what a marvelous way to start an outing."

In groups like these we usually find at least one practitioner of medicine. He usually claims to be a gynecologist or a pediatrician and thus can avoid having to work on anyone in the group by claiming, "that's not my field of speciality." Although he has been telling the others to watch what they eat, his own plate is piled high with a pound of fried ham, six beaten biscuits, three eggs, and plenty of butter and jam. He carefully explains this in a way that no one understands. Truthfully, no one cares. Let Doc have a good time.

The others are the usual mix—bankers, lawyers, salesmen, farmers, and general businessmen. But at Everycamp, circumstances change all that for at least a little while. Here, they are sportsmen and each is in search of some private destiny on this trip. Each will get one; whether it is the one he wants is always another question.

The outfitter who runs Everycamp is a wise and experienced guide. This, the first day, is for what he calls acclimatization to the altitude. For altitude, you can substitute whiskey, tent cots, the reunion atmosphere, new boots, saddle sores, and a rare sense of freedom and well-being. Some will take a nap, others will take a walk. One or two like chores and take to splitting wood and carrying water from the spring. The cameras come out and there is always one or two who will shoulder a rifle, mostly for show, and walk a little way off in hills—not quite out of sight of camp.

So the first day dwindles pleasantly to evening, and expectant ears listen for the strange and longed-for sounds of the high country night. Each remarks on the clarity and closeness of the stars and each wonders if any of the others sees what he really sees and understands what he really understands. For a minute, standing by the outside fire, waiting for the call from the cook tent, the years fall away so quickly and heavily you can hear them if you listen with your heart.

There stand small and wondering boys. You could almost cry at the magic of it. Each one wears something new in honor of the first day and wonders, inside, if all this is truly real and actually happening to him. It is almost too much to bear, standing there in the dark, on a mountain, with the comfort of fire, and the warmth of friends, and the magic of one of the wishes so soon come true.

Steak and home fries, apple pie, a smoke or so, and a little brandy have tended to the wrinkles of the mind and the soul and the belly. It's story time in Everycamp. "What's the chance, this year?" they ask the outfitter. As always, the outfitter tells them that both the good hunters and the lucky ones will get a shot and those that are both will take a trophy. Everyone knows just where he stands now, and the debate, as always, starts about taking the first good head or waiting for "trophies." The trophies, as always, have the nod. Just before the second wind hits his charges, the outfitter hands out the lanterns and sends them all off to their unyielding, unfamiliar beds. Long before you'd guess—just a goodnight joke and story or so later—Everycamp is a medley of snoring nightsounds that alarm the beaver and quiet the bark of the fox.

They say it doesn't take too long to spend a night in a deer camp, and long before the sun has crossed the Mississippi, the hunters of Everycamp have blended into the timber, smelling of coffee, cigarettes, and excitement.

Some will sit and wait while others will stalk the shadows and start at the cracking of twigs. Some are nervous with new rifles, others are confident with their old ones. But whatever their hunting style, each is waiting for that moment when the great change comes. First they will notice that their steps are a little softer. Then they will begin to see some things they hadn't noticed before. Sounds will identify themselves more quickly. They will sense a shifting wind and feel a darkening of the clouded sun. They are becoming part of the woods, not just men walking through it. They are becoming hunters. What they were yesterday is nothing; what they were a thousand years ago is everything.

As the hunters change, so does Everycamp. Things seem to get done with less effort. It seems natural to keep an eye out for kindling or notice that a stone has been moved an inch or two. Sleep is easier and deeper; the sounds of night are the right sounds and now comfort where they once startled. The land has become familiar territory and the hunters are swallowed deep into it long before light. These mornings they see the beaver and the squirrel before they themselves are seen. This is how the game is played; the hunters have learned many of the moves.

Some have turned out to be good, and others have been lucky, and game hangs from the pole. The splayed carcasses on the rack offer mute testimony that the men have been successful in what they came to Everycamp to do.

But now that the hunt is over, what has happened to the hunter? He has had his moments, his days and nights of knowing that what was put there in some ancient time is still there. He has felt the warmth of the cave and the satisfaction of meat. He has remembered something worth remembering, and the satisfaction of flourishing where others would not survive, while only a metaphor today, is still a comfort.

He came to Everycamp to be someone else, however too short the time, and he has looked for something and found that it wasn't entirely lost. Some men will always have to go back to their Everycamp and try to reawaken that bit of blood—the survival instinct—which at one time made them stand and fight with sticks and stones, understanding fear and the uncertainty that goes with fear. It is that bit of blood which makes some men take a step or two ahead of others who will not move. This is what Everycamp is for—to hear the echo of a triumphant cry born eons ago in Africa and Asia, that strange expression of pride in knowing something about yourself—the roar of the hunting lion or the cold call of the hawk that has struck and feeds. This is the pride that says: "I have hunted and I can live!"

NOVEMBER

Now that it's November, I feel a little less guilty than I have all summer about driving out from the house past the still unpainted barn, dodging still unfilled pot holes, passing still unrepaired fence, and a few dead apple trees that hold up their sere limbs like grotesque hands waving for my attention. But this is November.

A man can be excused for being a little lax about some things come the tag end of the year. After all, he has had guns to clean, boots to oil, shells to be sorted, dogs to run—and a hundred or so other little chores that have to be looked after while he sees how the rest of the world has been faring.

He has to go look at the mallards and the pintails, the gadwalls and the Canadas. He has to go down to the alder bottoms and check on the woodcock, and then, no rest for the weary, it's time to trundle up to the higher ground and see what has happened to the grouse in the months he's been away. It's just one thing after another, depending on where and when. Someone has to stand in the sunflowers for mourning doves and then, pacing himself very carefully so as not to overdo, it'll be bobwhites and pheasants, cottontails, chukars, or prairie chickens. Sometimes I just don't know how we do it all. But, this is November, and best we be at it.

The old dogs and the new ones know the calendar just as well. The Labrador who has spent the summer digging dusting spots under the rhododendrons and pine trees—the same one who would move only to find a shady spot—is up at 3:30 shoving a cold nose under the blankets trying to find a duck hunter to play with. The setters and pointers have been practicing their stiff-legged walks on the last robins to leave the lawn.

The women of the house don't need a calendar either. They can tell by the stuff that starts turning up on top of the mending pile. The heavy socks, canvas vests, and britches appear like magic. Thermos bottles, more than a few smelling like last year's coffee, are lined along the sinks, and the men folk are poking their noses into the ovens sniffing out the likelihood of brownies, pies, sugar cookies, and biscuits. The past summer's crop of brides tries to remember napkins for the lunches and little containers of mustard and relish. They ask, "Where are you going and what time will you be home for supper?" The wives of a few more seasons lean heavily on quantity and don't ask questions that require definite answers.

If I could ever design a perfect entry into November, I'd start a little early. I'd like first to be in Texas or Arizona in October to sharpen the eye with the dove season. Then I'd sort of drift over to Tennessee or Louisiana for some early season teal in October, and move to the upper reaches of Michigan in November for the woodcock and grouse gunning when the frosts have thinned the leaves. Then I'd like to cross the country, heading West for Utah and the heavy pintail flights for just a little bit. Heading back East, I'd like to sit in a blind on the coast of Maine to see how good I am at handling downwind broadbills or flaring black ducks with my broken-note duck call. And, if you'd let me steal a week or so from December and tack it on the end of November, right after Thanksgiving, I'd love to be back in Texas for quail or a ten-point buck.

I guess the ideal November ought to have at least six or seven weeks—and maybe it does for those of us who divide our year along the peculiar schedules of fishing season, hunting season, Christmas, more hunting season, and then the waiting for fishing season to start the whole year over again.

Did I ever have a real life schedule like that? Almost, if you'd let me spread it out over the two seasons instead of only one. In Michigan it absolutely poured. In Maine it was too hot, and I hit a "Norther" and damn near died from cold down in Texas. I had a week of three-dog nights (a three-dog night, in case you didn't know, is when you only have one dog sleeping on your bed with you, and you really need three).

Well, that is how it sometimes happens. But this year it's going to be different. This year is going to be like the week one of my friends had in Michigan, where on the *worst* day they flushed thirty-nine grouse and twenty woodcock! I'll be out of the duck blind after fifteen minutes or so, like my friends who went to Stuttgart to gun the flooded timber mallards. And who knows what will happen in Texas? I *do* know another hunting friend who, in one day, got a limit of quail, a good turkey, and a fat eight-pointer.

There are also some other things I plan to do differently this year. I plan to hit the skeet range a little more often so I won't do what I did last year when I *did* have a couple of Canadas turn to the call. I plan not to wait until the last minute to get my hunting license and find that the only close source is sold out. I plan on putting in a little more time with my retriever, so she won't pull the side of the duck blind over because I have to keep her on a leash. I plan to sight in my deer rifle for obvious reasons. I plan to quit playing poker in hunting camps, also for obvious reasons.

The way to look at it is that this is a completely new November. I see no reason why this one won't be the very best we've ever known. It won't be too wet or too dry, and it won't rain on weekends except after dark. The winds will be just the right mix of damp and soft, so the bird dogs will work their best. If it's a day for ducks or geese, then the breezes will have some bite and quarter in from the NNE. There won't be too many leaves in the upland coverts and what leaves are there will be just the right mix of brown, gold, and orange. The way I see it, most birds—or at least three out of five,—won't streak for the thickest cover, but will flirt with the openings more than usual. There won't be too many of those left-to-right shots, except for the left-handed gunners.

I see that the first of November arrives on a Monday—this year as it should. The Saturday and Sunday before we'll rake all the leaves, clean the gutters, take down the screens, put up the storm windows, and find the snow tires for the cars. When there's a November coming up as fine as this one promises to be, we want nothing but harmony when it turns the corner.

TOO MUCH AND NOT
ENOUGH

An oldtimer I like to yarn with was complaining the other day about life being unfair. "I don't see the sense," he said, grumbling, "behind the thinking that when you get old, you lose your hair and your teeth. There's a lot of other things I don't need that I'd trade off so my head would be warm and I could keep a better hold on my pipe." I had to agree with him, and it got me thinking about other things we have too little of and some we never have enough of.

October and November are too short and February is too long. Birthdays come along too soon and it's forever between opening days. Why is there too much rain around the beginning of trout season and not enough fresh tracking snow during deer season?

Why is that we never have too many good wool socks, yet there's a closetful of neckties? Why is your favorite brown sweater—the one that buttons up the front and has nice big pockets—always the one that you burn holes in but even the moths won't touch the bright green one that scratches your chin?

How come you never lose or break the stem off a pipe you don't like? And if you run out of tobacco, everyone else is smoking something that tastes like violets or orange rind? Why can't a woman who can whip up a four-course meal for six learn to make a decent sandwich for one? And whose idea was it to slice roast beef so thin you could read the game laws through it, or that only the Canadians could have decent bacon?

Why can't Labradors or bird dogs live to be twenty or twenty-five and cats only have one kitten every three or four years? Why can't canvasbacks have more babies and snakes a lot fewer?

We never have enough trap loads, or number 5's, or big red handkerchiefs, or good leather belts, or wide suspenders. You can hardly find a nice tweed or corduroy cap for love nor money, but every corner store is full of orange ones—made of plastic.

You won't argue that we have too many Mondays and not enough Saturdays, and that's even more true during hunting and fishing season, although I don't know why. Full moons seem to work the same way, and I'm sure you've noticed that the winds are too strong when you're trying to fly fish and not strong enough when you're sitting in a blind waiting for pintails.

I don't understand why a ten-point buck, live, is only eight points when you have him, or how a trout can shrink three or four inches and lose half a pound between the strike and the net. And what makes a 200-yard shot pace out at only around 135? Or why do the easiest pheasants turn out to be hens, and how come you can get three Canada's with only six or eight shells and the one you need to limit out takes four or five? Why is the twenty-fifth target at trap so much smaller and faster than the other twenty-four?

We never have enough flies or fly rods, or scissors, or those little reels you hang stuff from on your vest, or wading staffs, boots, or Thermos bottles, or big, flat rocks that don't wobble. Algae is unfair and so are certain trees when they're right where you need a long backcast. Mosquitoes and black flies are unfair and so are wind knots and trout that won't move three or four feet to hit a fly encircled by leader material. What about underwater logs and slippery stones, and deep holes that move around so they're not where they were last time you were wading?

You can never have too many dry matches, or too much pipe tobacco, or too many flashlights or pocketknives. It's unfair that you will have none when you need them desperately. The same applies to dog whistles, leashes, 16-gauge shells, pocket flasks (full), or a spare reed for a duck call (no one, in all of recorded time, has ever had an extra reed).

There's no such thing as too many good books or too many paintings and prints. Or bronzes of Labradors and pointers and Brittanies and setters. Or glasses with pintails and canvasbacks and salmon and trout flies. Or pictures of you and Charlie with old Duke and a limit of bobwhites, or a pair of muleys, or a half-dozen Canadas, or about a yard of rainbows. Or old decoys and duck calls. There are never too many good memories of days past or too many dreams of good times to come.

There's no such thing as too often when it comes to cornbread, cracklins, buttermilk, fried chicken, or homemade peach pie with hard sauce. Or sugar-cured ham, roast duck, stewed chicken and dumplings, fried rabbit, and squirrel. Venison chops, quail, doves, or fresh trout. Home fries, hushpuppies, hoppin' john, hoe cake, or grits with red-eye gravy. There's too much squash, okra, liver, and green tomatoes, but not enough fresh cinnamon rolls, apple turnovers, sourdough pancakes, or beaten biscuits—or little girls baking cookies for their father.

We don't have enough dirt roads, old orchards, watercress springs, or stands of wild grapes. Or hedgerows, swamps, waterfalls, partridge berries, or beech nuts. There's too much noise, barbed wire, and NO TRESPASSING. Too many broken bottles, empty beer cans, plastic wrappers, shot-up road signs, and spray-painted stupidity. There's too much anger and not enough thank-you's, too much taking and not enough giving. Too much taken away and not enough put back, too much shouting and not enough thinking. Too many "me's" and not enough "you's." Too many laws and not enough justice. Too much of what passes for education and not nearly enough commonsense.

There are never too many laughs, easy straightaways, or afternoons fooling with puppies. Or bass ponds, duck marshes, or wild rivers. Or good stories and fireplaces. We do have too much gray hair and too many eyeglasses on the men that took the time to talk to use about the important things—trout lies, bird covers, what to watch and how to listen.

I don't know of any world that doesn't have its balance of "too manys" and "not enoughs." And that's just right with me. Not that I would change it, because for the most part I wouldn't really know what to change. For sure I wouldn't want to have taken any more birds or any more fish. And there has been more than a little spice in the mix from the magnificent misses, the incredible wind knots, and the perpetual muddling of N, E, S, and W.

When you ask life to throw you a lot of straightaways and they don't come, you learn to get better on the sharp angles. When the best-looking covers don't hold any birds, you learn to adjust your thinking on "best looking." I guess the whole thing is some sort of learning process. And what you end up learning is that most of the time everything comes out about even—most of the time.

Why is it so difficult to explain, looking back, that if you add up a 20 percent bird shooter and a 60 percent bird dog, you get 100 percent. You could say that I'm a poor mathematician, but I've got a lot of proof that you'd be wrong. Some folks wouldn't factor in that there was a light frost this morning, which is another 10 percent, and that it's early December, which is also worth at least 10 percent. All of which reminds me that there are a few other things I ought to be doing now, if you'll excuse me. There are never enough light frosts at this time of year.

HOROSCOPES

Tired of those goody-goody horoscopes that avoid reality in the interest of making everyone feel better? Well, here's a zodiacal reading that pulls no punches, but dares to tell the plain, unvarnished truth. So read on...and try to guess which sign is the author's.

AQUARIUS: January 20—February 18:

You have a great imagination. If you're a fisherman, you tend to be more than a little loose with the facts. If you're a shooter, you are likely to add a target here and there to your trap scores or make unlikely excuses. You are often impractical in the face of unpleasant facts. If everyone is taking trout on No. 18 Adams dries, you insist on using a No. 8 Grey Ghost and blaming the weather, the Department of Fish and Game, and acid rain for your failures. You start things that you never finish. Somewhere you have a half-finished gunstock that needs sanding and a pair of waders you started to patch. Your retriever is not really steady to shot. You have forgotten your wife's birthday but can remember exactly where you were, to the yard, on the Brimstone Pool, what you were using, and who you were with and what they wore the last time you took a limit of brown trout. People like you because you make them look good.

PISCES: February 19—March 20:

You are a very hard worker at things you care about. You spend a great deal of time working on low house 5 or practicing the double haul when you should be home painting the living room. Your bird dog is probably overtrained and will be impossible at times, refusing to hear the whistle and running rabbits and occasionally deer. You tend to spend money buying new equipment in the hope that it will make up for your impatience with fundamentals. You like fads and have ruined your duck gunstock with spacers, add-on combs, adjustable recoil pads, and fooling with a rasp. Every so often you have a day when you shoot beautifully, usually when you are alone. These are the days when your retriever is faultless as well. You have a great tendency to upset canoes and wade in water over your hip boots.

ARIES: March 21—April 19:

You are quite intelligent and are quick to see the answers to problems, especially if they are someone else's. You know what's wrong with your friends' bird dogs, but you refuse to admit that your Maggie is dreadfully spoiled and overweight because you are always sneaking her table goodies. You can be a fine shooting coach but you don't follow your own advice. You tend to indulge yourself in fancy jackets, gloves, glasses, and hats, and then try to talk your gunsmith into adjusting the triggers and timing the ejectors on your bird gun for free. You get all the sporting goods catalogs and often forget what you have and then buy duplicates. You probably have at least three pairs of boots you've never worn; you tend to hide these things from your wife out of guilt. You give things away and then make your friends and family look for a week for them. You lose at least six pipes a year and at least three pairs of gloves. Gun clubs are forever calling you up and telling you that they have your hat or jacket. You are getting worse as you get older.

TAURUS: April 20—May 20:

You are uncommonly good looking and have all sorts of talent to spare. You are a born shot and an envied fly caster, and everything you do looks easy. You are a great natural athlete. You are liked everywhere you go but don't get a chance to travel as much as you should. You should write a great deal more because you are good at it, but you have a tendency to put things off. In spite of that, you would have been an uncommonly good surgeon, lawyer, explorer, professional hunter, or cowboy. It is a tragedy that you weren't born wealthy because you should have best grade English guns and a custom tailor. You have no discernible faults, and your wife should consider herself extremely lucky to have you. You are obviously a superior person, but overly modest. You are far too humble, and that may be your only shortcoming, except that you chew too much tobacco and occasionally forget to floss.

GEMINI: May 21—June 20:

You are a bit of a daydreamer and tend to get lost in the woods a lot. Details are often overlooked and you are seldom dressed warmly enough. You have been known to forget your shotgun shells and your fishing license. You are unable to fix anything and rely heavily on other people to keep your stuff working—everything from your reels to your pocketknife needs looking after. You get backlashes with anti-backlash casting reels, and none of your duck calls are in tune. You have chosen your close friends wisely—gunsmiths, dog trainers, mechanics, fly tyers, and people who are careful reloaders. You tend to ignore everyday economics and are constantly short of cash. You have to learn to resist bargains; you have too many decoys, duck guns, and down parkas as it is. Stay away from gin rummy games with people who make their money in finance, or else learn to add and subtract. Same with poker, only more so. You are easily led and spend too much time listening to stories about new streams and bird covers. You always avoid cleaning your share of fish and game.

CANCER: June 21—July 22:

You are basically very artistic, but this makes you seem careless or worse to most people. You are easily bored and as a result often do things the hard way. You should never attempt automobile repairs or carpentry. You will be the one who is casting 60 feet when the trout are only 40 feet away. The trap targets you miss are the easy straight-aways, and you are guilty of missing high ones at skeet because you won't pay attention. You often put guns away without cleaning them and have found yourself duck hunting with 8's and quail hunting with 4's because you are often rushing around due to forgetfulness. Every so often you have to buy two hunting licenses because you misplaced one. You will never save any money.

LEO: July 23—August 22:

Leo's are very outgoing and friendly. They usually have too many dogs and their clothes, lawn, and car show the results. They have a lot of friends who are the workers in gun clubs, field trials, and D.U. dinners. People are always borrowing their stuff and they are too polite to insist on getting it back. Leo's are the meek that ought to inherit the earth. They always let others fish the best pools, take the easiest shots, and sign up for the late squads when the wind quits blowing. Leo's should never make detailed arrangements for a hunting trip. They need to be taken care of. Leo men should have two or three daughters.

VIRGO: August 23—September 22:

You are one of those who would have been happy to have been born a hundred years ago. You love the old crafts and the tools. You collect knives, axes, and such trappings, but don't know how to use them. You have never really skinned an animal or cut more than a little camp kindling. You understand the art but not the function. Your guns and fishing tackle are beautiful to look at but next to useless in your hands. You love to trade and swap stuff and have a good sense of value, but your possessions own you. You like clutter, and you have married someone who is compulsively neat. When you find yourself saving newspapers and guarding 6-foot piles of old magazines, seek help.

LIBRA: September 23—October 22:

Libras are somewhat unlucky and tend to be frustrated. You would love to be able to call ducks but find that you're tone deaf. You admire woodcraft but tend to cut yourself and stumble noisily in the woods. Your homemade decoys float funny and your knots come untied. The varnish has never dried on your canoe paddle. The stuff you buy on sale rarely fits. You are the optimist who rarely learns. Everybody wants to play poker with you. You are the original guy who "should have been here last week." Whoever said "look before you leap" had you in mind, but you wouldn't have listened to him. You never have dry socks or an extra sweater.

SCORPIO: October 23—November 21:

You are the adventurous type who will try anything once. Your garage looks like a sporting goods warehouse—bows, muzzleloaders, kayaks, scuba gear, tree stands, spotting scopes, and an assortment of mysterious machines are gathering dust there. You are too long on enthusiasm and too short on patience or know-how. You are famous for trying to draw two cards to a flush and for leaving the deer stand before the drive is over. You probably throw away the best part of a cigar. If you've read this far, you probably skipped over all the rest. Take a little time to smell the flowers—very few of them hide bees.

SAGITTARIUS: November 22—December 21:
You are famous for being a spendthrift. Fortunately, you're rather successful and you can afford it, right down to the camouflage shoelaces. However, the fact that you pick up more than your share of the breakfast checks shouldn't entitle you to bore everyone else with your theories on decoy layout, dog training, and choke boring. You're generous with your help around camp, but you never let anyone forget who did the dishes and swept the floor.

CAPRICORN: December 22—January 19:
Women born under this sign are famous for their beauty and intelligence but tend to marry men who are almost totally devoted to bird dogs and shotguns. Capricorns are born financiers; they have to be or they'd be broke. You generally feed about five dogs and belong to six clubs. You will never be able to save any money because new models of guns are always coming out and all the local kennels know where they can get rid of extra puppies. Capricorns should insist that at least one of their children become either a veterinarian or a gunsmith, or marry one or the other. Capricorns are nice people who spend most of their life wondering what went wrong.

WOOD SMOKE

I don't know how it is where you live, but in my part of the country, it's suddenly starting to look like the farmhouse prints put out years ago by Currier and Ives. People are sporting huge woodpiles in their yards, and wraiths of fragrant smoke are flavoring the evening air. Everyone has rediscovered the absolute bane of my childhood—the wood stove.

My city-bred neighbors, who two years ago didn't know a copper beech from a paper birch, are now instant authorities on creosote content, flue sizes, and the BTU's you can wring out of a face cord of oak. Once our average cocktail party would feature heated arguments on choke boring and tippet diameters, or shorthairs versus setters; now folks are taking stands on air-tight combustion units, chimney fires, and cannel coal. Quaint and descriptive stove names float through conversations that once were reserved for comparing Parkers and Model 21's. Once you were below the salt if you couldn't name the fine points of the Lucky Strike or Shed of Arden's progeny; now it's the Kitchen Charm or some foreign import featuring soapstone or exotic tiles. OPEC started all this mess by jacking up the cost of heating oil to the point where we dream about a full fuel tank the way we used to grow misty-eyed over the impossible prospects of a Purdey or a Holland & Holland. But since both now run about the same in dollars, we've given all that up. Little armies have taken to the woodlots with axes and chain saws and wedges and peaveys. Until just a few years ago, the menfolk would have been sporting .30-30's or 12-bore pumps.

Ladies who formerly might have concerned themselves with stitches to the inch or some other fitting domesticity are now bragging about their husband's new chain saws or their own kindling hatchets. People are eyeing each other's wood-piles with the same looks once reserved for decoy collections or bamboo rods. I have no doubt that a lot of oldtime log skinners are in torment in their graves with all this chatter about back-cutting and felling and limbing, in much the same way Fred Kimble or Captain Bogardus must twitch whenever I get going on the proper way to lead a downwind teal or broadbill.

So far, I have stayed out of these born-again stove zealot discussions, largely because they tend to bore me and make me remember boyhood chores that I'd rather forget. Back then, on the farms, everyone heated everything with wood. We ran the furnace on it (coal was ridiculously high at eight dollars a ton), cooked with it, and used it to heat water. I don't recall any of us, especially the small boys whose job was to keep the wood-boxes filled, thinking this was fun, or even charming. It was never, to my recollection, the subject of much conversation over the evening coffee or cider. I wonder what today's woodpiles would look like if we replaced the gas and electric chain saws with 10-foot, two-man saws and the four-wheel drives with horses and chains.

I was only a little fellow, small for my age, but I made up for my size with a cunning aversion to hard work. I did, however, get captured often enough and long enough to work all day—day after day—helping to get in the winter supply. Even now, when I have to get out the ax and saw, I trudge out to my little woodlot with a strong mixture of caution and fear. A long list of friends who have had mishaps runs through my head, along with a list of "almosts" of my own.

I've always had a very high regard for a man who is skillful with an ax and a saw. I mean skills like being able to cut and shape a new ax handle that was just right for a particular ax *and* the particular man who would use it; skills like knowing when a saw wasn't working right and being able to sharpen and set it, and the ability to fell a tree so it landed just where it should, and what to do if, by chance, it didn't. Any day's work in the woods was physically demanding as well as dangerous. If I'm not mistaken, the term "widow-maker" came out of the lumber camps, and if I'm not mistaken again, it came out fairly often.

I've never seen a real professional logger at work, nor have I ever seen a north country log drive, but some of the old fishing guides I know used to work the river when they floated the timber down, and none of them ever seemed eager to relive that part of the good old days. Having seen photographs and heard the stories about working days in a row dodging logs and the ice floes that came down with them, I'll say *amen* to that part of our colorful history.

I must now admit that I too have couple of wood stoves, along with a couple of fireplaces, to occupy spare time once devoted to far less worthwhile and more expensive pursuits that took place at various gun clubs. Somehow it doesn't seem as bad as I remember, and I don't find myself homesick for the mumbling of the oil burner in the basement. I also have neighbors, named Howard and Jess, who are willing to donate a day or so of their expertise in return for my complete and totally honest admiration of their woodsmen's skills— and a few cold beers as we stand around and pleasure ourselves at the sight of a couple of cords of neatly stacked oak, hickory, and apple.

All in all, I think everyone agrees that this virtuous move back to older times is a good thing. There was a generation or so who came fearfully close to believing that milk came from plastic jugs, meat was born sliced and wrapped, and labor was just a political factor.

Not one to do things by half, which is another way of saying that I often bite off more than I can chew, I let my wife talk me into buying a chimney cleaning kit with a set of big heavy brushes and flexible rods. In theory, cleaning a chimney is simplicity itself. All you do is partially dismantle the stove pipes, move the stove (hernia surgeons love this part.), assemble the rods and brushes, and scrub away. In practice this occupies the better part of a day per chimney, and that doesn't include cleaning up the mess or frequently washing out the miscellany of particles that find their way into your eyes, nose, hair, etc. Having a bit of scholarly bent and a touch of the loafer, I went through some of my old books in the firm belief that there must be an easier way. The one I like best said that the best way to clean the flue was to drop a hen down the chimney a couple of times.

As an old country boy, this idea had a lot of appeal, and I came pretty close to visiting a neighbor who raises a few chickens for fresh eggs. I have a Labrador retriver who will, on occasion, indulge me in some odd ideas, but I felt that this would be a bit much to ask.

Right now I have a newly varnished gun stock swinging on a wire over my glowing Home Atlantic, and the makings of a hot toddy steaming in my old cast iron kettle that sits on top of the stove. The soft aroma of apple smoke is sweetening the evening air. Roughly figuring, my woodpile is worth a couple of cases of trap loads. We all know "it's an ill wind that blows no good." Thank you OPEC, whoever you are.

TAKING TURNS

Every so often someone writes to me and remarks that I tend to go on about missing the "good old days." Well, I don't mean to. I don't miss them, what little I knew of them, but, like most of us, I have a rather selective memory. It all depends what the conversation is. I'm glad that my girls had the chance to go to a much better school than my eight grades in one room. I'm romantic about farming, but that's because I don't have to get up at 4:30 to milk cows and then do another twelve hours of back breaking work before falling into bed for a few hours of sleep before all the same chores start again. I miss the old bird covers that I could get to my walking or riding my bike, and later on in my Model A Ford. But now I have the jetliners. Oldtimers never dreamed of hunting much more than an hour or so away from their own backyards—except for maybe a once-in-a-lifetime trip to some exotic spot like Maine or South Carolina.

I find it a little hard to believe that I never saw a Canada goose until I was about seventeen; now I have a couple of dozen in my pond almost all year long. And when I shot my first deer at age eleven, local whitetails were scarce enough that all the successful hunters got their names in the paper. I guess I do miss the kind of adventure and excitement that goes with turning eleven—the borrowed gun, hanging around with the grownups, Mom always worrying and Pop being somewhat surprised that I didn't get lost or fall in through the ice, since I was rather notorious for doing both with a fair amount of dimwitted frequency.

Since the time of my eleventh year and my first hunting license, I have had my share of deer and Canadas and a lot of other fish and game adventures in places more exotic than our old woodlot, but few of these adventures were all that more honestly exciting—all things, including being eleven, considered.

The good old days were good to me and I treasure them, but I don't miss them. They really weren't anything special, just the more or less normal excursions and outings of a rather typical country boy. I do dwell on the high spots when I have a captive audience, but there are no moments unique to me, only my personal places and private times.

To keep a balance, I don't miss the outhouse, the garden weeding, or mending stone walls. I don't miss waking up in midwinter before the kitchen stove was lit or having to go to church twice on Sundays, or cleaning chicken coops, or being terrified about catching polio or scarlet fever, or a few other similar horrors that are, thankfully, no longer with us. I don't miss having to work a churn, push a lawnmower, or carry water from the brook to the garden.

I do sometimes miss, as much for other little kids as for myself, sweet things like hay mows, sleigh rides behind horses, cutting bee trees, running trot lines for eels and perch, and maybe most of all, having a fine brook almost to myself and a very understanding series of dogs to explore it with me.

But, these are small things, meaningful to no one but myself. My day dreams were unambitious and common—catching a big bass or pickerel, having my own .22, enjoying a successful day now and then on the trapline, or having my father take pity on me and filling the kitchen woodbox while I dug for worms or went rabbit hunting.

What I do miss most—at the risk of being called cranky—is something I was brought up to take for granted: good manners. I suppose I ought to use the popular word—"sportsmanship"—but I think that a lot of people who ought to know better, and probably do, are confusing politeness with servility, or being "taken." I'm sorry to see this happening.

In what has come to be called the "good old days," when you went fishing or shooting with someone, you took turns, trying to give your pal the equal or the best of it, knowing that he would do the same for you. The phrase "taking turns" means a lot of things to me. I'd rather take turns with you in a duck blind than shoot the same duck you were looking at. I appreciate your willingness to let me run my dog a little more because it isn't as good as yours and needs experience. I'm delighted to row while you cast, or just wait and watch until your finished with that special spot. I like knowing that you won't pull over on my side of a covey rise, so I can take my time and pick my shots the way I want to take them.

Taking turns is a bit more leisurely approach than we seem to favor today. It's being a bit less competitive and says more about why we're out there together in the first place.

A perceptive reader reminded me recently that much of today's writing about field sports—mainly hunting and fishing—is concerned with the importance of manners and conduct and ethics, as contrasted by sportswriters who harangue us with reports on which athletes make the most money and who ranks where at the local, national, and international levels. Does this mean that as a group, hunters and fishermen have better manners? I leave that to you. But think what we would have (or not have) without such self-imposed and, I like to think, gratifying attitudes.

Taking turns is a way of being able to give someone something special—a few more minutes to fool around with a fish, another cast with his dog, a chance to see why he missed the last shot, or shot so well. I wish we'd get more competitive about seeing that our partner has a better day rather than concentrating on who has the bigger bag.

In the good old days, we seemed to have more time for one another. Maybe we're beginning to believe we don't have that kind of luxury anymore. I once ruined a pretty fair dog prospect by pushing him too hard and expecting too much. I've always been a bit ashamed of myself for that—and I hope I have never done the same thing to a friend. How easily a little greed or ego can turn us into petty tyrants.

Maybe the thought of taking turns—putting somebody ahead of yourself—is old-fashioned. But then again, as the kids like to say in a somewhat different context—if it feels good, do it!

A QUESTION OF
STATISTICS

The country, now in the hands of the computer people, has gone statistics crazy. I don't know about you, but I find that bar charts, graphs, and any kind of factions or percentages tend to make me dizzy. And, most of these statistics are totally meaningless anyway. For example, let's suppose you have a statistician operating a computer. He would know from past performance that in any given year, exactly 4,073 fly rods will have their tips broken—2,976 by screen doors and tailgate windows, 852 by fishermen trying to pull flies from trees, 120 by fishermen flogging their Labrador retrievers for chasing fly lines, 86 by being stepped on, 22 from being used to strike at snakes or bees or bats, 13 by taking a 9-foot rod apart in only 8½ feet of space, and four from "other" causes.

By July 4th, exactly 98,778 trap targets will be missed by right-handed shooters from post 5. Shooters whose last name begins with *H* will be among the big losers due to the inability to make up their minds whether to hold for the straightaway or start a foot or so off the corner. The majority of other misses will be caused by shooters wishing they had new guns with the currently popular high ribs or by shooters with the currently popular high ribs wishing they had their old trap guns back. The phrase "you lifted you head" will be used in 63,886 cases, and the phrase "I lifted my head" will be used in all others but 3; *that* phrase is not on the computer.

Of the 187,664 trapshooters, only four will feel that they had the right gun and that it fitted them perfectly. Each of these four will be, incidentally, a beginning shooter with less than 500 registered targets; three will be female. Of the last 36,972 high house one targets missed, eight skeet shooters will deny that there was anything wrong with either the puller or the line of flight of the target. Two of these shooters will insist that they just shot in the wrong place, while the other six will feel that new guns, reloads, or one of a variety of outside distractions caused the misses.

While the reasons given by skeet shooters who only missed one or two targets in the 100 bird events will tend to be too complicated, and those reasons given by those who missed 10 or more will be too obscene, the misses will seem, on average, to fall into a category classified as "an act of God." One shooter, thought to be a "Wayne Mays," will claim that he had "stopped his gun." Although this phrase is also unknown to the computer, it will later be determined that Mr. Mays' average had dropped to .99989 over 9,800 targets and the computer will attribute this to the probability of faulty ammunition.

In the Yellowstone Park region, it is estimated that 11 pounds of trout will be caught this summer by fly fishermen in 74,000 man hours of casting. A quick check reveals that this same effort would have mowed a lawn the size of Massachusetts or painted a house four times the size of the *Queen Elizabeth II*. The energy expended by bass fishermen pulling beer can tabs in only the water impoundments created by the TVA will be the equivalent of weeding a vegetable garden large enough to supply okra for five million gallons of gumbo!

In Texas alone, the bass fishermen will chew enough tobacco on the average Sunday to replace three months of OPEC oil if the expectorate could replace crude. These same fishermen, in the same amount of time, will use enough plastic worms to build a 3-foot wall completely around the cities of either Wichita Falls or Amarillo—but not both.

According to the computer, this coming dove season should be eagerly anticipated by Winchester, Remington, and Federal. Enough shells will be fired to pave the road from Brister to Zern. A great dove shot, who modestly refuses to be programmed by name in our system, anticipates that he almost averaged 50 percent! This is based on the fact that he almost averaged 50 percent last year and would have except for three factors: wind in the wrong direction, sun in the wrong place, wore green glasses instead of tan or gray. Shell expenditure per shooter will be the equivalent of a 10 percent increase in net income tax. Another statistic on the computer printout shows that the dedicated dove shooter will go through the dollar equivalent of a new linoleum floor for the kitchen and a trash compactor.

Quail hunters come out with somewhat different figures. To be fair, the expenses of dogs must be factored in along with ammunition, and miscellaneous items such as brush pants, boots, and side bets are grouped together at an average of $15 per hunter per season. This is intentionally low but offset by the numbers of beginning female hunters who are given their husbands' old clothes to wear. The high has been found to be in a 50-mile radius from Albany, Georgia, with the expenditure on bobwhite quail hunting determined to be the equivalent of the cost of a 747, fully fueled. The low, in contrast, turns out to be west Texas blue quail hunting in a 75-mile radius from Uvalde, with the expenditure being slightly less than three weeks' production of Lone Star beer estimated at wholesale.

Some of the more offbeat statistics are even more interesting and surprising. The most common nickname for a kindly old sportsman in all outdoor stories for the past thirty years is "The Judge." Everytime you read the words "pump gun," you will see the phrase "corn sheller" three times. If all the reels that "screamed" in Michigan last year screamed at the same time, 68 percent of all the windows above the third floor in Detroit would be broken. This statistic is based on a decibel average of both Orvis and Pflueger reels in good condition, i.e. not full of grit or sand.

Hunters and fishermen on trips have more flat tires after dark than other males age 35 to 55 by a ratio of 4 to 1, according to random telephone calls placed collect from public phones. Deer hair seems to cause an erratic effect on rifle bullets, whereas paper seems to have an opposite or "accurizing" effect. Air temperature may be a factor, but as of now our scientists are not willing to make a statement one way or the other.

Similarly, the displacement of air made by a large rising trout has a negative effect on the placement of a dry fly, but again, there are other factors involved that are under study. If all the bass boats in Tennessee, Alabama, and Arkansas were started and headed west at the same moment, the speed of the earth would be increased by .000076 mph. There are 23,964 more turkey calls in Florida than there are turkeys. In Wyoming on an average day in elk season (wind 9mph WSW, air temperature 28 degrees F), a mature bull can hear a saddle creak or a chew of tobacco being shifted for 3¼ miles.

I, for one, find none of this surprising, but it is interesting to see things that most of us already know examined in a more scientific light. But I'm still a little skeptical of a lot of published figures, no matter how long they've been around. If a trap load has a velocity of around 1,200 feet per second, how is it at all possible for me to shoot *behind* so many quartering angles? How can a 6-pound-test leader break on a 1½-pound trout? Maybe they ought to put disclaimers on some of these things, the way they do on car mileage estimates: *These trap loads will vary according to the age of the shooter and the amount of prize money at stake. Shooters named Kay Ohye will get more targets, and shooters named Hill should expect less.*

Just because it's in print or comes from a computer doesn't mean it's gospel. I think we all still have a lot to learn and we have to depend on each other. While statistics are amusing to those few who can remember things like their social security numbers and their license plates, in our fraternity we learn by observation and experience and questioning. As an example, even as superb a fisherman as Ed Zern once turned to me when we were fishing together and asked: "Hill, just exactly what in hell do you think you're doing?"

It takes a great man to be humble.

A MATTER OF PRIVACY

There are certain things that are best done when you are alone. One that will certainly bring no argument is the first shot of the season; another is the first cast on a trout stream. After several months of fooling around in the garden or replenishing the wood pile, we are never sure that any small skills we had may or may not have completely deserted us. The proper way to find out is with solitary contemplation as our companion, and with absolutely no possibility of witnesses who would, almost certainly, entertain friends for the rest of the season with increasingly embellished stories about climbing a birch tree to retrieve a No. 12 Adams or overshooting the classic straightaway by a yard.

The traditional opening day is really a beginning more than the taking up again of where we left off last year on closing day. Things are a little strange at first. The bird gun, unhandled except for a few ritual cleanings, hasn't settled down into its familiar weight and balance. The old gunning coat has to learn a few new curves left over from summer barbecues and the boots are still a little resistant after being removed from their dark and pleasant resting place. We know that everything will come around to where it ought to be and that one has to make the best of this settling in. In these first hours, about the last thing we need is a testing shot (and all first shots are testing, no matter how routine they seem to someone who isn't called on to make them). All we're really interested in is the pleasant fiddling with pipes and tobacco and gloves and glasses. It's housecleaning—putting things just where they belong in preparation for the days afield.

Fishing has its similar moments but it has always seemed a little easier to me just to sit along the side of a stream and sort of let things settle themselves out. It's only the amateur or the totally fishing-starved person who throws himself ravenously on the stream, threading his line through the guides even as he wades into the water and inevitably puts down every self-respecting trout within several hundred yards.

Some fishermen, and I'm not one of them, have profitably spent the dark days of winter sorting things out, putting away the late September salmon flies and replacing them with streamers and nymphs for opening day. My own vest is always a surprise package of odds and ends, and an early spring day stretched out streamside amongst the other early arrivals—robins, myrtle, and hopefully a woodcock or two, seems as good a place as any to do my spring cleaning. I hate to say that I'm here to *not* catch anything, since that wouldn't be wholly true, but I am here not to care about it too much, one way or another. My first casts are tentative as I settle myself into a new rhythm to match the lengthening days and the idling ways of the few feeding trout that occasionally dimple the water's surface.

Spare me the company of a more organized and ready person. I don't need or want a litany on what I should have done last month or last week. I am not well organized and I don't need any more reminders of that fact. I know the linesize marker has fallen off the reel, and that my leader tippets are too heavy, etc., etc., etc. This is my misery and I want to revel in my mess all by myself.

There are a lot of things a person has to do all by himself. Learning to whistle is one and, later on, learning to smoke a pipe or take a chew of tobacco are others. Trying out a new hat, fooling with a puppy, looking for slingshot forks, or making a willow whistle are private occupations that demand complete concentration. It seems to me the new generation feels that it's immoral to do something by yourself, and that the constant sound of another human voice is necessary for sanity. I totally and absolutely disagree. I didn't want anyone around when I was learning to set a number 1 trap. If you wanted to know where I'd been and what I had been doing, all you had to do was look at my thumbs and notice the little blue lines. I didn't want witnesses or advice when I was learning to ride a bicycle, stand on my hands, or do a one-and-a-half off the diving board. The list is long and a lot of it is private—as I'm sure yours is.

Maybe it's that I'm eccentric. But I can hardly believe I'm the only person who, when he's all alone, will talk to fish, or make a fool of himself rolling around on the floor with an old dog, or is still trying to learn to whistle with two fingers, or practice casting without a rod and shooting without a shotgun. And not being a paid professional comedian, I prefer to indulge myself in these harmless lunacies in total and complete privacy.

And so it is on opening days. I will not be at my best and I know it. I hunt and fish because I enjoy the places where these activities take place. I pleasure myself in the quiet, when I can control it. As far as I'm concerned, if you like spectator sports, go to a baseball game. I really don't mind if you come along, but don't feel bad if I suggest that you go your way and I go mine, and we meet for lunch back at the car.

To me, the great outdoors is mainly a private place. It's where you can go to try things out—a new idea or a new hat, a different gun or rod, or a thought that needs working on. It's a place to ask yourself important questions or look for answers, a place to wonder about the same things you wondered about when you were 12 and 20, a place to enjoy being older or to indulge yourself in the little sadnesses of age. It's considered trite and common to dwell on the questions and mysteries of bass ponds and duck marshes, but if they weren't there, I wonder how many of many of us would fish and hunt just to exhibit some small skills and come home with only something to eat?

Sitting in the dark is delicious if you're alone, but the mystery disappears the minute someone else enters the room. And so the alien presence of someone else can strip the daydreams of wilderness, or danger, or belittle the moments of missing, when the truth is you would just as soon have had it happen that way. Company often has a way of making us a little dishonest; it makes us seem to care about some things we really don't put any stock in, and it makes us too casual or indifferent about many things that are really important—privately.

You have your ethics and standards, and I have mine. Sometimes they're the same, and sometimes not. Sometimes you want to laugh with the loon, and sometimes you want to cry. An old friend of mine used to go out in the mountains every couple of years and just wander around until he was lost. He'd spend a couple of days sorting things out and then settle down. At least that's what he told everyone. Now I'm beginning to wonder what it was he went to lose and what he hoped to find. Who doesn't have a lot of questions he'd like to have answered? And who else can answer them better than he can, privately, alone, all by himself.

THE WAITING GAME

A drake mallard on the opposite bank watched me false casting. He would stand on one foot every so often and he looked like he was wearing orange baby mittens. He had a disapproving attitude, which I attributed to my casting stroke. I don't much care for it either.

I've often remarked, and often to the wrong people, that I thought much of the so-called mystique of fly fishing was nonsense. Not that I think it's easy, but it isn't neurosurgery either. It's just that I think too many people are taking the fun out of it by over-Latinizing, over-nomenclature, and over-everything.

One example: I was fishing the "fabled" Test a couple of years ago and my young English river-keeper was adamant about casting only to rising fish, upstream, with a dry fly. Fine, but at this period of the day there weren't any rising fish, so we were sitting on the bank telling each other lies. I took out my fly box and he asked if he could look through it. With more than a little disdain, he held up one of my favorite flies—a small Gray Ghost streamer.

"You actually use this?" he asked.

I told him that I'd caught more fish, including a few Atlantic salmon, on that pattern than any other. He smiled a bit condescendingly and said: "I rather think that our trout are a bit too sophisticated to go for that." Since nothing else was happening, I asked him if I could tie it on and make a couple of casts. "Why not," he said. I made three casts and caught three browns, the last one about four pounds. To my everlasting credit, I refrained from a little speech about big fish eating big flies, but we didn't get along very well after that.

My mallard kept following on the off-bank as I waded downstream. My guess is that some fisherman had been throwing bread crumbs in the water and the mallard was waiting for a handout from me. Trout fishing is not a spectator sport unless you're the mate of an osprey.

I am not a good judge of the quality of a trout fly, I can name only a few patterns, and I don't tie flies. I'm content with my tying friends' rejects and the few flies I buy in tackle stores. Nor am I an expert on the finer points of fly tackle. I do have a handful of bamboo rods. I absolutely cannot cast with one of them despite its famous name. There are four or five others, all from different makers, that I will never part with. My trout rods are all bamboo, and I use space-age-material rods for salmon and tarpon. But I can't rate any of my fly rods, just as I wouldn't attempt to grade a Boss shotgun against a Purdey or a Holland. No doubt I could use one better than the others for some indefinable reason of fit or balance, but they're all fine. It wouldn't be dollar snobbery either, because one of my "best" rods is an old Heddon, worth about half what I had to pay for my waders.

I just like to fly fish, even if I am ignorant, clumsy, and stubborn. I don't go for the vocabulary or the finer points of the art. If they won't take anything as big as a size 18, I leave the fishing to my betters and sit and smoke a pipe, or else I go off somewhere by myself and practice my casting, which is always rusty and not likely to get much better.

I like the dream within a dream in fly fishing—the quarry in one distant world probed best by the mind's eye, and you in another, acting as much the predator as the otter or the merganser, or at least trying to. I regard most of my catches as happy accidents and stand in pure awe of the skills I have seen exhibited by truly fine fishermen. But I don't envy them. I don't want to tie up a few cress bugs with my streamside outfit. I don't want to use an 8X tippet; I can't even see 8X. I will stay with my Adams, my Gray Ghost, and my Joe's Hopper, and the only thing I have to clean when I get home is my language.

I like watching my mallard, and I think he's enjoying watching me. I wonder if ducks get bored, or curious? Why not? Maybe he's a philosopher and will share with his wife a couple of laughs about my dress and what I was doing with a stick and some orange-colored string.

I wondered for quite a while about the fascination of fly fishing. Why is it that I can wade into a stream at 10 in the morning, look at my watch in a "couple" of hours, and find out that it's late afternoon. I really think it's like dreaming, only in reverse, where you have this long involved thing happening to you and you wake up and discover you've only been asleep a few minutes. It's like watching a water snake. The small boy in you says "throw a rock at him!" The growing-older man says "don't do that, it's waiting for something." You know that everyone and everthing is waiting for something to happen; we just don't know quite what or quite when. I imagine that the snake likes the feel of the warm rock on his belly and the soothing touch of the water on his tail. And so do I. We both like it here and we're both fishing for something—when we get around to it.

I like fly fishing, I guess, as a nice way to pass time; waiting. It is a respectable thing to do as opposed to being purely idle, stretched out in a hammock, or taking a nap on the couch. You at least look serious and industrious—a vest full of instruments, polarized glasses, wading staff and net, perhaps a small canvas creel, and the busy little hum of the fly line slicking through the rod guides. "There," you say, "is a serious man," if you should see me poised like a heron in some stream. Far from it. There you see an idler in costume, a man wondering where the time went. Not the past hour or so while exchanging nods with a duck or mulling a two-penny philosophy abut a mud-colored snake, but the past five or ten years. He is thinking about his work that has been left undone, his loves unknown, and that just yesterday he was only a boy.

To paraphrase a favorite silliness, I often think that life is fly fishing in miniature. Standing still in a current that is running past you, carrying with it the things you can only see for a flash of time. You keep casting and then, when you least expect it, everything goes just right. And, suddenly, without much having happened, the day is almost over. It is getting dark and the duck and the snake have gone to their mysterious resting places. The thin light of a summer moon seems cold and the night calls of the owl and the bittern sound hostile. It seems as if the whole world has something more important to do and the fisherman is in the way. With half regret and half relief the fisherman stands free from the water, cumbersome in his heavy waders on the land. He will come back tomorrow. Tonight, he will dream about what it was he was waiting to have happen.

GIVING AND TAKING

A year ago I was in Africa. Only a year ago, but it seems far more distant than time. I find writing about it strangely remote and unreal. How does one describe the way the lion tells you he is in charge of the night and how much you believe him? Nor can I properly express the combination of beauty and dignity, and the elusive shyness, of the great antelopes like the kudu and the sable, or put real meaning into the dark sullen tonnage of the Cape Buffalo.

The good writing about Africa, by Isak Dinesen, Hemingway, Ruark, and a few others, deals in the main with how the continent affects and changes the thinking of those who spend much time there. But their good words are like pebbles thrown in a pond—you see a little rippling on the surface, hear a splash, and then everything is just the way is was before. The country closes behind you as the writers take you through it. The animals move back a little, the baboons and birds resume their barking and singing. You are, in very short order, made to feel insignificant. As much as I've enjoyed sitting, as it were, at their campfires, looking over their shoulders at the stalk and the kill, it is not remotely like being there.

I could tell you, in detail, about stumbling into a lioness and her three cubs, and how frightening it was in an *absolute* way. But then, fright is not a strong emotion, secondhand. I could tell you about being chased by half a dozen elephants or almost walking into a hippo in the dark, but in print it's just another brush with a big animal. And if you wander around Africa, these things are bound to happen anyway. If you drive a car long enough, you are going to have a blowout or a skid or an accident. Who is going to know what you felt? Who cares about your life the way you do?

Enough of that. Let's hunt for a day I remember very well.

I have never felt quite so good after a week of walking all day, with the very comforting weight of my .375 riding on my shoulder. Back at the tent camp, I'd sit in front of the fire, have a little warm whisky, some good talk, a steak or two from the animal I shot yesterday or today, and then go to bed early to read for a little while. In the dark I'd listen to Africa, falling asleep with the soft voices of the camp help somehow cushioning the heavy bellows of the short-tempered hippos and the egotistical threats of a nearby lion.

In the morning it's cold, and you stand around the fire waiting for breakfast and the first light to extinguish the last of the stars. You check the rifles being put into the hunting car and go over your cartridge belts one more time. I slip four big 270-grain Noslers in one pocket of my shorts and a full clip for the 7mm Magnum in the other. Four more 300-grain solids for the .375 go in a shirt pocket, just in case. My old theory is, "if you don't have it in your hand or pocket, it might as well not exist." The professional checks the car one more time—extra gas, lunch boxes, water jug, spare tires, ropes. One rifle is tied with rubber straps in the outside rack; the other one rides up in front in my hands, three cartridges in the magazine and the bolt closed on an empty chamber. The ones in the rack are loaded the same way.

In the headlights as we leave the camp are the usual assortment of birds enjoying the warmth of the sand tracks, and now and then a rabbit or an elephant shrew. My binoculars are in a clip on the dash and I clean the dust off the glass and slip the strap over my neck. As we drive along the hunter and I play the old game. He says, "See that roan?" And I say, "Not more than 20 inches, maybe 21." That's a tie. We both saw it at the same time. You lose when you have to say "where?" I usually lose. He knows where to look, but I'm learning.

Today we're looking for sable antelope. And I'm thinking about yesterday when we must have seen thirty sable bulls and I turned them all down. Three days in a row before that, we hadn't seen one sable. But now we *think* we know where to start. It's an hour's drive past zebras, wildebeests, two giraffes, a family of warthogs, reedbucks, hartebeests, and one herd of at least eighteen elephants standing almost invisible at the gray edge of a stand of forest. The trackers, riding in the open back of the hunting car, are constantly tapping on the roof to make sure we see what they see. If we don't, we stop and ask "where?" Sometimes they don't understand why we pass by an animal that we were looking for a few days ago. They stop us now to point out a good kudu bull that neither the hunter nor I could see. I fool with the glasses for a full two minutes before I make out the ivory tips of horns, but the body of the animal is invisible. I already have my kudu and I hope this one isn't bigger because that's happened to me several times already. The hunter says, "He'll be a good 50 inches by next year if the poachers don't get him." By now the kudu has moved a step or two and I can see the white chevrons on his face. "Save him for me," I say. "Tell him not to go away until I get back."

About a mile from where we'd seen the sable bulls, we stop the car. I put a shell in the chamber of the 7mm, slide the glasses inside my shirt, and start to walk. We leave one tracker with the truck. The tracker with us carries my .375 and the hunter carries his own .458. All we need is a sable and all we see is an empty meadow. Disappointment is part of hunting, and the sudden vacancy is almost unreal. I still carry in my mind the picture of this field studded with the graceful black-pelted animals with their arching horns. I can so clearly see them clustered, it is almost like awakening from a dream not to find them there.

We turn and start the walk back to the car, the tracker in front and the hunter and me following behind, making plans about what to do next. The tracker stops with a low whistle and points toward the woods across from the clearing we just left. About half a mile away are some sables about to come into the meadow. Through the binoculars we can count eighteen, all cows. The hunter says there must be a bull somewhere. I tell him that I don't have anything better to do this afternoon and why don't we just walk over and take a closer look. Without too much optimism we start the stalk. With such a number of cows, it is sure, absolutely sure, that one of them will see us before we get too much closer. We crouch and freeze, run a step or two, and freeze. There is only one small stand of trees between us and the herd, and that still leaves about 200 yards of nothing but grass and thirty-six eyes. We drop behind a slanting tree and use the glasses. The hunter sees him first, standing in grass almost high enough to cover his back; all that is really visible is an arc of horn. But it seems high enough and far back enough. I rest the rifle on the tree, put the crosshairs under the front end of the horns, and wait. The cows are getting spookier and milling around as if waiting to be told what to do. The bull moves a step forward and I can see most of his front shoulder through the grass. The hunter nods at me. At the shot nothing much happens. The cows are milling a bit faster and the bull just stands there. The hunter shrugs and says "I don't know" to my unasked question. I shoot again and the bull and the cows walk back into the woods and vanish.

The bull is no more than 100 yards into the trees. We stop and I shoot one more time—the "insurance policy."

We get back to camp a little after dark and leave the sable in the capable hands of the skinners.

"It's a funny thing, isn't it?" the hunter said as we stood around the fire. "Hunting has a way of adding something to you and at the same time subtracting something as well."

I said that I'd taken a lot of animals before and hoped to get several more, but that it never got any easier.

"Would you throw him back?" the hunter asked.

"No," I answered. "We know there are twenty other bulls or more for his harem. I need him at home to watch over me, to remind me of some things I don't ever want to forget. Of Africa."

"Why wouldn't a picture do as well?" the hunter asked, and then answered his own question. "It doesn't, does it."

He held up his hand and I could see the scars that a leopard had put there.

"You should have asked the leopard to take your picture," I said.

"No," he said, "it wouldn't have been the right thing to do. There wouldn't be anything to this hunting business if you always won."

That night the lions somehow sounded closer than ever as I slept. The next morning I found out they had come into the skinners' tent and taken away my sable.

Africa giveth, and Africa taketh away.

A LITTLE QUICKER,
A LITTLE STRAIGHTER

I suppose that anyone who likes sports has "seen" himself in the spotlight as the crowd screams his name. The golfer sees himself stalking the 18th fairway of Augusta National, leading the Masters by five shots. The football fan sees himself throwing the bomb on 3rd and long, or picking his way past tackler after tackler. And there's the classic count of 3 and 2, 2 out, bases loaded in the last half of the ninth, the home team two runs behind, and you are at bat.

For the trapshooter, the dream takes place in Vandalia, Ohio. I can see the headlines now: "UNKNOWN SHOOTER DOMINATES GRAND AMERICAN!" Then come the details and the interviews. Ammunition companies who had before pleaded with me not to tell anyone that I used their shells are now promising me that my picture will be on their promotional T-shirts and that their brochures will read "Recommended by Gene Hill." Gun companies are asking what I would like in the way of engraving and how many extra sets of barrels if I would only use their gun in public for a round or two at the practice trap. Bob Allen sends out his personal tailor to fit me for a complete new wardrobe of shooting clothes, and the Hall of Fame asks if I would donate my old brown sweater.

The thing is to be gracious. Give credit where credit is due. I would admit that I've spent hours talking about the fine points with my old friend Rudy Etchen. I've also spent days watching the moves of Gene Sears and John Hall and have asked Kay Ohye to stand behind me to polish any rough spots that might have turned up.

This is no time to desert old friends. This *is* the time to be humble and to give advice as freely as it has been given to me. I apologize to the youngsters for setting a bad example by smoking my pipe for the last hundred straight and sneaking a chew between rounds.

I will submit to the demands of medicine and let the researchers test my incredible reflexes and eyesight. After all, I now belong to the public!

I will write about it, of course, filling in the details that we don't have time for on television news shows—the usual stuff about how any shoot is just one target at a time and that if you can break 25 straight and keep your concentration, there's no good reason why you can't go all the way. I'll freely offer the dimensions of my stock and my theories on choke boring, and I'll gladly demonstrate my stance from stations one and five. The only condition I'll insist on is that my past scores from the few registered shoots I've been in will never, never be made public!

I doubt if the life of a celebrity will be comfortable for me. I've spent too many years struggling to be mediocre, but I'll try to remain "average" and never forget that the road to success may be paved with hard work, but that a little luck in the right places has never hurt anyone.

The fact of the matter is, there's a little truth in all of this. I have spent a lot of time with some of the great shots and I have watched them carefully—though very little has rubbed off. I've got a gun exactly like Rudy Etchen's old Remington pump. I've got a gun like the one Gene Sears has. I've shot with Kay Ohye's and Frank Little's guns. The trouble is, I'm not an Etchen or a Sears or an Ohye or a Frank Little.

This reminds me of a story about a good friend who was and still is one of the most devoted target shooters I know. After one shoot in which he did fairly well, he went over to a long-time champion and introduced himself. The champion said that he'd been watching my friend and that he showed promise. My friend asked the champion if he had any advice and he said that he had.

"Just two things, my boy, and you'll be right there on top."

"What are they?" my friend asked.

"Be a little quicker and a little straighter," the champion said, with a wry smile. And the funny thing is that it's true, and almost impossible.

But what I wouldn't give to do well at the Grand!" "UNKNOWN SHOOTER DOMINATES GRAND AMERICAN," the headline reads. And there's a big picture of me smiling as I accept the check and the silver and the car. "Trap is almost all concentration," I'd say. "If you can break one target you ought to be able to break them all. It's just a matter of being a little quicker and a little straighter than the next guy."

No doubt they'd ask me why I'd never shot any sort of a really decent score in my life before now. That's the question I dread most. Who wants to admit that he just got lucky or spent a couple of days shooting so far over his head that he could hardly breathe? Maybe I'd say "It just suddenly all came together. I've got a new gun that fits perfectly and patterns exactly the way I like. And all the stuff I've been reading and listening to for years suddenly made sense. After all, the target is only a few inches wide and you've got a 30-inch pattern going for you, so it shouldn't be all that hard."

No doubt they'll ask me if I was nervous. "No, not really," I'll say. "I have a little trick of always putting a few extra shells in my pocket, and as often as not, I sort of forget when I'm getting near the end. I try to think of something else between shots to relax, like what I'll say to the reporters when I win!" That ought to get a little laugh.

If they ask me about the one I missed, I'll say that I asked the shell company to take a look at the empty and that they admitted it was bad. That ought to get another chuckle. People like you when you're modest in victory.

You bet I'd be modest. I think I hold the record for missing more first targets or more last targets than anyone who's ever handled a trap gun. I'm either not paying attention, or trying too hard, or suddenly fooling with something that just popped into my mind and which I've never tried before. I'm also superstitious. I hate starting on any position except number 4. I put the shells in the gun so that the maker's name is on top and everything is centered just right. I worry about how to call for the next target and I'm constantly changing where I hold the gun on station 5. About the only thing I am really consistent about is using a 12 gauge. I fool around so much it's a wonder that I ever break a 25, and when I do I have absolutely no idea why I did and prove it with the next round.

"UNKNOWN SHOOTER DOMINATES GRAND AMERICAN!"

What a chance to sit down and talk about choke boring, and stock measurements, and trigger pull, and rib widths, and points of aim and pattern centers, and all the other delicious stuff that all of us trapshooters thrive on. I've always wanted to try shooting with a barrel bent up a little, but I am afraid of ruining one of my too few guns. I've wanted to try a big rollover comb but don't have the money to get one. I've always wanted to fool with forcing cones and different chokes and stuff like that, but who wants to work on a gun for someone with my known lack of ability?

The truth is that I've shot the same trap gun (more or less) for over twenty years. Every once in a while it feels just right, but the trouble is I never know when that's going to happen. Oh, I have strayed now and then when a certain gun seems to be a big winner, but I've always come back to my old one. It's too heavy and I don't think it fits me just right, but we've gotten used to each other. I get mad at it every so often and threaten to sell it, but then it turns around and shoots a good score or two, and I accept the apology. No one ever offered to buy it anyway, and I don't need to ask why!

I do hope that some unknown shooter has his dream come true—that he has his picture taken by a new car, while shaking hands with the likes of Etchen and Sears; that someone, at long last, asks his opinion about 7½'s as opposed to 8's and light loads versus heavy ones; and that his wife and kids say truthfully that they knew he could do it all along. If it happens, there'll be someone as delighted with the whole thing as he is, someone who understands all too well how hard he worked and worried, and about the mystery of past shoots and the question marks about shoots to come.

He'll represent all of us for a little while, all of us who pore over the new catalogs and read the tips of the experts, and all of us who stand there trying to look like the guy who just ran 200 and backed it up in the shootoff, wondering just why we can't ever be just a little quicker and a little straighter.

ANOTHER
NOVEMBER SEASON

On any November morning you don't have to see it to know what's going on. A long row of gunners, making ghosts with their breath, moving through Midwestern corn stubble behind a pair of dancing dogs. A couple of men at the fringe of an alder cover in New England watching a little Brittany follow a wild thread that a woodcock has woven in the early morning breeze. A single pipe smoker sitting in a duck blind in a Southern marsh, sharing bites from a homemade sugar cookie with a slightly overweight Labrador. A young boy, no doubt a truant from school, watching a pointer puppy trailing 30 feet of borrowed clothesline toward a very special patch of honeysuckle that just may be the most important piece of land in all of Tennessee for the two of them.

On any November evening, you could guess exactly what's going on across the country. In Iowa, they'll be picking pheasants out behind the barn. Two little girls are saving the long tail feathers to make a centerpiece for the supper table; back in the kitchen, the ladies are fussing over cornbread and waiting for the giblets to make gravy. In New Hampshire, an orange-and-white bird dog has been smuggled into a motel room and is curled up in the softest chair. There is the faint sweetness of bourbon in the air, mixed in the earthy heaviness of muddy boots. The topic of conversation is whether it's late enough in the year to switch from light 8's to 7½'s. In Louisiana, a Labrador has sprawled out over the entire back seat of a station wagon. He is asleep, covered with an old canvas ducking jacket. The man driving is listening to the contented rumblings of the dog and adding a yard or so to the story he'll tell his wife about a crossing shot, and fixing the details of the retrieve in his mind.

About 60 miles from Memphis, the mother of a small boy is pretending she doesn't know about someone who didn't go to school and who now has a small dog sleeping with him under the covers. Mother is wondering which of the three of them is the happiest and hoping that the evening rain will be enough to wash the clay off the clothesline.

And so it goes in November season. It's a time for the pleasures and delights of the old traditions, the awakening of the young to the magic of bird and dog, and the reassurance to the not-so-young that deep contentment and satisfaction are near at hand, for a while, in a cornfield, on a hillside, and by the edge of the water. A hundred things are centered in these meetings with gamebirds and waterfowl. There is the anticipation that comes with buying a box of copper-coated 5's, the familiarity of an old cap, and the first wearing of a new wool shirt. And there is tuning a duck call, cleaning a shotgun, picking burrs from a bird dog, the relief of threading in a new pair of long-overdue boot laces, and all the Thermos bottles, pocket knives, shooting glasses, and gloves. These are the rituals of the hunter, who spends most of the year disguised as a salesman, dentist, farmer, or schoolboy, just biding the time until it's November season.

I don't claim to really understand it all. I do know that trudging along with a handful of shells banging around in a pocket, some kind of shotgun tucked under an arm or thrown over a shoulder, and a dog to please, seems like exactly the right thing to be doing. Nor do I think the whole thing ought to be overanalyzed. The dog knows what he or she is doing there, as much or more than I know what I'm doing there. We're looking for something—looking for something wild. Neither of us is searching for food; you can tell that by our shapes. An excuse to get into the woods? A little. A reason to pry loose and exercise an old instinct? Partly. To test our skills? Some of that. To be with certain people or away from certain others? Sometimes.

To lie on your belly and drink from a spring is part of it. So is making a small fire for tea. It is listening to a variety of comings and goings and watching Mother Nature put things away for the winter—sending her waterfowl South, urging the woodcock on in their bits-and-pieces flights, shaking the leaves loose so the trees can rest, and firing up some last minute urge in a variety of animals to fill the larder.

Behind the sorting of shotgun and rifle shells, the searching for vests and boots and dog leases, is the same compulsion. "Unto all things there is a season." We need no calendar to tell us this is November season. There is the trumpet-throated goose, the whisper of duck wings, the eerie whistle of the elk in the high country, and the soft notes of *bob white, bob white* in the low. The mornings have a hard and bracing edge, and the shortening days make every minute seem important.

And what will we take from November? Some will be lucky enough to show a boy or girl what it means to carry a gun and follow a bird dog, or the incredible satisfaction in knocking a rim of ice off the last decoy at pick-up time. Others have one sort of companionship or another to steep themselves in—the day alone to think those thoughts, and the day with friends to see some things through each other's eyes. There will be the delights of working with a brand new gun and the comfortable familiarity of an old one. There will be the misses, always with witnesses, and the successes, always with only a mute dog for an audience. We'll get wet, cold, hungry, and lost. We'll discover a new cover or two and find an old one gone to what passes for progress. It will be the last season for some dogs and the first one for others. Some special hunting boots will empty this year, and the once familiar faces will be there only in the evening stories. To some of us, the pheasants will seem smarter, the quail and grouse faster, and the ducks a little higher than we remember. It is not important that we do especially well; it is important only that we be there.

If you look carefully, you'll see a dog on point in the far corner of the field. It looks like it's a little springy there—good place for a woodcock, even a grouse. Not too far away, there's a man by himself, walking up toward the dog. I know what's running through his mind as his thumb rests a bit heavy on the safety. If he hurries too much, it'll make the dog nervous; if he doesn't hurry; then *he'll* get nervous. He's hoping it's a woodcock, because it'll hold, and afraid it's a grouse because it won't. He wishes he had 8's in both barrels instead of 7½'s and his 12 gauge instead of his 20. He's right beside the dog now, taking those small, careful steps, knowing full well that the flush will catch him on the wrong foot. From here I can only hear one shot. I see the dog disappear and then come back and sit. The gunner reaches down and takes a bird, looks at it for a moment, and slides it into his jacket pocket. I can't tell whether it's a woodcock or a grouse, but it doesn't matter. I doubt if it matters to the actors in the play, either. The circle was closed and that's all that there is to bird hunting—the man and the dog and the bird have come together.

The man is walking along another edge of the field while the dog dances ahead, almost showing off a little, doing a dog's version of shouting "hooray!" I'm not sure what's in the man's mind at this time, but if it were me, I know what I'd be thinking. In older times there was a common saying a man would often use when an old friend was leaving. So when I walk in what might be the last of this November season, I remember that saying. It's not a prayer but a thought asked of the wind, the wild, and the season. *Do not leave until thou has blessed me.*

SPECIAL SKILLS

Not long ago, I was idly leafing through a bundle of old issues of *Field & Stream*, picking out a hint here and a tip there to add to my rather lightly filled storehouse of woodcraft, shooting, and fishing skills. I found plenty, of course, by a very bright group of writers who could have earned a good salary and become responsible citizens if they had ever tried a responsible line of work.

Thinking about all that excellent lore, it occurred to me that I too rarely give my own readers any solid advice, like my secret for a long run of three or four on incoming doves, or how to cast a Grey Ghost weighted with split shot. I got to thinking about what I could offer you that no one else has and realized that I do have a few "secrets" I ought to pass along.

One of my great discoveries is, like many insights of genius, simple to the extreme once it's been explained and you've tried it for yourself. You've probably noticed (or you will now) that all the experts, real or self-styled, live to show off their skills. They treasure a dummy like me in camp as the ancients worshipped their gods. They vie for his attention and will do anything to show him "how this really ought to be done."

Which brings us to our first gem of advice: *Never, ever carry a knife!* I have spent hundreds of hours comfortably lounging around, enjoying a refreshment and smoking my pipe, while my current mentor was gutting and skinning my deer or picking my doves, or cleaning and filleting my fish, or doing some kind of repair to my equipment—all the while telling me that any other way of doing this or that is wrong.

But my relaxed pose is only a facade; I am constantly on the alert against the moment when my "teacher" might offer me his knife and ask me to try my hand at whatever he's been demonstrating. If you're a bit clumsy and careless, as I am, you can easily cut yourself or ruin a hide, or both. The real trick here is to be clumsy and careless with his treasured knife, which is something he cares a lot more about than your bleeding finger. If he insists that you have a whack at something, take his knife and test the edge by trying to slice a quarter or a dime, or trying to lob it into a tree. Tell him you admire the knife's edge or are taken with its incredible balance. Don't worry about losing him as a helper; there are plenty more where he came from.

Another great gem of advice involves those of you who really like to fish. All it takes is a little bit of restraint: *Never, ever admit to knowing how to row, paddle, pole, or run an outboard motor.* Long before I learned to forget how these things are properly done, I realized that it was always the other guy who was doing all the fishing. Why do you suppose women have become such fine fisherpersons? Because some man is determined to show his skills at rowing or whatever, and she's smart enough to keep smiling and hauling in fish. I don't mean to imply that I'm as smart about these things as the average ten-year-old pigtailed siren, but I'm not the slowest lad on the lake either. I figure I get in what amounts to about two weeks more solid fishing every year since I no longer fool around with oars, anchors, gas cans, or engine chokes. There's always the extra pancake and cup of coffee in the morning while the Skipper gets everything ready, the extra some-thing-and-water while he's putting things up in the evening. This is not to mention all the bad things that can happen to your body when you wrestle with a 25-horse-power motor or drag several hundred pounds of boat up on the shore.

I know that by now you're smiling and wondering why you never thought of these things before. Here's another gem: *Never, ever carry a camera.* Forget for the moment the money I've just saved you and think of the good will you're spreading among all the equipment crazies. I'll bet you've been on many a trip where some good soul had a new piece of photographic gimmickry he just spent a bundle on and couldn't wait to try out. He probably also had a fortune in film to go with his new toy.

Our photographer friend will take a zillion pictures, which will be at least ten times better than anything you'd get, and he won't rest until you have a set of the best ones. I don't know how you feel about going over a hundred overexposed, out-of-focus, badly framed slides, but I rank it with root canal work. But, deep down inside, don't you take a good deal more pleasure looking at pictures of yourself than at shots of Frank or Henry or Bernie? I thought so. And remember what all that stuff costs—equipment, film, processing, etc., etc? What would you rather have through which to view the world—a couple of cases of fine vintage wine, or a 28mm wide angle lens.

Actually, it's entirely possible, and probably very desirable, to go off on a trip taking nothing but stuff centered around your own personal comfort, leaving the excesses of hardware to the experts. Such an expert would be Dave Petzal. Were it not for the fact that he's left-handed and I'm not, Petzal would be the ideal big-game hunting companion. He's deeply committed to the ownership and use of any number of fine rifles—each of which is vastly superior to anything I might even dream about. Further, he is knife-crazy and addicted to cameras. I'd far prefer to use his custom-built, beautifully engraved, finely tuned stuff than the near junk that my spendthrift daughters have reduced me to.

Of course, Dave wouldn't dream of letting me touch one of his diamond-honed blades, and he knows that I haven't the vaguest idea what all the knobs and dials are for on even the simplest camera. The same goes for Zern and his exquisite fly fishing gear, and for Brister and his high grade, custom shotguns. While I wouldn't always count on it, these experts have been known to extend to me the best spot on the water, the best duck blind, or the most open spot on a covey rise.

The point of much of this is not that you should be selfish, but just the reverse. Not many people are thinking to themselves "I ought to invite old Gene fishing or hunting so he can use my Winston or Orvis rod, or maybe shoot my 20-bore Woodward." But maybe they just need a little urging to bring out their generous and thoughtful natures. It's not that I *can't* skin out a whitetail, it's just that it's obvious that some people enjoy that sort of thing more than others, and we ought to see to it that they are made happy when we can— even if it means a little self-sacrifice.

Just remember how much self-esteem you're allowing your partner when you let *him* wade across the river first to look for ledges and deep holes. You let *him* walk boldly up to the farmer's door past a BEWARE THE DOG sign, or take the shot when the dog's on point in the same field with the ton-and-a-half Hereford bull, or call your wife and tell her you've decided to spend the night. As they say, heroes are made, not born.

On the other hand, I happen to know that several of my friends' wives always carry knives, know how to row and fix shear pins, understand the intricacies of f-stops and depth-of-field, and know enough not to expect anyone to be home at the exact minute they said they would. I know a couple of wives whose husbands have Winstons and Woodwards too, but then I never promised you life would be fair.

I once made a list of equipment that the ideal hunting companion/ expert should have. Among the items on the list are a knife, 14½-inch shotgun stocks, his own canoe, medium-fast fly rods, and an extra pair of size 12 waders. A good quail lease and a duck marsh wouldn't hurt. And if I could have one more wish, he would be a size 44 Regular. I know one outdoor companion that could make him a very happy man indeed!

It's been especially hard for me to observe a few of my own *never, ever* rules—like mentioning a score I once shot at trap or skeet, my incredible skills at the poker table, a day in a Canadian duck blind I will never forget, and the uncanny skills of my Labrador retriever. But the lessons learned the hard way are the ones that hang in.

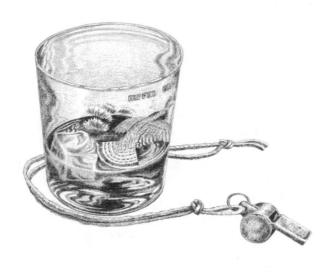

HOROSCOPE REVISITED

My first horoscope, which appears earlier in this book, was so uncannily accurate, so precise down to the last detail, that those who were quick to realize its potential won lotteries, caught fish on every outing, and raised their trap scores by an average of 3.9 targets. Most of my readers also had fewer backlashes, and only eleven failed to take their deer.

CAPRICORN: December 22—January 19: Capricorns are the great craftsmen. You can shingle a roof, fix faucets and even electrical appliances. You never lose small springs or screws on the floor. You are easily bored and seldom resist the temptation to fix things that aren't broken. None of your guns are in their original condition, and you tend to spend more money making fly rods than they would cost if you bought them. You must watch the tendency to buy tools you already have. Capricorns live for the sound of something breaking and tend to like to be around people who are known to be clumsy. Your lucky number is 7/16th.

AQUARIUS: January 20—February 18: Aside from a tendency to

be a little hard-headed, you can expect a fine year. You will have to get over being cheap and quit buying so-called bargains. If not, your waders will continue to leak, your leaders will turn brittle, and you will lose every fish over 2 pounds. Watch the tendency to run out of gas, and try to understand why you have so many flat tires. You're at the age where you *must* write things down! One of your biggest faults is putting things off. Get those triggers adjusted now and don't wait until the last minute to sight in your rifle. Stop making excuses, and work your dog a little more often; you could both afford to lose a few pounds. And give a little more thought to why you're everybody's favorite face at the poker table.

PISCES: February 19—March 20: Late summer and early fall look like outstanding periods, if you'll stick to your limitations. Avoid those right-to-left crossing shots at all costs and don't forget that your casting has more than a few problems; you have to live with what you are. The same goes for all those do-it-yourself projects you get involved in—either really pay attention or give them up. Be especially careful with your reloading, and think about buying your flies instead of trying to tie your own. Don't forget to wear a lifejacket or at least have one handy if you're around water. Buy a compass and learn how to use it; all your friends are worried about your being lost half the time. Don't ever go off all by yourself without leaving a note. Your wingshooting will be very good, for you, but curb your tendency to brag; your wingshooting won't be *that* good.

ARIES: March 21—April 19: Those of you who are bass fishermen can start taking bets! Stop fishing your partner's water and don't say "I'm not hungry" as you get into their food, and you'll be okay. You ought to buy a better rod; a new reel won't hurt either. You already have too many lures and odds and ends in general. You fuss with a lot of things you don't really understand—let your instincts take over. You have a lot of superstitions that are silly, and you tell too many old jokes. You could be a better listener. And fish more at night—you're not the sort of person that wives worry about.

TAURUS: April 20—May 20: If you can get your hands on a better trap gun and a case of practice shells, the boys at the gun club will be in for a big surprise! You are one of those rare natural shots, and only inferior equipment is holding you back. The same goes for fly fishing. You are a skilled woodsman, you have an incredible sense of direction, your duck calling and stalking techniques are outstanding, and you have an uncanny ability to play poker. You are obviously overtalented and underappreciated. Dogs worship you and people not only excuse but tend to find charming your occasional moments of forgetfulness. If there were more just like you, the world would be a better place. If you do have a fault, perhaps it's your reliance on others to keep you supplied with trout and salmon flies. You must, however, watch your wingshooting—it is far too easy for you to never miss.

GEMINI: May 21—June 20: You are far too reluctant to say "no." Every catalog seems to have something in it you can't live without, and you do too much work for every organization that asks you. You find yourself so busy with others that you don't get a chance to get out on your own as much as you should. People take advantage of you. You always remember the flashlight and you can be counted on to set the alarm. This is your year to enjoy yourself. You deserve to catch a trophy bass on your first cast.

CANCER: June 21—July 22: You are notorious for your willingness to change, and to a lot of your friends and family this is misinterpreted as fickleness or instability. You will probably buy or at least try out one or more new trap guns—but don't get rid of the old one. Remember that your lucky number is 23 and that your financial aptitude is not of the highest order. Your weakness early in the year is romance, which means that there may well be a new puppy in you future. Later in the year, it seems that you will have an educational experience and you could easily discover a potential to improve in an important area. This could mean a temporary mastery of station 5 or even getting your dog to come when it's called. The week after Thanksgiving will be very important, a fine time to take your vacation. Your wife will break the promise she made to leave you and will give you one more chance. Take it!

LEO: July 23—August 22: Contrary to popular opinion, Leos are exceptional woodsmen. They make ideal camping companions because they are eager to split wood, carry water, and certain to know the direction of true north. However, Leos are often too eager and tend to try tasks better left to others. Leos tend to burn pancakes and fry eggs too hard around the edges, and when they serve food, it often smells like kerosene. They are the only people who are born with the gift of coping with gas lanterns. Most Leos are indifferent fishermen and only fair shots, so they make ideal members of trap squads and excellent fishing partners. The rest of us look good by comparison, and our boats will never run out of gas. Leos make fine sons-in-law.

VIRGO: August 23—September 22: This looks like a difficult year, but you will handle it well. Small problems like leaking boots, backlashes, wind knots, and slight out-of-range waterfowl will be the pattern, but don't be discouraged. There is a new 3-inch magnum in your future and you'll do very well with it, in spite of an abnormal number of severe colds. Keep your equipment in tiptop shape and carry an extra spare tire. Your love life will suffer until the end of duck season, but things will be back to normal by the start of the trout season. Don't be too adventuresome—stick to the old paths and what you know best. But you might want to take out a little extra insurance—just in case.

LIBRA: September 23—October 22: Most good cooks are born under Libra. They are persistent with details and their knots never come untied. Libras make fine reloaders and fly tiers; they rarely get lost and never forget their rain gear. Libra wives are usually rare jewels who like to clean fish and pick birds; their husbands never have socks with holes in them. Libras would have made good poachers. They are a bit stubborn and bossy, and they often play strange games when it's their turn to deal the cards. Although poor gamblers, Libras are usually the first to try something new—often to their regret. People who shoot trap with bent barrels and open chokes are likely to be Libras. Libras still have a lot to learn.

SCORPIO: October 23—November 21: Scorpios are usually easily satisfied. They almost never have a really bad year because they see the bright side of everything. Scorpios believe in Santa and the Easter Bunny well after they should. If you see someone spitting on a hook or tossing salt over his shoulder, it's likely a Scorpio. Most "B" shooters are Scorpios, and they leave a lot of their flies in trees, but they don't really care. They should try to marry money, since they like the finer things and are great believers in traditions. Whoever first coined the phrase "good sport" was undoubtedly talking about one of you.

SAGITTARIUS: November 22—December 21: You are the merchant's dream—a born collector of two of everything. All the wish book mail-order companies ought to send you a birthday card. Every one of your fly rods has two tips and every gun has an extra set of barrels. You hope your waders leak so you can get another pair, or else use the new ones you already have. Your house is one huge closet, and you undoubtedly drive a van or a pickup—or both. Your friends joke about your net worth being in boots and wool shirts. The high point of your trip is packing. You were the first to wear camouflage underwear. When you are re-born, you will come back as a Supply Sergeant. Your lucky number is 9.98.

HAMMERS

I have this mental picture of me standing there holding a duck. In my other hand is a shotgun. At my side is Maggie, my black Labrador retriever—for once Maggie is not larking somewhere in the near distance.

The gun wasn't bought to shoot ducks particularly. I wanted it because it is beautiful. It has outside hammers, delicately engraved sidelocks, double triggers, and a straight-hand English stock. It was made, as best I know, on the backside of the 1900's; I'd guess around 1898. The full-choke, 31-inch barrels are fluid steel. The maker's name is H. J. Hussey. I know little about him except that he made as nice a gun as I have ever seen.

I wouldn't say that I shoot it exceptionally well, and there are other guns I'd take out first if I were a betting man, but I don't shoot it all that badly either. I just happen to be very fond of it and vainly dream of having another one something like it. Sometime I'd like to know just who had it made. It has 31-inch barrels, not 30, not 32. Was it some oddball shotgunner like myself who came up with his own against-the-tide idea of the ideal barrel length? Or did Mr. Hussey see in his customer a chance to prove a theory of his own? I envy them, going back and forth and deciding to go their own way and the devil with what the brothers Purdey were doing, or anyone else for that matter.

I have a suspicion that this gun was created for use in the live pigeon rings, where then as now, eccentricity is king, as long as you've got the money. I can easily imagine the owner wearing his five-button jacket of heavy tweed, a starched collar, and a hard crowned hat that we call a "bowler." I can see him opening the oak and leather case (and I wonder whatever happened to that...) and carefully fitting the gun together while those who knew him looked on with eager curiosity, wondering if, indeed, 31 inches might be the answer they were all looking for.

It might even have been a "challenge" match. Often, in those days, shooters used names like "Blue Rock," or "Venator," or just the name of their district—"York," for example—or something else so secret in meaning that it held significance only to themselves. The live bird ring was not held in social high esteem.

The notes in the sporting paper might read: *Blue Rock wishes to challenge anyone at 30 yards rise, 50 pigeons, with a stake of 100 pounds.* If the offer was accepted, and it usually was, especially if it was directed at a particular person, crowds of spectators would gather, their interests and opinions backed by their pocketbooks, and their conversations would be filled with facts and fancies over the relative merits of Skimmers versus Antwerp pigeons, Schultze nitro-powder, and whether or not Number 6 (British) shot was the best size.

Not too long after the turn of the century, live pigeon shooting was outlawed in England. Unless there was a secret match now and then, which wouldn't surprise me a great deal, the old hammer gun might have gone to the newer game of feather-filled glass balls sprung from a trap. Or, if the owner was really well-to-do, he might have used it on the Continent in the pigeon rings at Monte Carlo or Madrid.

Full-and-full guns weren't the choice of the better game shots when driven grouse and pheasant shoots became *the* thing to do. The choice for that was cylinder-and-full or cylinder-and-modified, but perhaps there was a second set of barrels struck, or maybe he just put his pigeon gun away and went gunning with something else. It's possible that the old hammer gun got carried out to a duck shoot now and then, before it was thought of as old-fashioned or a quaint antique.

It might have been traded in on one or a pair of the new hammerless doubles, or given to a young shooter so he'd learn safe handling with hammers he could see. Who knows? Somehow, it came to this country.

Anyone who ever used this old gun must have seen the same things in it that I do. It was kept oiled and cleaned, and except for a few scratches on the stock and a small nick in the splinter fore-end, Mr. Hussey would still be proud of it.

My guess is that over here, it was a duck gun, that full-and-full boring warming the heart of its owner. It would be fun to know what the gun sold for, if it was ever sold around. Hammer guns—no matter whose name was on them, no matter how fine and delicate the engraving, no matter how exquisite the checkering and how close the grain of the wood—were cut up for parts, left in the barn to shoot whatever was bothering the chickens, or made into lamps. Most of them had Damascus barrels and were considered unsafe with modern high-pressure loads. Even those with good steel barrels were considered "unsafe," and the upright hammers were as strange looking to gunners as the high silk hat. But the old gun survived, waiting for someone who would fully appreciate it.

I don't know exactly why—probably because one of the guns I wanted most as a kid was a hammer pump just like Pop's Model 97 Winchester—but my urge to own a hammer double has always been keen. I did find a pretty nice 20-bore hammer gun in an old country store, but the bank balance was too thin for even the piddling amount the owner wanted. But I decided that if I ever found another one that I really liked—bank balance, etc. factored in—I'd have it, as I do now the long-wanted Model 97.

Needless to say, any glorious moment the old Hussey was involved in will remain hidden in its past. But now and then, the dreamer inside me gives a little twitch and I can imagine a notice that might read: "Hill Country offers a challenge to Louisiana Rudy: 30 birds at 30 yards rise to be held at your club or mine; purse to be mutually agreed on. R.S.V.P." While waiting for the answer I would occupy myself by loading up the shells I'd need—48 grains of Schultze behind 1¼ ounces of Number 7 shot—and seeing to it that my brown derby hat and favorite tweed shooting jacket were cleaned and ready. A man shooting a bird gun with 31-inch barrels has to be prepared to be the center of some attention.

Having done his part, the dreamer disappears for a time and Maggie and I spend the odd afternoon in a local marsh, my old tweed cap a shabby substitute for a derby. Maggie is busy reassuring me that I can take Louisiana Rudy's measure between the trips she makes to shoo away blackbirds and herons, which for some reason she despises. Both of us love the solid business-like click of the artfully engraved hammers. The single greenhead that slid off to the right has tumbled into the long grass, and while Maggie is out fetching him, the dreamer is back at work shaking the hand of Louisiana Rudy, collecting the money, and answering his questions as to exactly why I went to a set of barrels 31 inches long.

Showing no respect at all, Maggie has covered me and all 31 inches of the barrels with muddy water. I try to tell her that this is no way to treat the man who just grassed a bird from 30 yards, but she's off flushing something out of the marsh, and to a man who's a little hard to hearing, the splashing of dog feet can sometimes sound not totally unlike the applause of a small crowd.

WHY IS IT...?

I forget just who remarked that "if God had wanted us to shoot an over-and-under, he'd have placed our eyes like that." Well, I for one won't argue with Divine foresight. I've been shooting trap with an over-and-under lately, and considering my scores, I'll take the advice from any direction. I often wonder if there are certain things my Maker wanted me to do or not do. For instance, if I was created to run English setters, why wasn't I given the ability to do 100 yards in ten seconds so I could have a little hand control over my dogs?

If I was needed to keep up the population of trained Labrador retrievers, why wasn't I given the ability to put my fingers in my mouth and whistle? Or throw a dummy more than fifty feet? Or do a little better on down-wind crossing shots? If I was carved out to spend so much time in duck and goose blinds, why do my hands and feet turn blue when the temperature drops below 50 degrees F.?

If I am supposed to spend a fair amount of time fly fishing, why is it that I'm not smart enough to wade for more than five minutes without getting wet? Why am I not able to tie an improved clinch in a 6X tippet without breaking it, or take a rod apart without either stripping a guide or pulling a muscle? Or remember any more Latin than *spiritus frumenti*?

If I'm destined to spend so much time in what passes for wilderness, why am I so often lost? Why is it that a Pacific Islander can canoe across the vastness of the ocean navigating with a pierced gourd, and I can't find the North Star or read a compass? I do, however, have the power to break a sizable twig by merely looking in its direction, and my scent can and does carry upwind, but this merely leads me to believe something's wrong somewhere.

One of the world's most eminent physicists was once asked: "If you could stand before God and ask Him one question, what would it be?" He thought for only a split second and replied: "I'd like to know why the ion has a charge of negative 1." No doubt this means a great deal to you physicists, but it doesn't appeal much to those of us who seem to stumble around tripping over more mundane problems. I've been a professional writer most of my life and I can't spell. I forget when the *i* goes before the *e*. My participles dangle like the hanged, and my infinitives are split as regularly as my wader seams.

What makes so many of us torture ourselves and teeter on bankruptcy trying to do things that are not clearly in the cards? If I can break the first twenty birds at trap or skeet, why do I do what I do on the last five? If I can cast a fly sixty feet or so in practice, why do I get wind knots, loop the line over the reel seat, and worse when I try to throw a fly to a fish only forty feet away? Will I ever learn how to hit an incomer in the dove field, make an easy double on quail, not miss high 1 on the skeet field, or look for the tell-tale porcelain insulators on wire fences? Why is it that I insist on paying to see one more card in stud poker or betting against the Dallas Cowboys? Would you believe my neighbor, who doesn't shoot, buys an old farmhouse and finds a Purdey in an attic closet? You know what's in the attic in my old farmhouse, Carpenter ants—and I wish them well.

I love the music Canada geese make, but my retriever winces when I blow a call. Why do the rings always fall off the inside tubes of my automatic shotguns? Do the line size stickers come off *your* fly reels too? I always put an even number of socks in the laundry and I always get an odd number back. Why?

It's not that I want to be any kind of an expert; there are more than enough of them around. My wife doesn't pin a note on me when

I travel or put *L* or *R* on the toes of my boots, but she does worry a little. I doubt very much if I'm the only one who has gone to the big D.U. dinner on the wrong night, or showed up at a .410 shoot with a 20 gauge. It's not that I'm absent minded or prematurely senile; it's just that I have a lot of things on my mind.

I'm even the wrong size. Hats marked L are too small and XL's are too big. That's bad because I have an uncontrollable passion for tweed caps. The stocks of factory field guns are too short and too low in the comb for me; and factory trap guns are the opposite. Yet when the average insomniac counts sheep to sleep, I count bobwhite quail or clay targets.

It's not that I'd be unhappy with being average either, but as you know, there's average…and there's *average*. I guess I get the average number of flat tires, and forget the average number of times that most gas stations are closed on Sunday. On the average, I'm too short for my weight and cannot touch my toes the average number of times. I am below average in remembering anniversaries and birthdays but way above when it comes to my dogs' ages, and hunting dates. I have better than average eyesight and below average hearing. I suppose I spend more than the average amount of time with outdoor catalogs and books, and less than average on daily newspapers. I am below average when it comes to fixing things and above average in owning things that don't work. My trap and skeet averages are a secret, but unfortunately, my birds-to-shells are not. I spend more than the average amount of time wishing the wind would blow the leaves off the lawn and out of the gutters, and less than the average with a rake or a ladder.

But lest you mark me down as a man railing against his fate, I will, in fairness, search for a balance. I don't get poison ivy, and bugs don't bite me very much. I haven't hooked myself with a plug or a fly in years. Dogs like me, but The Creator has instructed me in no uncertain terms to avoid both horses and domestic bulls. If He didn't want me to wade, I guess he wouldn't have made me a good swimmer. If He didn't want me to write, I'm sure I'd have been a surgeon or the sole heir to an oil fortune. I'm convinced that I'm a little deaf because I have a wife and two daughters.

I guess that I'm supposed to be a duck hunter because I have a passion for pump guns and Labradors. And if I wasn't destined to mess with quail and grouse and the like, I wouldn't be so addicted to side-by-sides, pointers, and alder covers. I can't look at a painting by

Maass or Reneson or Hennessey without seeing myself, and I can't pass a brook or a river or a stand of birches without a bit of wonder in my heart.

If we were average, we wouldn't collect hip boots, fly rods, old plugs, dog whistles, decoys, or pocket knives. Opening day would just be another Saturday, and frost or squalls wouldn't make us happy. We wouldn't fret about turkeys, or canvasbacks, or brookies, or striped bass. We wouldn't have dog hairs on the furniture or nose prints on the inside of car windows. We wouldn't have our minds cluttered with the ballistics of .30/.30's, theoretically leads, bloodlines of bird dogs, or mayfly hatch dates. Our wives wouldn't be saving for duck boats or outboards, and our kids wouldn't be "borrowing" our tackle and shells.

If just might be that we're here to understand and appreciate the importance of ducks, deer, pheasants, and bass, yet realize that not everything on this earth ought to be fully understood. It is important that there be men and women here who know about the rise of a trout or the soft sweetness of *bob-white, bob white*.

THE RESPONSIBLE
SPORTSMAN

It seems, often regretfully, that we are a nation of weighers and measurers, a people fascinated by even the most trivial of records. Can anyone put up with one more sports announcer telling us in all seriousness that so-and-so "has just set a record for being the first-baseman with the most errors committed on Friday the 13th," or some other such nonsense?

In general I don't like, or see the point of, the seemingly endless "my fish was bigger than yours" or "my four-point buck was ten pounds heavier than your four-point buck." First of all I have yet to have anyone tell me how to throw a plug or fly that will produce a bigger fish than yours when we're in the same boat or pool. I wouldn't listen anyway. I like competition—where competition belongs: on the skeet or trap field; in distance and accuracy casting tournaments; in golf and tennis, football and baseball, and a dozen other games that are competitive by purpose and design. But I believe in having a little time off from head-butting when I can.

If you insist on "firsts," I can think of some I'll agree are quite worthwhile. The day your little pal discovers that a shotgun really doesn't hurt. The time you were lucky enough to be the one to give someone their first pocketknife. Or show someone that a fly rod isn't all that hard to handle or that putting a worm on a hook doesn't require an M.D. degree. Or teach a bride to cast a spoon or a baby to row a boat.

And our own firsts that we can remember—sometimes with pride, sometimes with laughter. A puppy's first real point or good retrieve. That incredible longed-for twenty-five straight on the trap field, or the shoot-off where we broke eighteen just after running fifty targets. The hundred-yard shot in the wide open with our perfectly sighted-in .270 that cut a sapling three feet over the buck's back. The double on downwind broadbills in a twenty-knot wind. No doubt some of our sweetest evenings in front of the fire start out with someone saying "Remember the day that…," and along come the good stories of falling in, getting lost, four birds with four shells, first bucks, and buck fever.

I like to believe, and I really do, that hunters and fishermen have more fun laughing at themselves than any other sportsmen. It's not that we don't take ourselves seriously; we do, but only at the right time and for the only the right reasons.

I get a little annoyed at a lot of the outdoor writers who forget one simple thing: most of us are out there to have fun. We don't want to be perfect all the time. First of all we couldn't stand it, and secondly, we really don't care; perfection behind a fishing rod or a rifle or shotgun isn't the reason we fool around with them.

Too many proponents of this-or-that technique forget that most of us just like to go fishing and that doesn't exactly mean we're intent on catching fish. Nor do some of the best bird hunters I know bring home the biggest bags. I do think that we all enjoy learning something new, adding to our storehouse of lore and knowledge, but that doesn't mean we're not going to continue to fish with a No. 16 Adams most of the time because we just like fishing with a No. 16 Adams. Or that we're going to retire our old Model 12 just because something "more efficient" has come along. I know there *just has to be* a trap gun that I can shoot better than the one I use, but I like the cranky old thing, and while I may flirt with a new beauty every so often, it's the old love that gets the nod when I get the least bit serious, because we're used to each other.

I know our favorite successes very well, yours and mine. Like when we see a kid we've had the chance to help shooting in the middle 20's on the skeet field or putting out a nifty cast, time after time, right at the edge of the lily pads the way we taught him. Or the lady of the house just deciding to take the dog and hunt alone and coming back with a brace of birds. Those are the unforgettable moments that remind us of the first time we knew we could do it—all by ourselves— and did. We know right then that we have left a legacy without which there would never be the peaceful feeling of knowing that someone else will teach someone else in turn, and the whole thing is going to be carried on just the way it should be.

The thing we try to teach the young and the newcomers' young ought to be the philosophy of sport—The good manners, the sense of right and wrong and doing the right *when no one else is looking!*

A sportsman today is loaded with responsibility. There is the responsibility of being law-abiding and seeing to it that others are as well. There is the responsibility of courtesy—not only among ourselves but with everyone we come in contact with in our sport. We have to remember that "one bad apple" does indeed spoil the rest of us in a good many eyes. These are the things we have to teach by example and constant reminders.

The "macho" image every so often gets a little out of hand for our good public relations. No doubt you have a list of your own that disturbs you. My list includes hunters who insist on walking around in town with a hunting knife that's big enough to quarter a mastodon. The huge knife is silly enough in itself, and to wear it as a badge of "manliness" is even more ridiculous. Another example is attending a fair-sized trap or skeet shoot and "proving" your ruggedness by wearing a torn and filthy shirt with pants and shoes to match. While I agree that there are times and places to wear blaze orange, I don't think that the local diner or bar and grill qualify. I'm delighted to see more and more states discouraging the practice of draping cars and trucks with dead deer; it doesn't do the sportsmens' image or the venison much good. The less said about some "sportsmen's" T-shirts, the better.

Think for a minute about who is responsible for the stories about the town pond having a swan in it with an arrow through its neck, the intestines of a deer left in a schoolyard, the pet dogs shot during hunting season—and cows and sheep and horses and weathervanes and windows. We are responsible, my friends, whether we like it or not. We are the ones who leave stock fences open, who cut wire, who drive our pickups through standing crops, who litter streams, and who throw back small dead fish when we catch a bigger one.

I know you're the one who supports Trout Unlimited and spends a lot of time and work to clean up someone else's mess. I know that you and your wife work with your local sportsmen's clubs, you donate to D.U., you teach Hunter Safety courses, you get and show good outdoor films to your Rotary and Kiwanis Clubs. But when one of your neighbors loses his pet terrier to a nitwit gunner, you're the one who's got to apologize, one way or another.

I wish I knew the answers, but I sure don't. I don't understand why a perfectly respectable, hard-working person goes a little (or a lot) berserk when holding a firearm or driving an outboard boat. All I know is that I've been shot at and have come close to being swamped by a 200-horsepower crazy when my little rowboat was "in his way." And not just once either, and not too long ago.

I don't like to remember those times very much. I try to think of the hundreds of times when a real sportsman has proven to be just that. The man in a shootoff who told the referee that his bird was lost and that what someone else saw was just the wad. The lady who had drawn the best pool giving her rod turn to someone else who hadn't taken any fish. The small boy who fished along the edge of my brook and filled his creel with beverage cans that someone else had left—he didn't know I saw that, either. The guy who shares his last few shells with you, puts his good dog up so you can run the pup—the one that does the things that make us proud to be his friend. He's us too, I know. I just hope that the time comes when I can do some of the right things in my turn that you've done for me. Even if I'm all alone, and no one is looking.

ANNUAL REPORT
(FOR MOST RECENT
FISCAL YEAR)

The speaker has been standing at center stage for a few minutes as if expecting some recognition, perhaps even applause. Behind him is a rather statuesque blond lady. The speaker nervously clears his throat and, sneaking a look at the lady, who appears to be ignoring him, removes what looks suspiciously like a paper of chewing tobacco from his pocket and places some of the contents in his cheek. A frown crosses the lady's face. As the speaker begins, his voice is strong but low—as if he is afraid of waking up the men in the audience who have already begun to nod.

It would be a pleasure indeed to give a normal report like the cold delineation of your bank statement: so many dollars in, so many dollars out. I would like to be able to tell you: "In the months of October, November, and December, 78 shells in 20 gauge were fired, plus 143 shells in 12 gauge, and 167 shells in 28 gauge, and this resulted in our freezer stock which now contains twenty-four quail, eleven pheasants, thirty-four waterfowl (ducks and geese), four woodcock, and thirty-six doves." Of course, I cannot. I have no idea how many shells I fire, what's in the freezer as opposed to what should be, or what happened to my legendary ability to hit high incomers.

The Annual Report is a misnomer. I don't know what it *should* be called, since it's a mishmash of glossed-over misadventures, distorted emphasis, selective memory, and a very human inability to face any facts that seem harsh, or unpleasant, or postponable. Titles aren't really that important to me anyway. Mrs. Hill has long stopped referring to me as Mr. Hill and now uses the familiar *Gene*, even in front of guests and my children, who no longer rise when I enter the room. No doubt many of us are experiencing the same decay in manners in other areas as well—I see nothing to be gained by dwelling on the decline of better times.

As usual, the business at hand is trying to find some reasonable way to explain why times aren't as prosperous as they should be, why the cash flow has been diverted unsuccessfully, and other items that the old country stores used to label "sundries."

The place on the mantel reserved for the club trap championship is still occupied by the encrusted jar of sere holly berries and leaves. I know this is not startling news, but it is symptomatic of the sort of year it's been. The wooden plaque acquired for an eight-point or better whitetail is still in service as a table trivet. The 12-weight fly rod for tarpon has not hooked so much as a T-shirt or hat brim. The stock of one of our best shotguns broke clear through at the wrist—I might add that Management says we ought to have a category labeled *Losses* with the subtitle *clumsiness/senility* (this is the sort of statement that the Chairman considers witty). Our favorite retriever has had puppies out of wedlock and so it has gone, more often than I think is fair.

On a more positive note, we won six quarts of motor oil (10-40) at a D.U. dinner and a pair of ladies' gloves (work). We also won second place (coin toss) at a small skeet shoot and found a long-forgotten case of 28-gauge shells (No. 9's) while cleaning a closet in the garage.

You may recall that Labor had been requested by Management to take a much harder line with spur-of-the-moment expenses, and I'm pleased to report that this has been accomplished with less hardship than expected. One foreseeable problem is still being debated—the acquisition of present spending for future use. To wit, a new salmon reel that while not critical at the moment, was too good a bargain to ignore, and a new scope for a rifle (.222) that has yet to receive Management approval. (For those more technically minded than the Chairman, the .222 is needed both for turkey and miscellaneous. Those shooters among you will understand completely.)

An old dog has been lost and will be much missed. George (wire-haired pointing griffon) disdained fieldwork as such, although he did now and then join us as a curious spectator. He felt strongly about the arts, was a notorious fan of rock-and-roll music, and thoroughly enjoyed certain country-and-western singers, notably Willie Nelson, Tom T. Hall, and Lefty Frizzell. He lived in an upholstered chair in the garage where he could supervise much of what was going on without actually having to get involved in the kind of rough-and-tumble the Labradors are always into. George was interested in travel—by car—and tended more toward the mental pursuits than the physical. He prided himself on being an original thinker and tended to avoid sports, although he would watch the volleyball game on occasion, or take a swim on warm summer afternoons. He and the cat always got along very well and he would allow, or perhaps even invite, her to sleep on him when the weather turned cold. I think he always wanted to play Frisbee but felt it would be undignified. One of my daughters would talk him into jogging with her once in a while, but he stopped to sit and think so often that she finally gave up. The Chairman often discussed important matters with him and his unsurpassable qualities as a good listener and counsel seem irreplaceable.

The carp in the pond remain impervious to any of our angling techniques; the one attempt to net them was so pathetic and awkward that none of us involved are quite ready to try again or even to discuss what went wrong.

All in all, there is harmony around the farm. The cycle of losing things for months leads to the delight of discovery—the prodigal shooting glasses, the wayward box of 3-inch No. 2's. The spade comes out in the spring to plant the new, and the saw comes out in the fall to cut the old.

Speaking of things lost, the Chairman has instituted a new rule: Nothing can be declared "must be replaced" unless a year has passed or we have the remains in evidence. While some of us may see this as excess conservatism or the slanted view of Labor's general competence, it has been agreed to for the sake of harmony.

I see our time is finished. I thank you all for your interest and forbearance. I know I've said it before, but I sincerely believe that things will show a definite improvement in the next fiscal year.

I had hoped to deal a few hands of five-card stud, for instructional purposes only, but it seems that the Chairman has left my cards in her other shooting bag.

(Feminine voices are heard expressing sounds of relief and several men are being shaken awake. The muffled barking of dogs issues from the parking lot as the owners walk to their cars.)